A Raid on the Red Sea

A Raid on the Red Sea

The Israeli Capture of the *Karine A*

AMOS GILBOA

Edited and translated by YONAH JEREMY BOB

Potomac Books

AN IMPRINT OF THE UNIVERSITY OF NEBRASKA PRESS

Adapted from *Dramah ba-Yam ha-Adom: Tefisat Ḳarin A, oniyat ha-neshek ha-Palestinit, 3 be-Yanu'ar 2002* (Israel Intelligence Heritage and Commemoration Center and Effi Melzer, Inc., 2017).

Library of Congress Cataloging-in-Publication Data
Names: Gilboa, Amos, author. | Bob, Yonah Jeremy, editor, translator.
Title: A raid on the Red Sea: the Israeli capture of the Karine A / Amos Gilboa; edited and translated by Yonah Jeremy Bob.
Other titles: Dramah ba-Yam ha-Adom. English
Description: Lincoln: Potomac Books, an imprint of the University of Nebraska Press, 2021.
Identifiers: LCCN 2020025424
ISBN 9781640123571 (hardback)
ISBN 9781640124424 (epub)
ISBN 9781640124431 (mobi)
ISBN 9781640124448 (pdf)
Subjects: LCSH: Karine A (Ship) | Israel. Ḥel ha-yam. Shayeṭet 13. | Blockade—Gaza Strip. | Illegal arms transfers—Iran. | Military intelligence—Israel. | Israel—History, Naval—21st century.
Classification: LCC DS110.G3 G5313 2021 | DDC 956.9405/5—dc23
LC record available at https://lccn.loc.gov/2020025424

Set in Minion Pro by Mikala R. Kolander.

CONTENTS

ILLUSTRATIONS

PREFACE

At 0400 hours on January 3, 2002, the Israeli Navy Seals (Shayetet 13) clandestinely seized a Palestinian Authority freighter named the *Karine A* in the Red Sea at a distance of several hundred nautical miles from Israel. The ship was carrying fifty-five tons of high-grade Iranian weapons, including rockets that could destroy large Israeli cities, from the Islamic Revolutionary Guard Corps for the Palestinian Authority. The weapons, loaded onto the ship near the coast of Iran in the Persian Gulf, were headed for the Gaza Strip to help fulfill a joint goal of Iran, Hezbollah, and the Palestinian Authority of seriously escalating a campaign of terrorism (referred to as the Second Intifada) against Israel.

This operation marked the first time that Israel captured a large Palestinian cargo ship smuggling weapons. It was also the first time in history that any military force captured a moving ship with synchronized forces that both climbed onto the ship clandestinely from the sea and slid from helicopters down special fast ropes to the deck.

This thriller reveals the until-now classified intelligence, military operations, and diplomacy angles of the story. Israel's successful operation continues to shape sea-based conflicts over weapons smuggling between Israel, Iran, Hezbollah, and the Palestinians to this day. Generally, Israel is pitted against Iranian attempts to smuggle more advanced weapons to Hezbollah and Hamas for their use against the Jewish state.

A Raid on the Red Sea tells the story of how Israeli intelligence discovered the Palestinians had bought a ship to smuggle Iranian weapons as well as how it identified, located, and tracked the ship. The book also gives an exclusive, detailed description of the close working relationship between Israeli and U.S. intelligence in locating and tracking the ship at critical moments. This included the time when Israeli intelligence was concerned that it had lost the ship, meaning that months of effort had potentially gone down the drain. It gives an insider's view of how the daring capture operation was planned and how the Israeli Navy Seals had to make last-minute improvisations as they faced a torrential storm.

Brig. Gen. Amos Gilboa (Ret.) is the ultimate insider to tell the story, having served as the number 2 in Israel Defense Forces Intelligence (IDI) from 1982 to 1984 and having worked in other intelligence capacities for decades. In Israel, the Israel Defense Forces (IDF) Intelligence Directorate is by far the most powerful of the intelligence services. As such, his experience gives Gilboa far more influence and insight than even the deputy director of the U.S. Central Intelligence Agency or the Defense Intelligence Agency. Most critical to the story, Gilboa knows the key characters extremely well, including Hezbollah military chief Imad Mughniyeh, who was the likely mastermind of the *Karine A* weapons-smuggling plot. In 1984 Gilboa had briefed U.S. senator Daniel Inouye (D-HI) during a crucial and off-the-books visit, confirming and revealing aspects of Mughniyeh's involvement in planning the terrorist attack that had killed 241 U.S. Marines in Beirut, Lebanon, in 1983. At the time Inouye confided to Gilboa that the United States was still trying to understand what had occurred before forging its future Middle East policy. Gilboa's peerless knowledge of Mughniyeh was likely among the reasons that Israeli intelligence chose him to perform the classified operational review of the *Karine A* saga, which Gilboa is only revealing now.

This book also tells the diplomatic side of the story and its far-reaching consequences of the George W. Bush administration's calling for Yasir Arafat to be replaced as leader of the Palestinian Authority. This was part of a turning point in the U.S. administration's political strategy regarding the Israeli-Palestinian conflict and its grasping of Iran's broader role in promoting terrorism and instability in the Middle East. Iran's significance was highlighted in an August 2002 speech by U.S. undersecretary of state for arms control and international security John Bolton, who went on to serve in 2018–19 as the national security adviser to President Donald Trump, heavily shaping the country's Iran policy.

The book is based on classified intelligence materials, studies, minutes of deliberations, stenographic reports, original drafts of documents, and transcripts of the interrogations Shin Bet (Israel Security Agency) conducted of the *Karine A*'s crew. As part of his classified review for Israeli intelligence, Gilboa also conducted a long series of personal interviews with many of the book's intelligence and black ops heroes, from the most junior to the most senior. Portions of the chapters relating to the United States, Iran, Hezbollah, and the rivalry between Ariel Sharon and Yasir Arafat are based on interviews and materials that the book's English editor, *Jerusalem Post* correspondent Yonah Bob, gathered from high-level Bush administration officials, Israeli intelligence officials, and other sources.

The intelligence picture that the book paints is based on what Israeli and U.S. intelligence knew in real time, some of which was incomplete or even incorrect, as with any complex operation. After-the-fact interrogations of the *Karine A*'s crew revealed the full picture and filled in the remaining gaps.

ACKNOWLEDGMENTS

From the bottom of my heart, I would like to thank all of the many people who agreed to be interviewed for this book and contributed to it. Most prominently, I would like to thank Israel's naval forces, including all the different branches, though with special gratitude to Israeli naval intelligence.

A special thank you goes to naval captain Shlomo Gueta (Ret.), who helped me significantly in consulting on and producing the Hebrew version of the book, which served as the main basis for the English version.

I would also like to thank Lt. Col. Yoni Mann (Ret.), who significantly contributed to my understanding of the involvement of the Israeli Air Force in capturing the *Karine A*.

Another thank you to Almog Hajaj, from the Israeli Navy's hydrographics branch, regarding the maps he prepared, as well as to Zeev Eldar, graphic designer, for preparing the book's graphic illustrations.

A special thank you to Israel Intelligence Heritage and Commemoration Center chairman Brig. Gen. Dr. Zvi Shtauber (Ret.) and CEO Brig. Gen. David Tzur (Ret.), who made the publication of the book's Hebrew version possible.

Thank you to *Jerusalem Post* correspondent Yonah Jeremy Bob, who not only edited and translated this English version of the book but also wrote significant new portions of the book's English version relating to Iran, Hezbollah, Ariel Sharon, Yasir Arafat, and U.S.-Israeli relations.

In addition, I would like to thank my agent, Peter Bernstein, whose insight and experience helped shepherd the book's English version through multiple stages of evolution. He also made sure it crossed the finish line.

Finally, I would like to thank the many members of the Potomac / University of Nebraska Press staff whose professionalism and talent were obvious throughout and are apparent in the impressive final product. Thanks especially to Tom Swanson, our editor, whose enthusiasm and interest in the book carried us through from start to finish, and to Vicki Chamlee, whose tireless and meticulous editing improved just about every page.

Saving the most important for last, thanks to my wife, Dalia, who was instrumental at every stage, from the initial stages of the Hebrew book to the final stages of the English one.

DRAMATIS PERSONAE

Abdullah, Riad: Palestinian Authority naval officer, chief engineer on the *Karine A*

Akawi, Omar: top Palestinian Authority naval officer, captain of the *Karine A*

Ala, Abu (Ahmad Qurei): major Palestinian public figure, close to Yasir Arafat

al-Asalaki, Taysar: Jordanian, *Karine A*'s lookout

al-Diqs, Ibrahim: captain in the Palestinian Navy

al-Sankari, Salem: Palestinian diver and lookout on *Karine A*

Amit: head of the international commercial ships desk in naval intelligence

Anat, Lieutenant Junior Grade: analysis officer working on the counterterrorism desk in naval intelligence (the first analyst to foresee the *Karine A*'s threat)

Arafat, Yasir: chairman of the Palestinian Authority

Barak, Ehud: Israeli prime minister leading into the *Karine A* affair

Bassem, Haj: top Hezbollah lieutenant to military chief Imad Mughniyeh

Ben-Besht, Adm. David "Dudu": deputy chief of the Israeli Navy

Ben-Eliezer, Binyamin: Israeli defense minister

Benisch, Lt. Cdr. Michael: chief of staff to the chief of naval intelligence

Ben-Porat, Beni "the Weather Man": head of the IDF Center for Meteorological Forecasts

Ben-Shalom, Maj. Reuven: head of the helicopter desk in Israeli Air Force Special Operations

Blair, Tony: British prime minister

Bolton, John: U.S. undersecretary of state (later national security adviser to President Donald Trump)

Boucher, Richard: U.S. State Department spokesperson

Bush, George W.: U.S. president

Cheney, Dick: U.S. vice president

Clark: U.S. Defense Intelligence Agency's attaché to Israel

Dahan, Cdr. Shlomi: Israeli Navy Seals Academy commander

Dan, Lieutenant Commander: Israeli Navy seal

Diskin, Yuval: deputy Shin Bet chief during the *Karine A* affair

"Dudu": Israeli Navy seal

Feith, Douglas: U.S. Department of Defense undersecretary for policy

Friedman, Cdr. Dror: Israeli Navy Seals squadron commander

Gal, Lieutenant Commander: head of one of the counterterrorism desks of naval intelligence

Ghazem, Fathi: deputy chief of the Palestinian Naval Police and with authority over weapons smuggling

Gil, Captain: head of research for naval intelligence

Hagai: bureau chief to IDF chief Shaul Mofaz

Halamish, Col. Yuval: IDI chief of intelligence collection

Halutz, Maj. Gen. Dan: chief of the Israeli Air Force

Haris, Ahmad: Palestinian Authority naval officer, liaison to Hezbollah

Ido, Lieutenant Commander: bureau chief for the Israeli Navy's commander

Itamar, Lieutenant Colonel: Israeli Navy Seals intelligence officer

Ivri, Maj. Gen. David: Israeli ambassador to the United States

Jibril, Ahmed: Popular Front for the Liberation of Palestine leader

Khamenei, Ali: supreme leader of Iran

Kobi, Captain: head of naval intelligence operations

Kochavi, Col. Aviv: head of the paratroopers unit during the *Karine A* affair, currently the IDF chief

Kuperwasser, Brig. Gen. Yossi "Kuper": head of analysis for the IDI

Libby, I. Lewis "Scooter": U.S. vice president Dick Cheney's top adviser

Malka, Maj. Gen. Amos: chief of Israel Defense Intelligence at the start of the *Karine A* affair

Mann, Lt. Col. Yoni: head of Joint Special Operations for the Israeli Air Force

Marom, Rear Adm. Eliezer "Chiny": chief of the Naval Operations Command (later commander of the Israeli Navy)

Mashiach, Brig. Gen. Shlomo: head of the Israeli Air Force's Helicopter Operations

Meshita, Rear Adm. Yechezkel "Hezi": head of naval intelligence

Meshita, Yossi: deputy of the Operations Division of the Israeli Naval Operations Command

Mofaz, Col. Shlomo: IDF intelligence attaché in Washington DC

Mofaz, Lt. Gen. Shaul: IDF chief of staff

Mubarak, Hosni: president of Egypt

Mughniyeh, Imad: Hezbollah's military chief and one of the *Karine A* affair's masterminds

Mughrabi, Adel: head of the Palestinian Authority's smuggling network and manager of the *Karine A* affair

Myers, Richard: U.S. chairman of the Joint Chiefs of Staff

Peres, Shimon: Israel's foreign minister

Peretz, Hanania: civilian captain and external adviser to Israeli naval intelligence (and former naval intelligence officer)

Porterfield, Rear Adm. Richard: U.S. Naval Intelligence director

Powell, Colin: U.S. secretary of state

Rice, Condoleezza: U.S. national security adviser to President George W. Bush

Rothberg, Capt. Ram: commander of the Israeli Navy Seals (later commander of the navy)

Rubinstein, Elyakim: Israeli attorney general during the *Karine A* affair

Safavi, Sayyid Yahya "Rahim": Islamic Revolutionary Guard Corps chief

Sharon, Ariel: Israeli prime minister during the *Karine A* affair

Shimon, Lieutenant Commander: head of the naval imagery desk

Shkedi, Eliezer: head of Israeli Air Force Operations

Shlomi: husband of Anat

Shubaki, Brig. Gen. Fuad Hindi Hajdi: controlled Palestinian Authority's money, top official close to Arafat who oversaw the broad strategic aspects and financing of the *Karine A* affair

Sisso, Lt. Cdr. Yehuda: commander of the Israeli Navy's Red Sea Area

Soleimani, Qasem: chief of Iran's Islamic Revolutionary Guard Corps' Quds Force and one of the masterminds of the *Karine A* affair

Stephanie: U.S. Naval Intelligence attaché in Israel and key liaison during the *Karine A* affair

Tal, Lieutenant Commander: Israeli Navy seal

Tamir, Major: adviser to the IDF's chief for intelligence affairs

Tenet, George: director of the Central Intelligence Agency

Tiron, Zvi: pilot and head of the Atara Aircraft Project

Wolfowitz, Paul: U.S. deputy secretary of defense

Ya'alon, Moshe: deputy IDF chief during the *Karine A* affair

Yaari, Adm. Yedidya "Didi": commander of the Israeli Navy

Yaron, Commander: head of counterterrorism branch of naval intelligence

Yoki, Commander: head of naval intelligence collection

Zeevi, Rehavam "Gandhi": assassinated Israeli minister

Zeevi Farkash, Maj. Gen. Aharon: chief of Israel Defense Intelligence at the end of the *Karine A* affair

Zinni, Anthony: U.S. special envoy to the Middle East

Ziv: Israeli Navy seal

A Raid on the Red Sea

Introduction

On January 3, 2020, four U.S. Hellfire missiles fired from a drone engulfed two vehicles in flames as they were exiting Baghdad International Airport in Iraq. The target of the strike was so important that many feared the attack would lead to a general war between the United States and Iran, and possibly draw in Israel. The facts are still hazy, but it appears Iraqis and Syrians, and likely tips from Israeli intelligence, were also involved in an extensive months-long intelligence operation to take out the target. His name was Qasem Soleimani.

Soleimani was a chief nemesis of the United States and Israel for decades in his post as the leader of the Quds Force of Iran's Islamic Revolutionary Guard Corps. In this position, he served as the chief of Iran's intelligence, as the chief of its army special forces, and as the top adviser on all national security issues to Iran's supreme leader ayatollah Ali Khamenei. The former director of the U.S. Central Intelligence Agency David Petraeus said that six hundred Americans and countless others worldwide had died at Soleimani's hands and that his killing was more important than the killings of the chief of al-Qaeda Osama Bin Laden and the chief of the Islamic State of Iraq and the Levant Abu Bakr al-Baghdadi. A significant piece of Soleimani's and Iran's reign of terror has been conducted at sea and included attempts to transfer advanced weapons to proxies in the region.

Since May 2019, Soleimani was a key strategist of Iran's aggression at sea, where it attacked or captured ships connected to England,

Saudi Arabia, and other U.S. allies. In October 2019 Iran accused the United States and Israel of attacking some of its naval vessels. Led by Soleimani, 2017–20 also saw a marked increase in Iran's trying to smuggle advanced weapons to its supporters in Syria, Lebanon, Iraq, and Yemen as part of Iran's plans to expand and to destabilize the region. In June 2020 a battle intensified between Iran and the International Atomic Energy Agency over the latter's access to the country's various nuclear program sites. The Islamic republic is also pushing hard to remove a United Nations arms embargo that has held it back for years but is due to expire in October 2020. All of this occurred against the backdrop of recent years, in which radical Islamic terrorism—including by Iran, the Islamic State, and al-Qaeda—has become a central threat to the West. The role of the authoritarian Islamic Iranian regime as the central state sponsor of terrorism throughout the Middle East is unmistakable. It sponsors direct Israeli adversaries, such as Hezbollah in Lebanon and Hamas in Gaza, and supports proxy groups in Iraq, Yemen, and Syria. Iran's recent activities at sea relate to the standoff with the West over Iran's nuclear program, its hegemonic ambitions, and its goal to open new fronts for attacking Israel. In turn, following Jerusalem's successful 2002 commando raid on the *Karine A*, which was a massive Iranian-Palestinian ship smuggling weapons, Israel led more frequent operations against Iranian naval vessels in the Red Sea that were trying to smuggle weapons for use against Israel. Of course, for Israel, confronting an axis of Iranian-Hezbollah-Palestinian security threats is nothing new.

Both before and after its founding, Israel has been plagued by terrorism from various Arab neighbors with Palestinian acts of terrorism figuring prominently into the mix. Palestinian terrorism has even increased in certain respects since Palestinian leader Yasir Arafat signed a range of Oslo Accords with Israel in the mid-1990s. The Oslo Accords established the Palestinian Authority, which was given control of most of the Palestinian population in Judea and Samaria (the West Bank), as well as the Gaza Strip.

The Oslo negotiations between Israel and the Palestinian Authority to reach a final status deal failed. They reached a climax in July 2000 when President Bill Clinton brought Israeli prime minister Ehud Barak and Arafat to Camp David, Maryland, for a high-stakes summit. The summit failed despite Barak's offer of substantial concessions. After Sharon visited the Temple Mount on September 28 and people rioted the following day, in October 2000 a subsequent wave of deadly Palestinian violence against Israel broke out that was called the Al Aqsa Intifada. Its name referred to the holy al-Aqsa Mosque, which stands on Jerusalem's Temple Mount above the ruins of Judaism's two ancient temples and overlooks the holy Jewish Western Wall.

The wave of violence eventually grew into a widespread and sustained program of terrorism against Israeli civilians that the world would later refer to as the Second Intifada (the First Intifada covered the years 1987–91). The terrorists' primary method was leading suicide bombing attacks against groups of Israeli civilians. In the twilight of his time in office, the Clinton administration tried one last time to reach a deal or a cease-fire, but all of its efforts were in vain. The main reason was Arafat believed using terrorism was the best way to get Israel to surrender to his terms.

When George W. Bush succeeded Clinton as president, he had not articulated highly specific views about the Israeli-Palestinian conflict. He had expressed greater interest in nation-building at home than in investing himself in foreign issues. Still, he was known to be close to the Saudis and was expected to continue to encourage a cease-fire and peace negotiations. Thus, his administration, led by Secretary of State Colin Powell, National Security Adviser Condoleezza Rice, and Director George Tenet of the Central Intelligence Agency, started out with the underlying premise that Arafat still aspired for peace. Some of this perception would shift after the terrorist attacks of September 11, 2001, but the real changes would take place later as a central piece of our story.

In any case, Palestinian terrorism continued into the Bush era, and more and more Israeli men, women, and children were murdered in suicide bombings. Eventually, the numbers reached 1,137 dead, including 887 civilians.

Domestic political instability eventually hobbled the Israeli government, leading to elections in which Prime Minister Barak was defeated by Ariel Sharon. Sharon took office in March 2001. Internationally, many had misgivings about Sharon's background, though he would eventually win over some past critics. Within Israel he was one of its most storied military generals. A former defense minister, he was also known for his aggressive approach to fighting terrorism. Sharon had squared off against Arafat in Lebanon in 1982, and the conflict had sidetracked both figures' careers. Our story shows them in yet another grudge match of historic proportions.

A central component of the Palestinians' violent uprising was their efforts to smuggle high-quality weapons either to Gaza via the Mediterranean Sea or to the West Bank via Jordan. To accomplish this, the Palestinian Authority utilized Arafat's smuggling network, which was spread throughout the Mediterranean region. Arafat's right hand and moneyman, Fuad Shubaki, managed the network for him. Adel Mughrabi, the operational head of the network in the field, was also close to Arafat and had a prior background in terrorism operations.

On May 6, 2001, the Israeli Navy captured the fishing boat known as the *Santorini* in the Mediterranean Sea near the Lebanese coast. The boat was on its way to smuggle hundreds of rockets, mortars, and surface-to-air missiles from Lebanon to the Gaza Strip. The intelligence obtained from interrogating the crew indicated that the weapons came from Hezbollah. Intelligence also showed a tight connection between the Palestinian Authority's smuggling network and Hezbollah. That summer, high-quality intelligence came in indicating a clandestine meeting in the United Arab Emirates had been held with the heads of the Palestinian Authority's smuggling network, the Quds Force (led by Qasem Soleimani), and the Hezbollah operatives who smuggled by sea. Around the same time, a large volume of information started to come in about Iranian underwater experiments with equipment, but it was unclear if that equipment was connected to the weapons smuggling.

Lt. Gen. Shaul Mofaz, then chief of staff of the Israel Defense Forces, ordered Israeli military intelligence to prioritize collecting information on weapons smuggling and on trying to block it.

Israeli military intelligence and its collection agencies, including Unit 8200 (also known as "the Israeli National Security Agency"), was the central service in that regard. The intelligence units of the Israeli Air Force and Navy both reported to the military director of intelligence. Israeli naval intelligence, responsible for addressing all sea-based weapons-smuggling threats, over the summer of 2001 put together the following picture:

> The Palestinian Authority's smuggling network was seeking ways to smuggle weapons to the Gaza Strip via the Red Sea as opposed to from Lebanon via the Mediterranean Sea. This shift was based on its experience that the Israeli Navy tried to intercept smuggled weapons via the Mediterranean Sea.
>
> The Palestinian Authority's smuggling network was looking to acquire a large cargo ship (as opposed to a small fishing boat) to smuggle a large volume of weapons.
>
> The smuggling efforts would be coordinated with Hezbollah and likely with Iran.
>
> The operatives involved were trying to solve issues related to smuggling on a large ship to Gaza, such as how to unload the weapons from the ship and how to clandestinely get them into Gaza.

This picture led Israeli intelligence collection agencies—primarily Unit 8200 and the foreign-spying legendary Mossad—to throw a much wider net to uncover the where and the how of the smuggling network's moves to acquire a large cargo ship.

Time passed, but no single piece of intelligence confirmed that the Palestinian Authority had purchased a ship. The intelligence was too vague to decipher the full picture. The naval intelligence staff felt instinctively that something was happening—a smuggling effort involving large quantities of weapons was in motion—but it still had no real and reliable intelligence to go on. If the agents could not pierce the veil, they would fail to thwart the nefarious weapons-smuggling plot.

1

The Grand Scheme and the Ancient Grudge

Arafat's Plot

EARLY 2001

Yasir Arafat was feeling anxious but also free and unleashed. Through the Oslo peace negotiations track with Israel, the national leader of the Palestinian Authority (PA) already had gained control of the West Bank and Gaza—and a lot of guns—and he could still get something additional in the future. But at almost every major peace agreement signing ceremony, he had been uncomfortable. In one signing ceremony in Egypt, he was filmed throwing a temper tantrum, and Egyptian president Hosni Mubarak practically had to force him to sign the latest peace-related documents with Israel, documents he had supposedly already agreed to sign.

Now he could return to his comfort zone, falling back on his decades as a revolutionary, a fighter who always kept a gun nearby. The problem was guns were not enough against the Israelis. Now he had a new idea. What if his Palestinian forces could obtain rockets? If he could start firing Iranian-made Katyusha rockets on a large Israeli city near the Gaza Strip such as Ashkelon, then he could extract a whole set of new concessions from Israel about the future borders of Palestine. Then he also could return to the peace game with the new concessions and see if he could get enough of what he wanted or if he would have to fight again, maybe with even bigger rockets.

To make all of this happen, in early 2001 Arafat held a meeting with key senior PA officials who managed its weapons smuggling. Included was his right-hand and moneyman, Fuad Shubaki; Fathi Ghazem, who had served as Arafat's personal bodyguard; Adel Mughrabi, the operational head of the network in the field; and PA naval officer Ahmad Haris. The latter two would serve as liaisons with Hezbollah and Iran. Mughrabi was very close to Arafat and had wide-ranging experience in terrorism operations. He would recruit the PA's top ship captain Omar Akawi to command a ship for the operation, while Ghazem would manage some of its complex naval and diving aspects. As Arafat understood it, this enterprise represented a major opportunity for him to gain powerful weapons and financial and logistical backing from two arch enemies of Israel—Iran and Hezbollah.

For this plan, Iran and Hezbollah would pay for the weapons and transport them to a PA ship. Even Israeli intelligence is not 100 percent sure whether the plan first germinated from Hezbollah's military chief or from a top Iranian Islamic Revolutionary Guard Corps (IRGC) official, though it seems Hezbollah's military chief was the initial mastermind. However the plot originated, Hezbollah and the IRGC came up with an ingenious plan for outfoxing the Israeli Navy: They would pay for special floatable tubes to be designed that could hold the weapons. Then they would train PA personnel in Iran in diving and in how to use the tubes. The PA just needed to get a ship and hire a crew to pick up the weapons from Iran. In exchange, Arafat merely needed to look the other way and agree to let Iran place some of its proxies in the PA's areas. He would still have control and could always throw them out. It was an amazing deal.

How did the Palestinian Authority, Lebanon's Hezbollah, and Iran's IRGC start working together on weapons smuggling? This new axis did not develop overnight. The connection started in April 2000 with a series of Palestinian-Iranian meetings in Russia, Oman, and the United Arab Emirates (UAE), all of which took place with Arafat's specific approval. Subsequently, the Iranians prepared the floating containers for the weapons. Salem al-

Sankari was drafted for the smuggling operation for his diving skills and traveled to Lebanon, where he would be trained in handling the special Iranian floating containers. For the small price of letting Iran carry out some activities in the PA's areas, Arafat would receive game-changing weaponry. And in any event, he did not have much choice.

Only a few months earlier, in Taba, Egypt, in December 2000, Arafat had rejected Israeli prime minister Ehud Barak's offered peace plan, which had included a significant Palestinian foothold in Jerusalem. Now Arafat was stuck with new prime minister Ariel Sharon, his nemesis from the First Lebanon War in 1982. Sharon the "Bulldozer" knew Arafat. Back in his days in Lebanon, Arafat was known for sending flowers to the families of those Lebanese opponents he had killed. He had a sort of subtlety. Sharon just demolished his adversaries. He would be aggressive in countering any PA terrorism operations. Arafat felt the only way to turn the tables on Sharon would be to surprise him with high-quality weapons that he was not ready for—namely, rockets from Iran.

Arafat's top officers each presented different aspects of the weapons-smuggling plan. There were risks, but Iran was fronting most of the money and weaponry. By the time the ship smuggling the weapons was anywhere near Israel, it would have unloaded the weapons. And Arafat successfully had continued to shake off responsibility for a variety of terrorism operations that Israel had accused him of being involved in. He had convinced enough top officials in the European Union (EU) and even in the United States that he was a Nobel Prize–worthy peacemaker. This next scheme was a brilliant plan.

Arafat ordered Shubaki to gather and disperse the needed funds to buy the ships and hire the various crew members they would need. He ordered Mughrabi to begin recruiting key members of the crew, including Akawi. Also, he ordered Mughrabi and Haris to coordinate with Hezbollah and the IRGC on moving forward with their crucial pieces in the equation. Arafat believed Israel would never see this coming. He thought it was an opportunity to get some revenge on Israeli prime minister Sharon for Beirut.

Arafat and Sharon had become lifelong enemies in Beirut in 1982, eighteen years earlier. Each man had his plans derailed by the conflagration. Afterward each was forced off the main stage of making history and into a kind of political exile for ten or more years. The period in Beirut thus framed their conflict in 2001 as a sort of historic grudge match between the titans on the world stage.

In 1982 a much younger Arafat was at the height of his military power. He had led the Palestinians' national movement and a range of terrorism campaigns against Israel since the late 1960s. In 1968 Arafat's Palestinian Liberation Organization (PLO; the Palestinian Authority did not exist until 1993) had taken over large swaths of Lebanon, where the residents were mostly Palestinian. Hundreds of thousands of Palestinians had been living in refugee camps there following the Israeli-Arab War of 1948. The PLO fought the Lebanese military for control of these refugee camps between 1968 and 1969, eventually having their control recognized in the 1969 Cairo Agreement.

The PLO used these areas effectively as a Palestinian ministate within Lebanon, with Arafat as a dictator, and as a beachhead to launch infamous terrorist attacks across the border into Israel during the 1970s. In this period, the Palestinians also organized a series of airplane hijackings, and some nicknamed southern Lebanon "Fatahland" given the dominance of Arafat's Fatah faction of the PLO. Arafat remembered the time with some fondness. He did not have the same legitimacy he would enjoy in 2000, after he shared a Nobel Peace Prize in 1994 for the Oslo peace process, but he controlled significant territory and had significant forces at his command.

However, eventually he and Sharon ended up in a broader war that would link them forever. First, Arafat ordered multiple rounds of PLO attacks on Israeli civilians, and the Israelis countered with attacks on Arafat's forces. By August 1981, then defense minister Sharon was laying the groundwork for installing a pro-Israel

Christian-Lebanese government and for ousting Arafat. Responding to a Fatah plot to assassinate Israel's ambassador to England and wanting to eliminate the PLO threat, on June 6, 1982, Israel invaded Lebanon. Sharon ordered Israeli troops to go beyond a set line approved by Israel's security cabinet so that they could surround Arafat and place Beirut under siege on June 13, 1982. Sharon did not just want to hit back at the PLO; he wanted to end Arafat. Israel shelled portions of Beirut, and the Mossad reportedly sent agents to carry out car bomb attacks against the PLO.

When the United States proposed a cease-fire deal on August 10, 1982, Sharon ordered saturation bombing. Some experts say he was trying to eliminate Arafat before the cease-fire went into effect. On August 12 the Israeli cabinet stripped Sharon of authority to order attacks without its approval, and American officials pushed through the cease-fire. According to the deal between Israel and the PLO, Sharon was forced to allow Arafat and his followers to leave Lebanon for Tunis. Sharon said in a 2002 interview that having had Arafat in his grasp, he would have liked to have taken him out in 1982; however, the Israeli security cabinet had essentially tied his hands. After the cease-fire, Sharon got into trouble with the Israeli cabinet for exceeding his authority in the Lebanon invasion to target Arafat. He also got into trouble because his invasion led to Israel-affiliated Lebanese militias' massacring Palestinians at the Sabra and Shatila refugee camps in Lebanon that September. Sharon ultimately was forced out as defense minister and was abandoned to the political wilderness from 1983 until 1998.

Sharon emerged from the sidelines finally in 1998 when then first-term prime minister Benjamin Netanyahu appointed him foreign minister. Then he took over Netanyahu's Likud Party when Netanyahu lost the 1999 elections. Sharon completed his remarkable comeback in 2001, winning election as prime minister. In a 2002 interview as prime minister, Sharon made it clear that he thought a huge number of Israeli lives would have been saved from terrorist operations if he had been able to end Arafat's reign in 1982. All of this bitterness was fresh in Sharon's mind when he confronted Arafat's Second Intifada in 2000.

"Expulsion" to Tunis, meanwhile, had left Arafat more removed from the Israeli-Palestinian neighborhood for years. He remembered them bitterly and desired his own revenge; however, he remained the unelected consensus Palestinian leader and made his comeback years before Sharon had.

One important twist came out of Arafat's expulsion from Lebanon: it left a twenty-year-old, rare Lebanese Shiite member of Fatah unemployed and looking for a new direction. This young Shiite was no ordinary recruit, as Fatah was a Sunni-dominated Palestinian organization. Despite his being neither Palestinian nor Sunni, the young Shiite had risen quickly in the ranks to Fatah's elite Force 17, where he was assigned to guard Arafat and other top Fatah officials from assassination. The name of this young Lebanese Shiite operative was Imad Mughniyeh, and he would become the most unbeatable enemy of the Central Intelligence Agency (CIA) and the Mossad for around twenty-five years.

Born in 1962, the Lebanese Mughniyeh became close with Arafat in the short time when Arafat was still in Lebanon and when Mughniyeh was just old enough to join a military unit. (These close ties from their Lebanon days would prove crucial eighteen years later when Mughniyeh helped hatch a weapons-smuggling plot to help Arafat.) When Arafat left Lebanon, Mughniyeh did not stay unemployed for long. Iran recruited him to become part of an elite unit guarding then Hezbollah leader Ayatollah Mohammad Hussein Fadlallah. So as far back as 1982, Mughniyeh was already a unique individual whom fate had given special ties to the trifecta of Arafat, Hezbollah, and Iran.

From his elite bodyguard positions, Mughniyeh learned to pay incredible attention to detail and to exercise caution to avoid detection and assassination. These strengths would be crucial for his avoiding numerous Mossad and CIA attempts to assassinate him as he climbed the ladder to become Hezbollah's military commander and the mastermind of its most audacious terrorist attacks worldwide. Mughniyeh and Iran's Qasem Soleimani became a nearly unstoppable tag team over the years. But as Mughniyeh become one of the world's most high-profile terrorists, Arafat, for a time, took a different path by entering historic peace negotiations with Israel.

When Arafat attained a global status as a warrior turned states-man with the 1993 Oslo Accords, he achieved a new kind of high. Meanwhile, Sharon, whose comeback did not occur until the late 1990s, watched from the sidelines. He seethed with anger at the hand that history had dealt him and at Arafat's acceptance in the West. But the latter did not last. While the Oslo process had seri-ous momentum for some years, it eventually came apart. How-ever, the peace process had created new facts on the ground: it had established Arafat's Palestinian Authority in Judea and Samaria (the West Bank), as well as the Gaza Strip.

Thus, Arafat's ability to project terrorist operations against Israel was unprecedented both in his having received a plethora of new weapons for the PA's police force and in his proximity to the Israeli border. According to the Israeli narrative, later endorsed by most U.S. officials, Arafat balked at making a final peace deal. Instead, he opted for a bloody terrorist campaign against Israel from 2000 to 2005 to pressure it into better terms. In this period, Arafat and Sharon were destined to face each other for a rematch in their struggle of wills.

This bruising historic rivalry was the context in which Arafat's meeting to bring a huge weapons-smuggling ship into the pic-ture took place in early 2001. Knowing he was militarily weaker and facing a grudge match with Sharon, Arafat worked out deals with Mughniyeh, Hezbollah, and the IRGC to raise the level of terror that the Palestinians could rain down on Israel's civilian home front. He hoped his new friends (with whom his former bodyguard Mughniyeh connected him) could even the balance of forces or gain him an advantage over his nemesis, Ariel Sharon.

Enter the Iranians

EARLY 2001

In a rare public moment on January 7, 2020, Iran's supreme leader Ayatollah Ali Khamenei cried and his voice shook as he mourned in front of millions of Iranian television viewers. He was grieving after the U.S.-led assassination of Qasem Soleimani, commander of the IRGC's Quds Force, four days earlier. Soleimani was Iran's dominant figure for spreading terror in the Middle East. The Quds Force is Iran's version of the CIA, although Soleimani had far more authority to promote revolution in foreign countries.

Despite his modest beginnings, Soleimani rose rapidly up the IRGC's ranks for bravery and daring during the Iran-Iraq War of 1980–88. Much of the war was a bust for Iran, but Soleimani had pulled off a couple of rare victories by planning, by using creative strategy, and by pure force of his personality. A truly self-made man, Soleimani's resourcefulness and mythic abilities spawned pro-Iranian movements, seemingly from nothing, in countries throughout the Middle East. Until his assassination, he was the point man for Iranian proxies in Lebanon, Iraq, Syria, Yemen, and elsewhere. On January 6, 2020, former CIA director and general David Petraeus said that the killing of Soleimani was even more important than the killing of former al-Qaeda chief Osama bin Laden.

In 2001 Soleimani, at the age of forty-three, was a legend, one Khamenei had at his employ to work wonders against the Israelis. The general was deeply involved in planning how to get advanced weapons to the PA to attack Israel and in gaining Khamenei's approval of such an operation.

Khamenei, then sixty-two, had already ruled the country with an iron fist for twelve years, yet he had much greater ambitions. He had the secret AMAD nuclear program about which the West knew very little. There were also Shiite groups throughout the Middle East that could eventually be turned into Iranian proxies to tip the scales in favor of Shiite Islam. After hundreds of years of the region's being mostly dominated by Sunnis, Khamenei hoped to make this happen.

Hezbollah in Lebanon was already an example of fantastic success. But in 2001, Khamenei thought what would really make him, and Iran, a star would be his becoming the godfather of the Palestinians' sacred cause to cleanse Israel from the Holyland. He wanted to restore the Haram al-Sharif and be rid of that rotting beggar wall where the Jews prayed known as the Wailing Wall. To accomplish these goals, Khamenei, a man of religion, needed to count on men who were less religious but were men of action.

Luckily, he had two legends working for him—Soleimani and Hezbollah's Mughniyeh. Mughniyeh had already outwitted even the Mossad and the CIA for around twenty years and would continue to do for years to come. The wizard-terrorist had more than nine lives. Israeli intelligence knew that Mughniyeh had traveled to Iran sometime after Israel withdrew from southern Lebanon on May 24, 2000. He had gone to Iran to rally the IRGC's support for establishing a far more threatening front for Israel from Lebanon. With the Israel Defense Forces (IDF) out of Lebanon, Israel would find it much harder to interdict the movement of large rockets to Hezbollah. Also, short of these rockets being fired on Israel, the IDF would not want to start another round of conflict over the mere movement of rockets. The purpose of its Lebanese withdrawal was to extract itself from an ongoing tit-for-tat with Hezbollah. Without Israeli interference, Iran's sending large rockets to Hezbollah would make it the sword on Israel's neck. Years later, Israel would learn the hard way, with hundreds of Israeli civilians killed, about the cost of failing to prevent the Mughniyeh-IRGC plan to arm Hezbollah with powerful rockets.

Mughniyeh's Mischief Making

EARLY–MIDDLE SUMMER 2001

In the summer of 2001, Israeli intelligence reported that either Mughniyeh himself or his top lieutenant, Haj Bassem, met with IRGC and PA representatives in the UAE and in other locations to plot the weapons-smuggling scheme. Earlier meetings had taken place in Moscow and Oman in April 2000, according to Israeli intelligence, but Israel's spy agencies cannot be certain about their timing or the exact messenger. Yet since Mughniyeh generally delivered important messages only in person, either he or Bassem likely returned to Iran in 2000–2001 for additional meetings about smuggling weapons to the PA.

Khamenei would have been waiting in his own offices as Mughniyeh met with top IRGC officials. As the head of state, he was not expected to meet directly with Mughniyeh. But while proxies of the IRGC normally met with its top deputies, Mughniyeh expected to be granted a direct meeting with head of the IRGC's Quds Force, Qasem Soleimani, and the IRGC chief Sayyid Yahya "Rahim" Safavi. One of the leaders of the Iran-Iraq War who was involved in Iran's external operations, Safavi rose to become the powerful chief of the IRGC in 1997 and held the post until 2007. (Since then, Safavi has acted as a senior personal adviser to Khamenei. On September 23, 2019, Safavi warned the United States and Israel that "our force of defense has reached the Mediterranean Sea, and it stretches from the Persian Gulf to the Indian Ocean. The strategic navy of the Islamic Republic is now in the Indian Ocean.") He and Soleimani would then directly update Khamenei. But the link between Khamenei and Mughniyeh was as direct as possible without their actually meeting. Mughniyeh was a huge part of Khamenei's success in spreading Shiite revolution and terror throughout the region.

Mughniyeh was not a religious man. In some ways it was strange for Khamenei and Mughniyeh to have become such close allies. What made Mughniyeh different was that he did not just propose and carry out a tactical operation; that was the narrow-mindedness of normal military commanders. Mughniyeh's daring brilliance was in his broader strategic vision to alter the rules of the game and the balance of power. His smuggling plan built on his success in convincing Iran to send its top-line Iranian rockets into the hands of Hezbollah and the PA right when Arafat had finally come to his senses and was revving up to wage a sustained conflict with Israel. With Iranian rockets, Arafat could potentially ravage large Israeli cities such as Ashkelon and even farther away. And in 2001, the Israeli Iron Dome missile defense system was not even a pipe dream. This plan, if successful, would be a strategic game changer and would bring Israel to its knees more than any event since the Jewish state had turned the tables on the Muslim world in the 1967 Six-Day War.

Mughniyeh himself had jumped on the U.S. and Israeli intelligence agencies' radar screen literally with a boom: He was the mastermind behind Hezbollah's suicide car bombings of U.S. and Israeli bases in Lebanon in 1983. When 241 U.S. Marines were killed by a truck loaded with 5,400 kilograms of TNT, Mughniyeh is said to have been watching with a telescope from a high-rise building. Some credit Mughniyeh as being the father of modern suicide bombing. (When the author, Brig. Gen. Amos Gilboa [Ret.], met with Daniel Inouye in 1984 to describe who Mughniyeh was, he also informed the senator that the Mughniyeh case was personal for him. CIA Near East director Bob Ames, who was killed in the bombing, had become a close friend of Gilboa's from their regular intelligence cooperation.) A crucial interlocutor between Hezbollah and Iran, Mughniyeh was involved in a variety of masterful terrorist operations in the region and worldwide over the years. After the terrorist attacks of September 11, 2001 (9/11), some would call him Hezbollah's Osama bin Laden. Numerous efforts by the CIA and the Mossad to assassinate him were all foiled over the decades through his brilliant tactics and famous disciplined intelligence tradecraft.

Once the Second Intifada started in 2000, Mughniyeh and the IRGC's Soleimani helped convince Khamenei to build a new alliance with Arafat to escalate attacks on Israel. In public speeches, Khamenei waxed propagandistic and philosophical. He gave historical lectures about "the graceful Iranian nation displaying glory, sovereignty and dignity" and about the United States' foul influence in making the country "move backward" during the pre-Islamic rule of the Pahlavi family. He proved his regime's popularity based on the significant turnout at pro-regime rallies.

However, behind closed doors, the leader was viewed as getting right to the point. After Safavi and Soleimani had conducted meetings with Mughniyeh or his representatives, Khamenei would have noted that Mughniyeh and Soleimani were asking for large amounts of time, money, and resources. He would have wanted assurances that the potential prize was worth the cost. IRGC officials Safavi and Soleimani clearly convinced Khamenei that gambling again on Mughniyeh, this time to help Arafat, was absolutely worth it. They told Khamenei all Muslims of the Middle East would praise his daring and his vision. Safavi and especially Soleimani had their own visions of spreading a much bigger Shiite crescent across the region. Arafat would provide a major new footprint for them.

Mughniyeh would have gone into detail with Safavi and Soleimani to make the sale. Many of Khamenei's generals, who had become establishment figures and comfortable since the revolution twelve years earlier, had become risk averse. By contrast, Mughniyeh, Soleimani, and Safavi were always ready to gamble and to put themselves personally on the line; this was part of what convinced Khamenei. The risk, however, was not small. The Israeli Navy had improved its capabilities, and its catching of the *Santorini* boat in May 2001 showed it was on guard against weapons smuggling by sea. But Mughniyeh was one of the few operatives who had succeeded at times in outsmarting the Israelis and even the Americans. His new daring idea—to drop the weapons sealed in special floating tubes off the coast of Egypt before the point at which the Israeli Navy was capturing smuggling ships—was genius.

Khamenei would have been shown one of the tubes for effect. Mughniyeh and Soleimani would have also described elaborate plans to obscure the name, flag, destination, and travel history of the ship that would be used. The plan was not without risk, but it had a real chance of succeeding by using the elements of surprise Mughniyeh and Soleimani had devised. Israeli intelligence believed that Khamenei also appreciated Mughniyeh's covering his tracks; no Iranians would be on the ship at any point. There would be no full-proof way to connect Iran to the ship if somehow something went wrong and if the Israelis nabbed the weapons. And Khamenei was a gambler too. When the revolution's founder, Ruhollah Khomeini, died, it was not obvious that Khamenei would succeed him. There had been ayatollahs of higher religious rank and experience, but his daring and fast action had left his more circumspect competitors in the dust. Khamenei gave Safavi and Soleimani the green light, which they would pass on to Mughniyeh.

Mughniyeh and his "project manager," Bassem, held a clandestine meeting with PA smuggling network chief Adel Mughrabi and Soleimani in the United Arab Emirates. In June 2001, under orders from Arafat via Mughrabi, Omar Akawi acquired a fishing boat in Egypt. Along with another boat he had acquired at some indeterminate date a few months before, Akawi, Mughrabi, and the other planners decided to use these boats for receiving the Iranian weapons and moving them to Gaza. In July 2001 Hezbollah and Iranian operatives conducted joint activities to make floatable sealed containers that could be dropped and store the weapons just under the water's surface until fishing boats could collect them. At the same time, they made efforts to find divers. Israeli intelligence knew in a very vague sense that the Iranians were conducting underwater experiments with equipment, but the Israelis could not connect it to the smuggling operation.

In August 2001 the PA's weapons-smuggling network started looking to purchase a large cargo ship. Eventually, it bought the ship RIM K on August 31 from a Lebanese company, with the actual purchase carried out by an Iraqi middleman on Mughrabi's behalf. Meanwhile, Mughniyeh knew Israeli intelligence agents had heavily penetrated PA circles; however, his strategy with Iran was to keep smuggling a steady stream of weapons with the assumption that portions would get by Israeli defenses. Given the ship's importance, he assigned his top lieutenant, Bassem, to personally handle the delivery of the Iranian weapons to PA captain Akawi.

Israeli intelligence, with naval intelligence in the forefront, was still stumped. The agencies could instinctively feel that the PA had a major weapons-smuggling plot running with the involvement of Iran's IRGC and Hezbollah. The Israelis grew frustrated with their inability to obtain solid and actionable intelligence, and worried that a failure to crack the puzzle would lead to disaster.

2

Picking up the Trail

There's a "Tub" but No Ship

MID-AUGUST–SEPTEMBER 2001

Israeli Navy lieutenant junior grade Anat's "office" (more like a closet) was befitting to her lowly rookie status. Nobody knew who she was outside of the immediate subunit of a subunit within Israeli naval intelligence, though maybe some of her immediate middle management commanders were starting to get to know her.

Some low-ranking junior officers had to go through every inane piece of intelligence (aspects of intelligence collection were pretty incoherent and unimpressive) just to be sure nothing was missed. That was Anat's job—sifting through intelligence at the bottom of the line. She might sit for hours, days, or weeks without coming up with any kind of lead that was actually practical.

Sometimes during these stupefying hours of going through intelligence that led to nowhere and meant nothing, she would stare at the few pictures she had in her tiny closet of a room. There were pictures of her with a few female friends when she had just finished the junior officers' course and when she had finished the entry-level intelligence officers' course.

The room had no windows for her to even look at some of the large, imposing concrete buildings of Israeli military headquarters in Tel Aviv. Unlike her friends, whose offices had windows, she could not peek at the nearby Bor, the underground "pit" that top commanders sometimes accessed to follow important operational situations.

When she grew bored of staring at her few photos, sometimes in her head she would run through some musical pieces from her flute that she had once played. Or she would imagine herself in the historical stories she loved to read. Or she would daydream about exotic places she had been. Her upbringing had been far more exotic than this room.

During her childhood, she had spent time on a naval base at Sharm El-Sheikh in the Sinai Peninsula before it was returned to Egypt in a peace deal in 1982. She had some vague memories and images of that time, though probably much of what she remembered was from the photos her parents took. She had also spent two years as a teenager living in France when her father had a position there for the Jewish Agency, which promotes relations between Jewish communities worldwide and Israel. But that was all in the past. These days, she was leading a relatively boring life as a glorified paper sorter in naval intelligence.

But the boredom was about to lift. One day, while looking through a particular intelligence intercept—pulled from somewhere in the middle of the endless pile she had to go through—a light went on in her head.

"This tub is the ship! This tub is the ship," Anat said, practically hopping with excitement. She only recently had been accepted as an intelligence officer in Israel's Naval Intelligence Command. With two months as an officer under her belt, she was, in some ways, considered a rookie, but then again, in other ways, she was not typical at all. Yes, she was the lowest-ranking officer around, but she had been promoted and was now in charge of following Lebanese and Palestinian terrorism for the Naval Intelligence Command.

A little after 7:00 a.m. on August 15, 2001, Anat calmed herself down and started to meticulously jot down the main points of intelligence that had just come in. Israeli intelligence had intercepted an important telephone call and transmitted its substance in an intelligence cable that said Hezbollah had appointed Adel

Mughrabi, the chief smuggler for the PA, to inspect a "tub" and take notes about its specifications.

The Israeli defense bureaucracy might not have had any idea that this cable was significant, but Anat's brain was already racing. She thought, "I know that Adel is currently in Egypt. I know him well from many past operations and from following his exploits. I also know that his network has been searching for two months, with the help of Hezbollah, everywhere it can to find a ship. No doubt 'tub' is code for a 'ship.'"

At 8:30 a.m. the morning update was with Naval Intelligence Command's Research Division head captain Gil. This was the routine five days a week. Anat felt the pressure build within her. For once, she was going to have to make the presentation instead of her middle management bosses. Why couldn't her first random day making the presentation have happened on a typical boring day? Commander Yaron, the head of the counterterrorism branch, was going to be absent, and Lieutenant Commander Gal—the head of the branch's counterterrorism desk who reported to Yaron and was over Anat—was running late. Anat was going to have to step up and make the presentation herself in front of much higher-ranking officers. It was intimidating. When Gil questioned someone, it could practically become a contact sport. She would have to have laser-fast and exact responses. If she missed anything, she might be embarrassed. "What? You didn't catch that crucial piece of intelligence? Why did you forget to mention it?" And now she actually had to present data about something that could have enormous significance. She prepared herself as quickly as possible. She checked in to make last-minute clarifications with multiple intelligence collection agencies, spoke with her colleagues in the Research Department of Israeli Defense Forces Intelligence, and kept going over the relevant reports.

At 8:29 a.m., she gathered a large volume of intelligence information and ascended the stairs to Gil's office on the first floor. The first floor held the offices of naval intelligence's top officials: the bureau's commander, Rear Adm. Yechezkel "Hezi" Meshita, and his two deputies—Captains Kobi and Gil, the heads of the Operations and Research Divisions, respectively. She passed the secretary's desk and walked into Gil's office. Everyone was already seated, including their aides. Gil had headed the Research Division for a full year and had previously filled a diverse variety of roles in naval intelligence. When Anat entered the room and they exchanged looks, several unspoken messages passed between them. Gil could sense that she was nervous, but there was something unusual about her. It was not quite a swagger, as Anat was not into grandstanding; rather, it was an audacity, a confidence that she knew better than the others. This attitude did not come from seniority, which she did not have, nor did it come from pride. Anat simply knew that she had actually dug deeper and longer than the others had into the ocean of intelligence information that poured into the office. The main difficulty was sorting through what was important and connecting the dots. In this area, Anat was a natural from day 1.

Anat's preparation paid off. In a matter-of-fact but powerful way, she presented an incisive picture of the links between the tub and Haj Bassem, whose name kept coming up in related pieces of information. A series of complex data items with corresponding conclusions rolled off her tongue as if they were obvious. But she did not have sole control of the microphone.

"What do we know about him?" asked Gil. Other questions followed.

Anat stood her ground. "He's Lebanese and a senior member of Hezbollah with command over the intelligence unit and is the operational liaison with the Palestinians. He's among the leading smugglers for the Palestinians; everything around him stinks of smuggling. According to the Counterterror Division experts from the IDI's Research Department, he is very close to Imad Mughniyeh, Hezbollah's military chief. You could call him Hezbollah's project manager for smuggling. The IDI says that Mughniyeh always gets things rolling and then leaves Haj to do all of the dirty work."

Hearing the name "Mughniyeh" and that of his top lieutenant Bassem was enough to set off alarms. "Tell me, did Bassem take part in this conference in the United Arab Emirates around two weeks ago?" asked Gil. "All of the smuggling network regulars were there, including the Iranians, and probably also Hezbollah representatives."

"There have been all kinds of hints that Haj Bassem was there, but we don't have clear evidence to confirm that," Anat responded.

"We assume with a high level of certainty that he was there," interjected Commander Yoki, head of the intelligence collection branch of the Operations Division of naval intelligence. "Wherever we see smuggling and Iranians, he's always there. He's an expert at preparing 'crates,' and who knows what they might be doing with them?"

Some part of intelligence gathering was doing the best you could slowly and empirically to piece together a massive puzzle with an almost scientific level of detachment and objectivity. But some of it, such as Yoki's comment, was more about gut instincts that developed after years of experience with how the world worked and about being able to sniff out a trail from small hints that only meant something to the initiated.

"The problem is that we don't really know what happened at the UAE conference," Gil cautioned. "We're giving our best estimate, and I think we're probably correct: the Palestinians, Iranians, and Hezbollah are planning something big with smuggling weapons in the near future. But what will they be smuggling? Who? How? Where? We have no answers." Israeli intelligence knew that the Iranians were developing some kind of new underwater capability but did not know what kind of weapons it related to or how the new development would impact Israel.

"And they have Adel working on locating a ship appropriate for smuggling," Anat added.

Gil was most concerned about the Haj Bassem–Adel Mughrabi connection with the most advanced of the smuggling efforts. He ordered a review of all earlier material linking the two as well as the tracking of Adel's expected upcoming travels from Egypt to Lebanon to meet with Bassem. Also, Omar Akawi's name came up in Egypt in connection with Adel. Gil said the IDI and the Mossad would need to step up their surveillance efforts of these associates and issues. Gil knew that Akawi was a top Palestinian ship captain.

Anat returned to her tiny room. The update had run for ninety minutes, but she felt as if she had survived a ninety-year battle. Her adrenaline was still running, like a car whose wheels could not stop spinning, but she was physically and mentally spent by the experience.

Many people in similar situations retreated to whiskey or vodka. At least while still in the office, she resorted to the security of a caffeine high from her cola bottle, which was always on standby.

Having survived the trial before Gil and the other officers, her mind began to drift. She started to envision the Sbarro Restaurant in Jerusalem. Almost a week earlier, a suicide bombing at the Sbarro pizzeria at the corner of King George Street and Jaffa Road had killed 15 people, including 7 children, and injured about 130.

The suicide bomber had concealed explosives in a guitar case, which he had carried with him into Jerusalem. He entered the restaurant just before 2:00 p.m. and detonated the five- to ten-kilogram bomb. Packed with nails, screws, and bolts to ensure maximum damage, it completely gutted the restaurant and killed the terrorist. His controller had been on a list of wanted terrorists that Israel had submitted to the PA the week before the attack. Hamas and the Islamic Jihad both claimed responsibility for the attack.

Esther Shoshan, one of the victims, described the mayhem from the attack:

> Then there was an enormous blast. The place went dark. People started screaming: "Pigua! Pigua!" [Terror attack! Terror attack!] But at first, I didn't believe it. People shouted: "Get out! There may be another blast." Finally, we ran downstairs. There was a terrible stench. I saw body parts everywhere—here a limb, there a head. . . . I searched for my children. My two daughters who had gone to the car-park arrived seconds later. The older one came inside and found Miriam and Yocheved. They were on fire. She managed to put out the flames but was then rushed away by rescue workers.

Anat couldn't stop thinking about the tragic events. President George W. Bush had responded with a strong public condemnation:

"I deplore and strongly condemn the terrorist bombing in downtown Jerusalem today. My heartfelt sympathies and those of the American people are with the victims of this terrible tragedy and their families." Secretary-General Kofi Annan of the United Nations (UN) also condemned the "terror attack by a suicide bomber in Jerusalem," saying he deplored "all acts of terror" and was "deeply disturbed by the terrible loss of life."

This bombing, however, was nothing compared to the disaster Israel might face if Anat's suspicions were correct about the size of what the PA, Hezbollah, and Iran were planning. Mughniyeh's involvement was particularly disturbing.

Then Gal's voice broke her concentration. "Maybe the tub isn't even a ship," he called out in the informal manner in which he ran the desk. He was her commander, but their close interactions made them more like equal partners. Lifting the large file of intelligence, she went next door to see what he was talking about.

Gal had been busy reading through the intelligence information about the tub. As part of the navy's elite intelligence section, he also had been coming into the office early most mornings during his six months running the counterterrorism desk.

He was not a navy man. Rather, he was an Arabist, an expert in analyzing intelligence regarding the various Arab neighbors of Israel's. He was also a techy and an alumni of the IDI's Unit 8200, which gathered the IDF's signals intelligence and was considered the Israeli version of the U.S. National Security Agency. Now he was applying those skills to thwarting terrorists' smuggling efforts by sea.

The problem, as is frequently the case, was that the intelligence coming in had provided a mixed picture. Gal said, "Adel and Haj Bassem know something here about a ship which we still don't know. So the intelligence doesn't make any sense to us. We need to get into their heads."

"I can't tell if they purchased a ship or if they are looking at one seriously but are still undecided and are still looking at other ships," said Anat.

"Let's wait for Yaron. He won't be here until tomorrow," Gal concluded.

Anat nodded her head. Commander Yaron was Gal's boss and was viewed as the maestro when it came to counterterrorism issues. She left the room, dropped off the file, and went up the stairs toward the bathroom, since she did not have one nearby on her floor.

Late that night, Anat left the naval headquarters building with her husband, Shlomi, a major in the Operations Division of naval intelligence. They had met in naval intelligence.

Anat's father, whom she had idolized, had spent his career in the navy. Her father eventually reached the high rank of captain and served as the deputy commander of Israel's prized naval base in Haifa as well as the commander of the Naval Academy.

Growing up, she did not see her father frequently due to his regular naval deployments. However, once she was a teenager and he retired from the navy to take a desk job at the Defense Ministry, he regularly took her touring around the country and helped her with homework. She identified with his genuineness and ironclad commitment to what he believed in. Ever since she was a schoolgirl, as long as she was positive that she was right, Anat exhibited a persistence and stubbornness in the face of others who might disagree with her judgment.

Joining the navy was in her blood. After her father spent his military career in the navy, her brother, older by four years, joined the navy and served on a submarine. Her younger sister would eventually join the navy as well.

So maybe it was not a surprise that she fell for a navy guy such as Shlomi. When they met, she was still an enlisted soldier fulfilling her required service time of two years, just as the vast majority of Israeli adolescents do. Shlomi was a junior officer.

It was socially acceptable for junior officers and enlisted soldiers to mingle in the mess hall, in the corridors, and in some of the grassy areas that were only a few minutes' walk from the navy's headquarters. But it wasn't love at first sight. Shlomi pursued Anat repeatedly before she relented to his advances. She was not easily impressed. But eventually he won her over.

One fringe benefit of being married to someone working in the same building, if not the same naval unit, was being able to easily return home together from work. They went home to their rented apartment. In three more months, a new home they were building would be ready. Ever one to dream in multiple directions, Anat thought to herself, "It's time for a child." Eventually they would have four children together, but that was far down the road. Given their careers at that moment, children just were not practical.

Another positive of their both working in IDF intelligence was that they could share work issues with each other. Both had top secret security clearances.

"You know that Palestinian ace ship captain Omar Akawi's name came up at work this morning?" she said to Shlomi.

"Okay, so what?"

"I know him really well. In the naval intelligence officer's course, my project was to look at what kind of intelligence could be collected from conferences relating to studying bodies of water. Akawi attended these global conferences using the title chairman of the Maritime Association of Palestinian Authority Ports as his ticket to get in. He also went frequently to top fish restaurants in northern Israel near Haifa."

With a hint of mischief of an intelligence officer who has invested endless hours studying an adversary, she talked about Akawi in quasi-relationship terms. "We had a 'break,'" she said, alluding to a period when she was not following Akawi's exploits, but now she was "back 'with him' again in combating smuggling." Despite her pride at being an expert on Akawi, Anat shared that she was having trouble unraveling some of the mysterious communications that Israeli intelligence was intercepting relating to Akawi and a potential smuggling operation.

"Do you know ship captain Hanania Peretz?" Shlomi chimed in without much explanation.

"No, but I think I heard Yaron mention him once."

"You don't know him? You should definitely get to know him! He's our guru for understanding ships," said Shlomi. He thought

Peretz might be able to cut through some of the mysteries Anat had not yet been able to crack relating to Akawi's smuggling plans.

Anat's eyes closed from exhaustion. Soon she would meet Hanania Peretz and understand just how valuable he was to Israeli naval intelligence.

"My friends, we are here right before the Jewish holiday of Yom Kippur. The holiday of Rosh Hashanah is behind us. A month has passed since we learned about 'our tub.' Have we gotten anywhere? What do we know today that we didn't know last month regarding Adel's smuggling plans?" asked naval intelligence director Rear Adm. Hezi Meshita, opening the meeting on September 25, 2001.

Meshita had served in his position for two and a half years, but he felt as if much more time had passed. His background was not in intelligence. He was a missile boat man. As such, he had commanded squadrons of the small naval combat vessels that made up the majority of Israel's modest navy. When he was tapped for a top position in naval intelligence, it was mainly due to his experience and stint as head of the planning branch in the navy's Operations Division. Meshita also had the benefit of having been exposed to broader perspectives as the Israeli Navy's attaché in Washington DC. Dedicated to overcoming any shortcomings in his résumé regarding experience in the intelligence world, he had thrown himself fully into studying naval intelligence materials and dilemmas.

The division heads at this meeting had become a cohesive team while they were following and pursuing a prior weapons-smuggling ship, the *Santorini*. Back then, they had huddled together for untold hours, developing their group chemistry and common language. The meetings had become a melting pot for the leading staff of naval intelligence. Meshita's secretary brought refreshments to the table, including hot and cold drinks and a sprinkling of fruits and cookies. Once again, no alcohol. For Meshita, Gil, and Kobi, she brought their favorite drinks in their personal mugs.

Gil was facing the wall that had a map of the world and a blown-up picture with models of all of the Israeli missile boats. After hesitating for a moment, he said, "The truth is that there isn't much new to add. We know that Arafat's lieutenant, Adel, and Mughniyeh and Iran's lieutenant Haj Bassem are in Egypt. Bassem is the go-between for Adel and the Iranians. But what's he planning to do? We don't have a clue, and we've been racking our brains trying to guess."

Yaron picked up from where Gil left off, delving deeper into the details. A walking encyclopedia of knowledge, memory, and history on counterterrorism, Yaron was unrivaled. He had over six years' experience as the assistant to the head of the counterterrorism desk and had served as the head of the desk since July 2001. He referred to intelligence reports of the Iranians doing some kind of underwater training for outside operatives, probably Hezbollah, but the details of exactly what they were doing underwater were still hazy. "As you know, we are also racking our brains over the issue of underwater equipment and training in Iran," Yaron continued. "Gal is preparing a working paper on the issue right now."

Meshita looked over at Gal, his eyes full of questions.

"The intelligence could be understood in ten different ways," Gal said. "I had extensive discussions with the head of the Iran desk from the IDI's Research Department. We tried to crack the riddle together. Their view is that Iran has a clear interest to supply weapons to the PA but without being caught."

"The bottom line?" Meshita asked.

"The IRGC has recently trained Hezbollah's naval commandos in Iran to use certain unidentified underwater naval weapons. We assume that following the training, they will start manufacturing these weapons and bring them to Lebanon potentially to be used against us."

Silence fell over the room.

The Israelis still did not know that the underwater equipment experiments were a key piece of Arafat, Mughniyeh, Soleimani, and Khamenei's plot to bring Israel to its knees. The anti-Israel axis had developed tubes that could hold massive amounts of weapons and still float near the water's surface. Using these tubes, the Iranians' plan was for a ship's crew to drop the weapons in the water at a preset area where nondescript fishermen's boats would pick them up—all before entering the Mediterranean Sea. Using this tactic, they hoped to transfer the weapons to the PA before a point at which the Israeli Navy was likely to engage the ship. But even though the best Israeli analysts saw multiple plots happening, they did not necessarily connect them.

"What are we doing in terms of intelligence collection?" Meshita asked, looking at Kobi. Kobi had been running naval intelligence's Operations Division for two and a half years. He had served previously as a naval intelligence officer for Shayetet 13, also known as the Israeli Navy Seals (sea, air, and land team), as well as in a variety of other naval intelligence roles. Kobi looked over at his deputy, Yoki, who was a graduate of the ship captain's course.

Yoki replied, "We are holding regular meetings with the intelligence collection arms of the IDI and the Mossad. We are working twenty-four/seven at trying to find key nuggets that we can focus on for intelligence coverage and going operational."

He continued, "We are focused around three key persons in Arafat's smuggling network: [Fuad] Shubaki, Fathi [Ghazem], and Adel. In my opinion, we need to add Omar Akawi, the director of Palestinian ships. Since the Second Intifada started, he has left the territories, and all signs are that he's become the key conduit for smuggling by sea. I'm about to issue an official priority request to the different intelligence collection agencies."

Meshita needed a smoke. He glanced over at Lieutenant Commander Shimon from the imagery desk who was also a serious smoker. "So what does imagery have to say?"

Kobi looked over at Shimon and thought, "My guy did great work in helping catch the *Santorini*. Thanks to imagery's research, he was able to locate the *Santorini* in a mishmash of thousands of ships in the east portion of the Mediterranean Sea and seized the PA-bound weapons."

"Commander, there is no concrete ship, so there is no imagery," said Shimon with a half smile.

Meshita nodded his head. "Something is happening under our noses, and we don't know what. Let's hope that we'll have a better idea after the Jewish holidays of Yom Kippur and the fall harvest Sukkot holiday."

The meeting ended, but when everyone rose to leave, Meshita raised his hand, signaling that they should sit down. "I want to remind you all—and I know I'm not saying anything you don't know, but still—two weeks ago we witnessed the largest terror attack ever when al-Qaeda terrorists took four airplanes and destroyed the Twin Towers in New York, crashed into the Pentagon, and killed almost three thousand people. This is our point of reference with the United States and the world. We are in a new era—part of the United States' global war on terrorism. I still don't know how this will impact us. But my estimate is that Palestinian terrorism will increase and that the PA's motivation for smuggling advanced weapons will go up. And it is already high."

After the office had emptied, Meshita finally got to light one of his Marlboro Lights cigarettes. He called his wife, Revital, and said, "I'm leaving for home now."

"Sounds good. Someone wants to speak to you."

"Dad? We won our basketball game tonight, so we get to advance to the higher division!" he heard his oldest son's voice.

"Way to go! Way to go!" Meshita said to his son, a star basketball player with his hometown team south of the Lower Galilee. It was good to remember what he was fighting for.

An Epiphany but Still No Ship

EARLY OCTOBER 2001

The eve of the Jewish fall harvest holiday of Sukkot fell on October 1, 2001. Shootings and other terrorist attacks had occurred in the meantime despite Israeli foreign minister Shimon Peres's having reached a cease-fire with Palestinian Authority president Yasir Arafat leading into Yom Kippur only a few days earlier. Everyone in Israeli naval intelligence was getting ready for the extended weeklong national vacation that came with Sukkot. Gil was preparing to leave work for his house in the country's center, about thirty minutes away from naval headquarters in Tel Aviv. He was just taking one last look at his computer monitor when surprisingly Yaron called on the telephone. "Gal and I are coming up to you."

"Come on up!" answered Gil, a bit startled.

Gal arrived out of breath and told Gil, "We have intelligence information from a good source that says Adel Mughrabi is flying to Sudan with eight Egyptians."

Gil was buoyant. Finally, concrete information from a good source! But where would it lead? "What does Adel need with Egyptian fishermen? What business does he have in Sudan? And where in Sudan?" asked Gil, starting to interrogate the men.

"Something sea-based is planned from Sudan, probably smuggling. Remember, the intelligence information from a few days ago said that Sudan has a weapons stockpile earmarked for the PA," Gal responded.

"Maybe we are on the verge of getting somewhere," Gil thought out loud. "Gal, can you pop into the office during the vacation period?"

"For sure," said Gal, while privately thinking that he would pay for this on his family's end of things.

When Gal came into the intelligence operations center over vacation, he picked up the material that had been left for him and went up to his office. It was a depressing day. That evening, the Palestinians had penetrated a West Bank settlement, killing two people and injuring fifteen. Also, on October 2, 2001, U.S. president Bush had announced his vision of a Palestinian state alongside Israel. "The idea of a Palestinian state has always been a part of a vision, so long as the right of Israel to exist is respected," Bush told reporters. This was music to Arafat's ears and a blow to Sharon.

Since becoming prime minister seven months earlier in March 2001, Sharon had worked tirelessly to turn Bush against Arafat and recast the PA leader from respected statesman to disgraced terrorist. Sharon had not only failed, but with Bush's formal endorsement of a Palestinian state, the Israeli prime minister also would now have to cope with U.S. momentum empowering Arafat with even greater legitimacy.

But Prime Minister Sharon's problems at the statecraft level were not Gal's concerns. Gal was focused on his job. He started to read some newly received information: "Akawi was given pictures of the eight Egyptians as well as of Riad Abdullah and Ibrahim al-Diqs."

He read it a second and third time. The names were well known to him. Riad had been a chief commercial ships' engineer and a *nakiv* (captain) in the Palestinian Naval Police who was known for his connections with Mughrabi, Fathi, and Akawi. He was connected with Akawi's smuggling operations, and he lived with his family in Jordan. Ibrahim was a ship captain, a graduate of the Libyan Naval Academy, an officer in the Palestinian Navy, and a close associate of Riad's and Akawi's.

Suddenly, Gal started to connect the dots between the many different pieces of intelligence information. In place of the dark haze, a partial picture started to form: Mughrabi—meaning Arafat and the PA—was gathering together a ship's crew. It had to be for a commercial ship because the crew had at least ten people, and at least one of them had the profile of a chief engineering officer. The group was connected to weapons smuggling because Palestinian Naval Police officials who were often involved with smuggling were part of the crew. Gal was overcome. It was all coming together.

"Adel has already tried to smuggle four times, and now he is trying a fifth time," Gal thought as he started to dial Yaron's house. "But will the smuggling come from Sudan?" he asked himself as he started to report his findings to Yaron.

Later the Israelis would learn the stop in Sudan and the goods picked up there were part of an elaborate fake-out plan by Arafat's Mughrabi, Hezbollah's Mughniyeh, and Iran's Soleimani. For the time being, that deception was working perfectly as a smoke screen to distract even the best efforts of the Mossad, Unit 8200, and the naval intelligence analysts to crack the scheme being hatched.

"Gal," Yaron sighed after hearing the news, "it all sounds good, but we don't have a ship!"

That was the work of intelligence officers. Even epiphany-type moments often still added just one more piece in a puzzle that seemingly took forever to solve. But they did not have forever.

A Game Changer Waiting to Happen

During the daily update in the intelligence officers' conference room at navy headquarters following the Sukkot holiday, everyone was talking about the Americans' attack on Afghanistan on October 7, 2001, that had started only two days before. It was less than a month after al-Qaeda led the 9/11 attacks on the United States. President Bush had given the Taliban an ultimatum: hand over Osama bin Laden and the leadership of al-Qaeda behind the attacks and destroy al-Qaeda's bases. The Taliban had refused.

President Bush then altered the direction of his presidency from nation-building and avoiding foreign entanglements to retaliating with devastating power against al-Qaeda and the Taliban. In fact, the U.S. search for bin Laden would later help Israel in crucial ways with stopping the smuggling plot. (This convergence of U.S. and Israeli interests may not have been all that different from what led to the assassination of Qasem Soleimani on January 3, 2020.)

But Israeli naval intelligence was not that far along yet in its quest to uncover the PA-Hezbollah-Iranian scheme. "Is there anything new regarding Adel and his crowd who were in Sudan?" Gil asked in opening the officers' meeting.

"No," Yaron responded, "but we have a lot more intelligence information about their purchasing ships. On its face, the information that has come in is about a Jordanian fishing company and about doing legitimate and regular business in Yemen. But it's all a cover for the smuggling network."

Not long afterward, on the evening of October 9, one item of intelligence information leapfrogged to the top of the pile:

Fathi Ghazem is in Egypt: In the last two weeks, he paid $800,000; he is interested in a house and in a small car in Egypt; and he needs a little bit more money, but he can't request it.

Ghazem was Mughrabi's superior in the smuggling network and even closer to Arafat. His presence in the field was even more alarming than all of Mughrabi's activities.

Anat entered Gal's room. Amit, head of the international commercial ships desk, was already there.

"So, what do you think?" Gal said as he lifted his eyes from his computer monitor.

"Obviously, it's clear that the money is not earmarked for a house and a car," Anat answered, penetrating the cover story with an ease that she was known for. As she sat down, she added, "The reference here to an $800,000 purchase refers to purchasing a commercial ship—our tub. And the 'house' and the 'car' are really referring to small boats."

Gal thought and continued to stare at Anat as if he was waiting for an answer.

She continued, "I think it connects everything we have followed since August: Adel, who is in Egypt, makes a request to purchase a ship. You remember the intelligence information about our tub? Adel then recruits an Egyptian crew and drops them off in Sudan. Adel brings Riad Abdullah and Ibrahim al-Diqs to Sudan. Akawi is involved somehow. And now they are purchasing a commercial ship or possibly even paying for a ship that they contracted for already in August!"

"Meaning, he has a ship and a crew in the Red Sea for smuggling," said Gal, half declaring and half asking.

"Yes!"

"But where is the ship?" Gal asked as if interrogating her. "Maybe the smuggling network wants to buy it in Sudan or even in Yemen? We have a report that the network is searching for a ship in Yemen. And where are they going to bring the weapons *from*? From Sudan? Yemen? Eritrea?"

As good as she was, Anat still had no idea.

"Okay, let's keep following it, and we'll go in to see Yaron later," said Gal.

The next day, Anat barged into Gal's room. "Have you seen it?"

Gal knew exactly what she was talking about. He typed quickly and pulled out the intelligence information:

Riad Abdullah was in Egypt, and on October 8 he had set sail with Omar Akawi and Ibrahim al-Diqs.

"We have another connection, another confirmation," Anat said with visible satisfaction as her sharp and incisive eyes zeroed in on Gal.

"You're right. The picture is starting to look clearer. But all of our questions and uncertainties still remain. Anyway, send out a priority intelligence request to the Mossad, Unit 8200, and other collection agencies. But also make sure to throw a wide enough net regarding Palestinian smuggling trends so that we don't miss anything with an overly specific collection request," said Gal. As always, the art was for the intelligence collection units to get specific enough information to nab the prey but general enough that they did not miss the target.

"How do we piece together all of these stories regarding Abdullah, Sudan, the eight Egyptians, and large amounts of money?" Yaron asked himself. It was making him crazy. The overall intelligence picture was complex, fragmented, confusing, and full of gaps and contradictions:

> The PA smuggling network was busy purchasing commercial ships and was buying and selling blankets, computers, and similar commercial items. Was this a cover? Was it legitimate?

> The network was busy buying sailboats—nominally for the Association of Jordanian Fishermen, which sold commercial goods in Jordan and Yemen. What was this? A straw company?

> Shubaki, the head of the network, was the owner of a commercial company with the name "Eastern Arab." Was that a straw company? He wanted Arafat to approve the transfer of title for the Palestinians' oil company into his name. Why? As a cover for smuggling or for raking in some new personal riches?

"And maybe this entire story was no story at all, and these were just a bunch of random disconnected events," he thought to himself. "Maybe there is no connection between Riad and al-Diqs and the eight Egyptians. Maybe there is no connection between all of that and purchasing an $800,000 tub."

His eyes returned to a picture of a 2002 Porsche in a car magazine he had been reading. For a few moments he was able to forget his sorrows of trying to crack the unsolvable smuggling puzzle.

On October 17, 2001, a terrorist from the Popular Front for the Liberation of Palestine murdered Israeli minister of tourism Rehavam "Gandhi" Zeevi at the Hyatt Hotel in Jerusalem. In response, the IDF entered the Palestinians' "capital" of Ramallah, the major northern West Bank city of Jenin, and other cities in the West Bank. The U.S. government then pressured the IDF to withdraw from these cities.

By October 29 of that year, intelligence information had accumulated that was connected to the story of the tub and filled in details:

> Riad Abdullah and Ibrahim al-Diqs were in Yemen as of October 29. High Arafat lieutenant Fathi Ghazem was also again in the picture.
>
> At first, the ship had not been allowed to enter Yemen.
>
> The ship was in awful condition and needed a broad range of renovations.
>
> Insurance for the ship was $40,000 and was still unpaid.

"We still have lots of questions and gaps in our information," Yaron said at a meeting that he chaired, "but there's already a critical mass of information. I think we can finally send out our first intelligence bulletin about the situation."

On October 30 the counterterrorism branch issued an intelligence bulletin with the following main points:

> The PA's smuggling network has purchased a ship that is being used by PA Naval Police personnel who are known for engaging in smuggling.
>
> The ship is about to enter a port in Yemen.
>
> Our estimate is that the ship is connected to efforts to smuggle weapons via the Red Sea.

Weeks later, the intelligence bulletin still had not drawn the attention of either the IDF chief of staff or the top echelons of the navy.

What had entered the mix of conversation was that the Palestinians were attempting a range of tactics to smuggle weapons. Also, Meshita, a navy operations man, had not yet really absorbed the significance of the situation. He carefully read the internal memorandum Yoki had sent around about considering positioning a missile boat in the Red Sea. The same memorandum also advocated putting together a new capability for the Israeli Navy Seals to thwart weapons smuggling in that area, but the missile boats and the navy seals operated in the Mediterranean Sea, not the Red Sea.

"Yoki, is a graduate of the ship captain's course. He always thinks operationally and out of the box," laughed Meshita in a complimentary way.

"Who is this Ismail character?" Gal inquired about the memo during the morning update on November 18. "It's the first time I'm hearing about him."

"We had a bunch of Ismails in the past," Yaron said, racking his brain. "But they don't match up with this Ismail." Ismail was a new name that came up in connection with Mughrabi.

"We know that he's a ship captain from a family of ship captains, that he lives in Syria, and that he is connected to Bulgarian shipping officials," Yaron continued. "But the most important thing is what came up from other information: the ship arrived at Dubai in the United Arab Emirates in the Persian Gulf on November 16.

"Were Abdullah, al-Diqs, Akawi, and the eight Egyptian 'fishermen' on that ship? Was this the ship that had been in Yemen? I don't know," said Yaron, answering his own question. He continued, "Adel himself is expected to arrive in Dubai on November 18. It appears he is coming from Egypt."

"We need to keep track of the connection between Adel and this Ismail, and to try to understand which ship has arrived in Dubai," concluded Gil.

The night of November 21, Anat was getting ready to go home, and Gal had already left. Suddenly, she nearly went into shock. A new item of intelligence information popped up on her computer monitor about a seemingly routine issue, the kind she constantly saw throughout the week:

Riad Abdullah has arrived in Oman. He is going to arrive in Dubai
with a ship on November 24.

Anat felt a rush of satisfaction. The pieces of the puzzle were
connecting to form a coherent whole. The ship, which first came
up in an intelligence report about the tub, was the same one that
had sailed from Sudan to Yemen, and it would arrive in Dubai in
the Persian Gulf within a few days. "This ship was the one Adel
bought," she thought, "with the eight Egyptians as its crew, with
chief engineer Abdullah, and maybe the ship's captain was Omar
Akawi. And we also knew that Adel went to Dubai. Sure, the intelligence information said that the ship had arrived on November
16—which now seemed off by a week—but that didn't really matter."

Anat was considering with whom she could bounce the new
information off when the red secure telephone rang. Lieutenant
Junior Grade Itzik, a counterterrorism intelligence official in the
IDI, was on the line. He dealt with everything related to Palestinian terrorism, including smuggling.

"Did you see it?" he asked. The two junior but highly professional intelligence officers—the real backbone of the intelligence
apparatus—had a wide-ranging conversation. They had worked
together on an internal intelligence community memorandum that
was directed mainly at the Mossad, Unit 8200, and other intelligence collection and research officials. At that point, they knew
that the PA's smuggling network was preparing to smuggle weapons on a ship that appeared to have left Egypt at the start of October. It had been in Sudan and Yemen, and was expected to arrive
in Dubai on November 24.

On November 22 Gil concluded the morning update meeting by saying, "We still don't know: Who is supplying the weapons? What smuggling method will they use? What kind of crew
is manning the ship? When will the smuggling take place? Is this
really weapons smuggling, or is this just a commercial ship arriv-
ing in Dubai? But the most important thing that we don't know
is the name of the ship. And what does it look like? Without that,
we can't start planning anything operational.

"Amit, try to locate our tub," Gil said to the head of the international commercial ships desk. When everyone had left, Gil took a peek at the newspapers. The headlines were about the expected arrival of retired American general Anthony Zinni in Israel on November 26. Working with a plan developed by CIA director Tenet, President George W. Bush's envoy was trying to secure a cease-fire for Israel and the Palestinians. Now Israeli prime minister Sharon had demanded a full week of quiet—no terrorist attacks—as a precondition to any talks.

Amit was an academic naval officer whose recent appointment as head of the international commercial ships desk made him responsible for researching how these ships might transport weapons for terrorists, what courses they might take, and which ports they might use. He was also responsible for following movements of foreign navies in the region. With one other officer and a noncommissioned officer, he squished into his embarrassingly tiny room and hunkered down. His job was to check the databases to see if the suspicious tub of Abdullah's was registered as having visited Yemen, Oman, and Dubai. Nothing showed up in his review. "I have no idea what kind of tub it is or what its cargo is, so what am I even looking for?" Amit asked himself.

On November 29 at 11:00 a.m., General Zinni sat in the conference room of IDF deputy chief of staff Moshe Ya'alon. One day earlier, Zinni had met with Arafat, and now he was meeting with the IDF high command. The former commander of U.S. Central Command, whose area of concern includes the Middle East, had retired from the military in 2000. In November 2001 Bush appointed him as his special envoy for the Israeli-Palestinian conflict, and later he became the special envoy to the Middle East. Zinni had come to Israel to secure a cease-fire, yet the level of violence had only spiked. During his visit, serious shooting terrorist attacks had occurred near the Lower Galilee and in Gush Katif near Gaza, and very recently there had been a suicide bus bombing near the well-known army base Camp 80, also near the Lower Galilee. Zinni was following the PowerPoint presentation being run by the head of the IDI's Research Department Brig. Gen.

Yossi "Kuper" Kuperwasser about Arafat's worldview. The envoy was trying to digest it.

Already when he had arrived at the airport, Kuper had begun presenting information to him about Arafat's character. "General Zinni, you've promised him that he'll be the president of the State of Palestine. If that's already been promised to him, then why should he stop the terrorist attacks?"

The thoughtful Zinni was absorbing Kuper's words. He turned away from the presentation and toward the general. Kuper had taken his current position in July 2001, but he was a longtime and unmatched expert regarding the Palestinians. He had been the intelligence officer for the IDF's Central Command, which deals with the West Bank, and had served the previous six years with distinction as the top aide to the previous head of the IDI's Research Department. That experience had led him deeply into all strategic and tactical issues relating to the Palestinians.

Zinni responded in angry overtones, "I told Arafat that if he did not stop the wave of terror attacks, he would not be president."

"Do you know," Kuper started to respond with a glint of playful skepticism in his expression, "how many people have already said that to him? What he's hearing from you is that he will be the president, and that's what is important to him. And we have tons of intelligence information that he is constantly trying to smuggle weapons into the PA's areas."

Zinni did not respond; obviously he was furious with Kuper's sentiment. But Kuper was right about the suicide bombings continuing. They even became larger. In Jerusalem, Haifa, and Gush Katif, 26 Israelis were killed and 270 injured. Hamas took responsibility. Zinni leaned on Arafat to stop Hamas, but the terrorism did not subside. It was a tense time with no end in sight.

Maybe in order to lift everyone's spirits, a variety of helpful intelligence information came in to Israeli naval intelligence:

> Some of the documents relating to the ship, which had arrived in Dubai, had been shredded when the ship was sold to Mughrabi.

There was a chance that the ship would arrive at a European shipyard in two to three weeks.

Captain Ismail worked in the shipping company that sold the ship to Mughrabi.

Even after that helpful information, Meshita was not complacent. On the evening of December 3, he started energetically grilling his two top deputies. "Okay, everyone, so what the hell is happening with this ship?"

"The destruction of documents is a very incriminating sign for our ship. It greatly strengthens the assumption that we're dealing with a weapons-smuggling ship," said Gil.

"That's true, but don't forget that we still don't have any information that directly connects the ship to weapons smuggling," Kobi pointed out.

"Just now, information is coming in about the ship's cargo, and this strengthens the idea of it being a weapons-smuggling ship even more," said Gil.

"It's clear to me that this is a ship with a large cargo. We have to identify this ship, we have to!" said Meshita excitedly as he grabbed one of his Marlboro Lights.

"We'll try to identify it using our databases and publications relating to ships," said Gil.

On December 4, like a refreshing breeze, a series of concrete and dramatic intelligence reports dealing with the ship's cargo and its crew arrived. Gal, Amit, and Anat held meetings and debated the issues before Yaron. They mostly agreed: The information showed that the ship's cargo was not commercial and was not even really camouflaged; the cargo was weapons. Further, the ship was illegal and was leaving soon!

"We're standing at a turning point, where the smuggling operation is moving from the planning stage to the action stage," said Yaron. "This is already a new situation, and our job is to provide a warning once we have the ship's name and before it is too late."

IDI issued an intelligence bulletin later that day regarding the statecraft-strategic perspective:

These actions of the PA combine with its efforts to increase and diversify the kind and quality of its weapons and represent the overlapping interests of Iran and the PA in light of the conflict in the territories. Iranian involvement ties into Iranian actions on other fronts to try to inflame and escalate the conflict.

For Gil and the others in naval intelligence, it was a nice piece of strategic writing but nothing more than that.

"As long as we don't have the ship's name, we can't even begin to plan a counter operation to thwart the smuggling. Who is going to get us the ship's name?" Meshita asked Gil.

Gil put the same question to his research staff. The staff members still didn't realize that they already had the answer, sitting smack in the middle of a huge pile of old intelligence information. This "golden" piece of intelligence information only required an inquisitive mind to reveal its game-changing significance.

3

An Intelligence Coup

The Ship's Old Name Is Discovered

DECEMBER 4–6, 2001

On December 4, 2001, at approximately 7:30 p.m., Gal was serving his turn in the on-duty rotation in the interagency intelligence operations room. He was watching CNN's coverage of the Gaza Strip. The reporter was describing the resulting destruction after the Israeli Air Force's helicopters attacked Arafat's helicopters and that the Hamas spiritual leader, Sheikh Ahmad Yassin, was under house arrest.

Gal's eyes jumped back to the computer monitor. Another intelligence report appeared, and another and another, but contained nothing important. Suddenly his curiosity was piqued by a report from December 3. Though it had been delayed a day and a half, it was marked extremely urgent. The subject line of the report said: "Terror / Syria / Palestinian Authority."

Gal started to read it and almost stopped breathing after he saw the second sentence in the report. He read the entire report with excitement. It was about problems in a shipyard with repairing an unnamed ship and the competing offers from different repair service providers. At first glance, this report was boring and insignificant. Who would be interested? But one sentence, written as if barely relevant, seized Gal's interest: he saw it twice mentioned the name *RIM*. Moreover, the report connected the ship needing

47

repairs to its being purchased by the PA in Lebanon last August, just when Israeli intelligence started to track an uptick in its smuggling network's activities.

Gal's heart beat feverishly, his imagination racing. In his brain, he reviewed all the reports that discussed "their" ship, which intelligence agencies had been following already for over six weeks. He lined them up with the report about repairing this ship, currently in Dubai. In this report, names of people who he knew were connected to Adel Mughrabi, the project manager of "their" ship—which he believed was in Dubai in the Persian Gulf—were popping up. He felt a rush: maybe RIM was the name of the ship Adel had purchased?

"That's it! I've got it!" he practically shouted. After a minute, he had calmed down enough to pick up the telephone to call his boss, Yaron, at his house. "We have the name!"

Yaron was just entering his house at that moment. "What?"

"We have the name of the 'singer,' its name!"

"What? How? From where?"

Gal explained in code, using the code word "singer" for the ship, and told Yaron, "I am going to start looking over the books."

But was there even a ship named RIM? Gal started to search through books in the intelligence center at a fevered pace. He found a few oil tankers and reefer vessels (refrigerated cargo ships) with the same name. Ultimately, he had a list of three ships:

RIM, which flew a Maltese flag

RIM K, which flew a Lebanese flag

REEM, which flew a Saudi Arabian flag

All three ships had undergone an ownership change in 1998. He remembered, out of hundreds of reports, that their ship also underwent an ownership change. Which of the three ships was their ship and was docked in Dubai? The expert in that area was Amit, the head of the international commercial ships desk and Gal's counterpart within the broader branch.

It was Wednesday at 6:00 a.m. "RIM is 'deer' in Arabic. Another name for a deer in Arabic is 'gazelle,'" thought Amit. "So I'll start checking the industry books and our database for a ship with the name *Gazelle*."

He struck out looking for the name *Gazelle*. Amit then checked all the ships named RIM or something similar and found seven. He disqualified all the ships that could not be used for smuggling and was left with a list of general cargo ships, outfitted with derricks, and ships with large cargo containers. Ruling out ships that were not traveling through the Middle East region, only two ships were left:

REEM, flying a Saudi flag, with a capacity of 1,600 tons

RIM K, flying a Lebanese flag, with a capacity of 4,028 tons

Now he was close. But which of the two was it?

Gal was shaving at the time, but he and Anat, who was hopping with excitement, were about to join Amit in the high-stakes complex search. Anat went back and cross-examined members of Unit 8200's signal collection staff who had gathered the intelligence: "Are you sure about the name? One hundred percent sure? There could be no mistake?"

Amit checked the names of the two ships in the databases of traveling ships and of the shipping companies, and reviewed the reference books. Like Gal, he was wavering. But both of them were homing in on the RIM K.

"Its recent movements would take it from the Mediterranean Sea to the Red Sea," Amit explained. "In Sudan, it disappeared. Unless there is a change in its flag, name, or its title regarding ownership, *a ship does not just disappear*," Amit emphasized.

Gal noticed Amit was on a roll. Amit was spontaneously tossing out insights and immediately added enthusiastically, "And this works perfectly with the reports about Adel and the eight Egyptians who traveled to Sudan, and this fits with our October time frame."

"We're cutting through the outer layers and are closing in on the PA's real plans," Anat said.

"We also have the Lebanese shipping company, the registered owners of the ship, 'Diana K Shipping,'" pointed out Amit. "We know it is involved in smuggling between eastern Europe and Lebanon."

Amit sent out a request to intelligence collection agencies for a general intelligence status review regarding everything related to the ship RIM K. He drew together all possible data regarding the ship and took out a picture of a "sister" ship named the *Tanga* from the commercial ships book *Jane's Merchant Ships, 1998–99*. The *Tanga* was of a similar make and structure. "That's it! We can see how the ship looks. It's the first time that 'our' ship has an image, a face, a bow, a stern, sails, and a funnel," said Amit. Its length was around a hundred meters, its capacity was around four thousand tons, and it had a two-pronged large derrick in the center of the ship. The ship's picture was immediately transferred to the imagery section, whose dark room lab started working at breakneck speed to prepare visual aids of the ship.

Shimon, the head of the imagery desk, closed himself off in his tiny room. He felt the magnitude of the challenge physically reverberating throughout his body. Once they knew how the ship looked, his job was to locate and identify the critical ship. According to the data available, it was in Dubai and could leave any day. He needed satellite coverage of the Port of Dubai (known as Mina Rashid). The Intelligence Collection Division of the IDI, headed by Col. Yuval Halamish, had approved coverage of the Port of Dubai for December 7. An Israeli company's Earth Resources Observation System (EROS) satellite would perform the surveillance. An American company owned a higher-quality satellite, but its price was higher and obviously could pose a problem with information security. Would the Israeli satellite discover the ship?

Gil, the Research Division head, was reading about the RIM K and feeling relieved for the first time in a while. Finally, there was a ship. But at the same time, doubts tormented him. "Did we make a mistake in identifying the ship," he thought, "or a mistake in attributing weapons smuggling to an innocent commercial ship? Son of a bitch! The intelligence still did not have one word about weapons!" He not only was excited about the partial confirmation of being on track but also needed to address new uncertainties and doubts. This was just part of life for the counterterrorism group in the naval intelligence branch.

In the afternoon, Gal, Amit, and Anat met with Yaron in his office. Yaron opened the meeting. "Let's say that we are correct, and RIM K is the name of our ship. Great! But if they have really destroyed the ship's documents, then for sure Adel and his coconspirators also changed the name of the ship. Now it has a different name, which is also standard after a change in ownership."

"At least we know how the ship looks—even without its name," Amit offered.

"That's true. But in any case, from an intelligence collection perspective, we need to know its new and current name," said Gal. "Plus there are tons of things we don't know: When will the ship really leave Dubai? What is its destination? Where will it unload its cargo? And don't forget that we could end up seizing it and find ourselves in for a surprise in the end that the ship is an innocent commercial ship."

Suddenly the door swung open. Hanania Peretz peeked in, asking, "Am I interrupting?"

Hanania was a man of the sea. He was a sailor, a captain, and a shipping agent. Since 1973 he had performed reserve duty in naval intelligence and was considered the father of the art of naval intelligence regarding ships. Hanania was ready to be called in at any moment, usually on a voluntary basis. The mix of naval intelligence's up-to-date expertise along with Hanania's knowledge of ships always led to stellar results. Generations of intelligence analysts got to know him, became his students, and were educated from his professional knowledge and incomparable experience. Anat's husband, Shlomi, had been encouraging her to meet him and get his help with some of her unsolved mysteries. Yaron had called on Hanania only a few days earlier to consult with him. He had not expected Hanania would return the same day that the name RIM K came up. In the biblical Jewish terminology that often crept its way into Israeli culture, his appearance was "the hand of god."

Everyone in the room turned their attention to Hanania's chuckling face.

"Come in and sit!" said Yaron, looking pleased. Amit immediately gave his chair at the conference table of Yaron's small office to Hanania and left to bring himself another chair.

"I've just come from meeting with Yoki [the head of the naval intelligence collection branch], and he's already given me the general picture," said Hanania, with a twinkle in his eye.

"Great," said Yaron and asked his secretary to bring coffee. "Now I'll give you a more detailed picture." He described the ship's weight, likely crew complement, the ports it had visited during its journey to Dubai, its expected course back to Bulgaria, its deteriorating condition, and the destruction of its insurance documents.

"I understand that my friend Captain Akawi is also part of this operation," Hanania interjected.

"Yes, but we still don't know what his exact role is," Yaron answered him. Everyone knew that in the past, Akawi had been the commander of the PA ship *Jyndalla* at the port of the large northern Israeli city of Haifa. They also knew he had become close buddies with Hanania at the shipping agency; they had even frequented Israeli fish restaurants together. All of this, of course, was before the Second Intifada, which had torn apart many Israeli-Palestinian friendships.

"Where are the ship's schematics, and where is a picture of it or of its sister ship?" Hanania asked.

Amit presented him with the picture and the schematics.

Hanania looked them over, taking some time to ponder the implications. He then asked a few clarifying questions. "Give me a few minutes," he said as he started to jot down a series of calculations on a piece of paper.

As he was completing his calculations, Gil entered and exchanged warm greetings with Hanania. Hanania returned to his work for an additional period of relative silence. Finally, he raised his head: "I did all of the calculations of the ship's cargo, gas, salary, port taxes, registration, insurance, bribes, self-pocketing of funds, repairs, and other issues. Listen up: This is the most uneconomical business I have ever seen. Every ship owner wants to maximize profits. Every one! Here, the thrust is the opposite: maximum losses! To send a ship like the RIM K to the Persian Gulf with the expenses it requires, that is liking taking a wad of money and flushing it down the toilet."

Gil cut in, "Hanania, can you elaborate?"

"For sure. Look, according to my calculations, the transportation costs of the RIM K reach around sixty dollars per ton of storage. This figure is much higher than the twenty-five- to thirty-dollar average cost of transportation per ton of cargo on the Sudan–Persian Gulf line for a similar ship to the RIM K."

"Meaning the cost of our ship is double the cost of a regular commercial ship," Gil added.

"Exactly," Hanania laughed. "You know what? Even if the cargo of the RIM K was gold—I mean actual gold—this trip with this trajectory would still make no sense economically because of the large expenses."

The room went silent. Hanania started to scrawl various sketches of the ship.

"Hanania!" Gil yelled, breaking the silence. "You're saying this proves that this is a weapons-smuggling ship?"

"A variety of clues point to that conclusion," added Yaron. "They include suspicious signs, such as the involvement of Adel and his staff. Now Hanania has arrived at the same conclusion using a commercial shipping analysis."

They returned to drinking their coffee, but a few moments later Hanania asked, "Tell me, where do they intend to load the weapons?"

"At the Port of Dubai," everyone answered as if part of a chorus.

"And how will the weapons get to Dubai?" Hanania continued with his questioning.

"It's a gigantic international shipping port, and the weapons could arrive there from anywhere, even from the Far East," Amit answered.

Hanania took this in, continuing the whole time to scrawl sketches. "Can I offer you a different analysis? I don't believe that they'll load the weapons in Dubai. The location is exposed, out in the open, and it is a well-run port with oversight. It would be impossible to just cavalierly load such weapons. It would be an inconceivable risk."

"Maybe, but our intelligence materials say explicitly that the ship arrived in Dubai and is waiting for its cargo and for the inspectors who are due to arrive," Yaron immediately responded. He added, "We also had information about containers. All of this shows that they are loading weapons in Dubai."

All eyes focused on Hanania.

"Friends, let's talk about these 'containers'—assuming they really are containers. By the way, you need to realize that a lot of the time, the intended meaning of the word 'containers' is 'tools.' Anyway, I'm telling you this as a ship captain: there is no logic to smuggling weapons in containers. Why? Because that would require them to open the containers in a well-run port, and that makes no sense to me."

"So what's your opinion? What's happening here?" Gil pressed.

Hanania turned his gaze to a map of the Middle East hanging on the wall. He pointed toward it. "Look, Dubai is close to Iran. As a captain, I would go out to sea, take a northern angular path to the Iranian port of Bandar Abbas or to one of the many nearby islands, and I would do the loading there. That's around 138 miles and ten hours of sailing. There is no way I would do the loading in the Port of Dubai!"

A debate erupted. So then what are they loading in the Port of Dubai? The intelligence explicitly mentioned "loading." Maybe Hanania was right, but there was no indication of that in the intelligence. (Despite the real-time intelligence, after capturing the ship, Hanania was proven to have been right. The whole Port of Dubai idea was a head fake to throw Israeli intelligence off the trail of the ship. In real life, the ship was anchored at the UAE port of Ajman, north of Dubai. From there, it would travel toward Iran to receive the weapons from the IRGC and Hezbollah.)

As with many such debates, this one also ended without a conclusion and with no breakthrough insights. But everyone left the room thinking one thing: the analysis that the RIM K was not an innocent ship was on stronger footing.

As Hanania was leaving the office, he shared the following: "Based on the picture of the ship and all of the schematics I received from Amit, in my spare time I'll start to prepare first drafts of sketches of it, and we'll see where we go from there."

That same day (December 5), the commander of the navy held his weekly status check. Gil presented the weekly intelligence report. He noted it appeared that "we have a specific weapons-smuggling ship that is potentially expected to leave the Persian Gulf in the coming days." The reaction to the report was not unusually enthusiastic; it was just another report in a string of intelligence reports. And the Persian Gulf looks far away. It was decided that naval intelligence should "continue to follow" developments related to the ship.

On December 6 the morning update took place with naval intelligence director Hezi Meshita. "We are holding the threats forum later today," he opened. "The naval intelligence bureau chief will let you know about the exact time of that meeting. In that meeting, we'll delve into the details of the RIM K issue. Right now, just give a general outline."

At the conclusion of the meeting, Meshita summarized, emphasizing, "We need to send out an intelligence memorandum regarding the ship and request maximum intelligence collection coverage. Let's see what the EROS satellite brings us tomorrow from surveillance of the Port of Dubai."

A special and detailed critical intelligence request was sent to the Intelligence Collection Division of the IDI, the Mossad, and Unit 8200. At the top of the list of priorities was discovering both the RIM K's new name and when it was going to leave the port. Obviously, they also needed to learn what was being loaded onto the ship; what the security arrangements were surrounding the loading, including how the security officials were armed; who the members of the crew were; and when the ship would reach the Suez Canal, among other questions. This critical operational intelligence request had a singular purpose: capturing the ship. In differentiating between higher- and lower-priority intelligence, the highest priority would be anything usable for real-time naval operations intelligence.

But—and there was always a "but"—Gil and his staff of analysts were not 100 percent at peace with the conclusion that the RIM K was really their ship. Some small doubt could always gnaw at you. Amit began searching through all of the ship and database documents about the RIM K. He looked at all of its technical specifications, its movements, and its history regarding its name, flag, and owners. He discovered its name was issued on August 2, 1998, and that its prior name was the *Luba*. That same day, it was also registered under a Lebanese flag. This information intersected with all the intelligence reports regarding Mughrabi's purchase of the ship and his plans to load it with cargo soon at the Port of Dubai.

Feeling excited, Amit quickly took his revelation to his commander, Yaron, who rushed to tell Gil. Buoyed by the feeling that they were on the right track, Gil was still plagued by the next round of questions. "Now the questions are, What is the new name of the ship, and when will she leave the port?" Gil thought out loud.

"Now I see for the first time a report estimating that the ship will leave tomorrow, December 7," Yaron responded.

They were still talking when the intelligence dispatch alert was brought in for Gil's final approval. The memorandum would be sent instantaneously to all the intelligence bodies, to the naval high command, and to the IDF's head of operations. It contained two main points:

Senior Palestinian Authority and military agents of Hezbollah and Iran are currently making moves to send out a ship called the RIM K from the Port of Dubai in the Persian Gulf.

The ship is loaded with an unidentified cargo and is projected to be leaving Dubai in the coming days on its way to Bulgaria.

The evening threats forum was meeting in Meshita's office. Beforehand, Meshita approached the refrigerator in the small kitchenette next to his office, took out a bottle of mineral water, and started to drink. He then washed his face and returned to his office. His clerk brought in pots of coffee and tea. His secretary brought the personal favorite coffees and mugs for Meshita, Kobi, and Gil.

"I don't know what all the attendees like," she always said, "but I do know what the triumvirate likes."

As she left, Meshita spoke to the assembled group. He was taken with Hanania's economic analysis. His confidence in his team's diagnosis of the issue was growing. As Shimon, the imagery guru, started to report on the expected satellite images for the next day, Friday, December 7, Meshita was able to envision a real-world operation to address the weapons-smuggling challenge before them. He said that from an operational perspective, there were a few possible scenarios: they could conduct an operation in the Red Sea, in the Gulf of Eilat, or in the Mediterranean Sea.

Since an operation to capture the ship was now becoming a real possibility, Kobi quickly moved to coordinate a meeting with the planning branch of the Operations Department on Sunday morning, December 9. So the first operational seeds started to germinate in the navy's Operations Department. The navy's security branch also issued a code for intelligence activities connected to the ship: "Milk and Honey."

Afterward, Meshita continued to read the intelligence material that had accumulated on his table during the meeting. He picked up the telephone to call his wife, Revital. Adi, his daughter, answered the telephone. "Tell Mom that I am going to be home a little bit late," he told her.

Everyone knew what "a little bit" late really meant.

An Operation's First Steps

DECEMBER 6, 2001

Lieutenant Colonel Itamar, the intelligence officer for the Israeli Navy Seals, was engrossed in a meeting with the navy seals' commander, Capt. Ram Rothberg, when his telephone rang. They had been discussing targeted killing operations against Palestinian terrorist cells. This work had been the focus of most operations for Itamar since he had assumed his position in July. A bit embarrassed by the interruption, he answered his telephone.

"Itamar? This is Gal! Do you have a secure red phone you can get on? Let's continue talking from there."

"I'll get on the red phone in a minute." He left the room, picked up the bureau's red phone, and started to take notes in his notebook.

"Listen," Gal said, "we came out of the special counterterrorism forum just now at Meshita's office. Here's the story: there's a commercial cargo ship named RIM K expected to leave Dubai on December 7—"

"Dubai in the Persian Gulf?" Itamar cut him off quizzically. He didn't understand what a ship on the opposite end of the Middle East had anything to do with him.

"Yes, yes, from Dubai. It's eventually supposed to travel to Bulgaria. The ship's crew may include up to twelve people, including members of the Palestinian Naval Police. We are trying to follow it as the cargo may include dangerous materials."

"Anything else?" Itamar said, growing more curious.

"That's what we have as of now. That's for your ears only. You can't discuss it with anyone in your unit."

"Okay, I get it," said Itamar.

Itamar was born in Uruguay, where the love of soccer was passed on within the family. A former combat fighter on a missile boat, he had filled several roles in naval intelligence both in research and operations, as well as serving as the intelligence officer for a variety of naval units. He didn't hesitate for a moment and immediately rang Amit. In the past, Itamar had headed the commercial ships and foreign navies desk. That was also where he had first met Hanania Peretz.

"Hey, buddy," Itamar started, "did you find the ship in the books? Did you find all of its technical-tactical information?"

"Of course!"

"So read it off to me!"

Amit read to him what he had found.

Itamar's next call was to Kobi of operations. They were close.

They were both "Reds"—that is, hard-core fans of the Hapoel Tel Aviv soccer team—and shared a mutual professional respect, even as Kobi was the senior of the two in terms of rank and authority.

"Listen, you got me just as I was about to leave," Kobi answered.

"What's going on? Why are you leaving work so early?" Itamar snickered sarcastically and peered at his watch, which read 10:00 p.m.

After Kobi responded, they discussed operational ideas for dealing with the ship. At the end of their brief talk, Itamar asked Kobi if he could speak about the ship with the commander of the navy seals, the commander of the combat fighters, and the weapons commander. Kobi hesitated out of informational security concerns but eventually gave his approval. "But remember, only to those three at this point!"

Itamar galloped over to the commander's bureau. The hour was late. Tomorrow was Friday, December 7. He knocked lightly on the door and opened it. Peeking in, he asked, "Ram, do you have a minute?"

In using his name instead of "commander," Itamar went against the general custom in the IDF. Captain Rothberg sat toward the end of his office, talking with two of his officers—Cdr. Dror Friedman, his subcommander for all of the navy seals' combat fighters, and El-Chai, who was responsible for the navy seals' weapons and equipment. Ram, who grew up on Israel's east coast just north of the Tel Aviv region, was not interested in the IDF's strict formalities and hierarchies. He was a man who loved being out in the field with his men. His brain was wired to always use initiative, surprise, and creativity to analyze situations. While others thought "outside the box," Ram tossed the box out the window.

He started his military career in the elite paratroopers' unit and climbed up the ladder through the navy seals. Next, he went through the ship captain's course, commanded missile boats, and served as the commander of the Duvdevan Unit's undercover special operations for infiltrating Arabic-speaking areas. Ram's experience included hundreds of operations under his belt. He had only taken over command of the navy seals four months earlier after returning from advanced military studies in the United States.

But since he had taken up his post, his navy seals had been mostly involved in special operations missions against Palestinian terrorists in the West Bank and Gaza while continuing their naval special operations. His navy seals were at 100 percent combat readiness. He had just returned from an operational planning meeting with the elite Shin Bet (Israel Security Agency), which is the Israeli version of the U.S. Federal Bureau of Investigation but is significantly more powerful. Shin Bet special operations agents going into battle also did not wear suits and ties.

"Is there new intelligence?" Ram asked Itamar. Ram's eyes lit up with obvious curiosity as they rotated away from a map he had been looking at while going over operational plans with Dror and El-Chai, and turned to Itamar.

"No, I still don't have intelligence about 'the business' we are working on with the Shin Bet, but I have intelligence about a completely different issue, very sensitive. It's about a weapons-smuggling ship slated to come to the PA," Itamar said.

"What are you talking about?" asked Ram, surprised.

"I need a map of the entire Middle East to explain," said Itamar.

"So let's go to [Deputy Commander] Ori's room. He's got a big map," Ram said.

In the deputy commander's room was a giant map of the Middle East. Ram and his officers entered the room, already brimming with curiosity. Itamar closed the door and clued them in on the secret developments as they looked over the map. The Persian Gulf area of the map was blocked by a large hanging plant. In a comical moment, Itamar fought with and tried to move the plant to the side so that the commanders of Israel's elite unit could zone in on the Persian Gulf area, eventually meandering to the Indian Ocean and to the Red Sea.

Itamar was still speaking and presenting intelligence data when Ram's wily brain went into overdrive. He started to think about how they would capture the ship. His eyes danced from the Persian Gulf to the Indian Ocean to the Horn of Africa near Yemen and north to the Red Sea. More than a thousand miles of water separated the Indian Ocean on one end to the Suez Canal and the Sea of Reeds, which Moses famously split in the Bible, on the other end.

"It would be best to capture the ship in the Red Sea," Ram said, uttering his heresy out loud. The small and limited Israeli Navy operated in the Mediterranean Sea, close to home, not in the far-off Red Sea. An adventurous, almost romantic spirit overcame him. He could barely contain his excitement. "Look at how many islands there are near Yemen and Eritrea, islands of *Robinson Crusoe*— barren of people and full of wonders."

Later, during a conversation about the alleyways of Palestinian refugee camps in the territories, he shifted to discussing the different possibilities for taking over the ship that was coming north toward the Red Sea. It was close to midnight, and his operational idea started to crystalize: they needed to bring small boats to the area of the islands, where the navy seals would then capture the weapons ship.

"When is the ship expected to leave Dubai?" Dror asked.

Ram added, "And what's its name anyway?"

"I don't know," Itamar responded. "And, in general, I have very few answers to even basic questions. On Sunday I should already have a picture of its sister ship, and we'll start to get a better sense."

"So we'll continue to prepare on Sunday, and then I'll also speak with Yedidya," said Ram, wrapping up the conversation and referring to Adm. Yedidya Yaari, the commander of the navy. Ram then returned to thinking about his combat fighters who were carrying out operations in the territories.

A Ship Takes a New Name

DECEMBER 7–11, 2011

On Friday, December 7, the question was: Was the ship even in Dubai?

Shimon, head of the imagery desk, was looking over the satellite footage taken by the EROS. The footage covered about eleven square kilometers and had Dubai in the center. He was trying to find the RIM K in the congested port area among all the ships. Next to him were pictures of the RIM K's sister ships and all of the ship's data and measurements. The resolution was poor and hard to sort through, among other related challenges, but Shimon and his staff did not despair. They had to find the ship. Kobi, his boss, kept calling in and asking, "So have you found the ship yet?"

Nothing. But then they found a cargo ship that might match the length of the RIM K. Shimon checked it repeatedly, did comparisons, and eventually said, "No, I can't say that this is the ship."

After one last review, Shimon told Kobi, "There is one suspicious ship at the port, but I can't tell you anything definitive."

"Fine," Kobi responded with disappointment. "Issue a report and make an urgent request for another round of satellite imagery of Dubai—and this time with high resolution!"

Shimon's answer lowered Kobi's spirits but also motivated him. "We need to do an intelligence collection push. We need to utilize all of our collection abilities with this 'Milk and Honey' issue," Kobi muttered to himself as he headed north of Tel Aviv to his home.

On Sunday morning, December 9, Ram was gearing up for action in the Palestinian territories and would return to the navy seals' base near Haifa in the afternoon. Saturday had been the first one he had spent with his family in a while. He rarely had the chance to spend time with his wife, Michal, and his three children: Zohar, Amit, and one-and-a-half-year-old Assaf. He lived with his navy seals unit day and night, just barely grabbing some hours to sleep here and there in the wee hours of the night, and thought constantly about waging battles. He called Itamar.

"Itamar, you're my point person right now regarding this ship issue. Get all of the possible intelligence you can. Then think through scenarios with El-Chai and our intelligence friends for capturing the ship when it comes through the Horn of Africa to the exotic islands. Tomorrow, Yedidya returns from overseas, and I'm going to discuss the issue with him."

Following their call, Itamar telephoned Kobi, who was meeting with the head of the navy's operations branch, Yossi Meshita. Also known as "Little Meshita," Yossi was the nephew of Hezi Meshita, the head of naval intelligence. Israel is a small world; some say tiny.

"Kobi, what are you doing planning-wise for a navy seals operation to take over the ship?" asked Itamar as the two launched into a conversation about operations details. "How are you going to throw a big enough net to collect all of the intelligence needed about the ship itself, the potential ports, and the potential courses that might be relevant around the Strait of Hormuz [bordering Iran and the Arab Gulf States], the Horn of Africa, and the Suez? We'll also need a life-size model of the ship for the seals to train on. We need to know: How high is the highest deck? What are the obstacles on the deck? What is the exact height of the derricks in case we need helicopters? What is the layout for the bridge and the other rooms? My head is hurting from all of the details I'll need to present to Ram and the seals."

"We've already scheduled a meeting with the Mossad, Unit 8200, and the other intelligence collection agencies to work through the best way to approach the collection issue," Kobi responded. He had also been an intelligence officer for the navy seals.

"Tell me, when are you going to send the schematics regarding this ship?" Itamar asked.

"The intelligence community is trying to get this," answered Kobi, "but anyway, soon we'll have three-dimensional pictures of the ship from every angle. Hanania is working on sketches of the ship based on its sister ships, data we've collected, and his own knowledge. You know each other well, no? He's going to be working with you."

"Great! Now, tell me, is there anything new with the ship? Do we even know when it's setting sail?"

"According to the most recent information we received, it needs to leave today, Sunday, December 9. But all of that is only a best guess," Kobi answered.

(In the months after capturing and interrogating the crew of the ship, renamed *Karine A*, the Israelis would learn that on December 8, the ship had already left the port north of Dubai and sailed to an island off the coast of Iran. On December 9–10 the *Karine A* met up with an Iranian ship after Haj Bassem, Mughniyeh's lieutenant, broadcasted the code word "Sultan." During those days, operatives of Soleimani's from Iran's IRGC as well as of Mughniyeh's Hezbollah loaded the crates of weapons onto the ship. The weapons had been flown in or otherwise brought in from Iran. As talented as Israel's intelligence team was, it had missed the *Karine A*'s sneaking out to receive the weapons from Iran. The entire conversation about when it would leave was a costly wrong trail, which the intelligence analysts would not discover until later in December.)

"What do we know about the ship's crew?" Itamar continued, reviewing a checklist in his brain.

"A crew for a ship like the RIM K would include ten to twelve members," Kobi said. "We don't know who the ship's captain is. It could be Ibrahim al-Diqs from the Palestinian Naval Police. The engineer and Palestinian Naval Police force member Riad Abdullah is definitely on the ship. Captain Akawi is connected to the ship, and maybe he's in command. It appears that they have eight Egyptians who are technicians and will handle general crew duties. We don't have any information about whether the crew is armed."

"And what the hell is the name of the ship?" asked Itamar, raising his voice.

"We still don't know the ship's new name, and without that it will be very hard to keep an eye on it. What sucks the most is that we might already be staring at its new name in our intelligence information without us knowing that it is our ship, the RIM K!" Kobi replied. His spirits began to sink.

Itamar said, "Today is the first day of the Jewish winter holiday of Chanukah. Tonight, we light the first candle of Chanukah, and in the end, you'll find the ship's new name. But let's forget about that for a moment. The navy seals have a plan for taking over the ship near an exotic island near Yemen."

When Kobi heard this, he perked up. He went to Meshita and tried to get him on board with the idea. But Meshita countered, "The plan regarding the exotic island isn't realistic. But I agree with Ram that, in theory, it would be better to take over the ship in the Red Sea than in the Mediterranean Sea."

In the navy's Operations Division, Ram's idea of the Red Sea operation had come up, but the majority was dead set on taking over the ship in the Mediterranean Sea. The navy had long-standing experience with capturing hostile ships in the Mediterranean. Its central fighting force featured the crews of missile boats that would encircle a hostile ship and order it to halt. After the ship dropped a ladder for the seals to climb, the navy seals aboard the missile boats would board the ship. The seals would then inspect it and escort it to either the port of Haifa or the port of Ashdod if they found the incriminating cargo on board that intelligence had predicted was there. This series of maneuvers was part of the navy's regular drills and had been successful in the past.

The last ship that had been captured this way was the *Santorini*, which was caught near the Israeli-Lebanese maritime border in May 2001 while trying to smuggle weapons into Gaza. The operational concept for capturing the RIM K was to follow this tried-and-true approach. The ship would need to traverse the Suez Canal, enter the Mediterranean Sea, and head toward Gaza, though its eventual expected destination was a shipyard in Bulgaria. The secondary option was to take it in the Gulf of Eilat if the ship appeared to be moving toward the Jordanian port of Aqaba instead of toward the Suez Canal. In that scenario, the navy seals would be the main force to capture it.

"But how could they follow the ship's movements if they still didn't even have its current name? And when would it leave Dubai?" thought Itamar. "The picture was still obscured in darkness. Would the light break through? Maybe the light of the Chanukah candles would bring redemption and an answer."

At 10:30 a.m., Monday, December 10, Amit picked up a call from Second Lieutenant Zohar of the collection agencies.

"Amit?"

"Yes," he answered, hearing some excitement on the other end of the line.

"We have the ship's new name!"

"What??"

"Yes. Its name is *Karine A*."

Zohar sounded choked up. Amit thought for a moment that they had been disconnected. A few seconds passed, and he heard the voice again, full of energy: "We backtracked through old intelligence information on file on the ship *RIM K* and found two pieces of information from the middle of October 2001."

As she started to read this crucial information to him, Amit was beside himself. These pieces of intelligence information were uncelebrated and routine. Out of millions of cables regarding technical and unexciting ship insurance issues, one gave the name *Karine A* as replacing the name *RIM K*. It was managed by the Karine A Shipping Company with a Yemen-based address and flew a Tongalese flag.

In October 2001 the information had no significance and was tossed into piles of other meaningless items of information. No one had comprehended that it was related to the PA's weapons-smuggling flagship. The key information was not reported, but it was saved and stored. After December 5, when the Israelis made a connection between the ship Mughrabi had brought from Sudan to the Persian Gulf and the name *RIM K*, October's pile of garbage had effectively become December's pile of gold. Context had given the information significance. And what would have happened if the information had not been properly stored in an efficient system for checking later?

Amit practically leaped out of his office and barged into Yaron's office next door. Yaron immediately reported the information to Gil, who flew over to Hezi Meshita's office. The good news struck the Naval Intelligence Command and Naval Operations Division like lightning. Gal and Anat, the research officers responsible for the issue since August who had been razor focused on the ship and had little by little narrowed in on it, skipped up the stairs to Yaron's office. One could feel a sense of accomplishment in the air. "This was it! We're on the right track!"

Some people would have jumped out of their seats or pumped their fists at this moment, but Anat was more cerebral, experiencing the exhilaration internally. Still she wore an easy smile on her face from ear to ear. Her excitement and relief came from two places. First, on a personal level, she had invested an insane amount of time, energy, and emotion into this file with a roller coaster of ups and downs, wrong turns, and forks in the road with an unclear path forward. Knowing she had chosen the right path at every key point gave her major satisfaction and an electric feeling. The second level was more on the plane of patriotism and values. Anat was young, but she had a rock-solid, old-fashioned commitment to helping Israeli security, serving her country, and making her navy-focused family proud. She felt as if she was joining her father in the annals of Israeli naval history and was no longer just the young daughter living in his overwhelming shadow.

Once everyone gathered, Yaron dispassionately analyzed the situation: "Let's calm down a bit. We have the ship's current name, and it works in perfectly with all of the information we've received since October—the critical month. And maybe what's most important now is we have a basis for organizing our intelligence collection efforts. We have the name of the ship and of the ownership company. But we still don't have proof to validate the theory that the ship is smuggling weapons."

"I'm 100 percent positive that the ship is illegally smuggling weapons," Anat interjected, smacking her hand on the table.

Yaron laughed and looked with understanding at the animated Anat. He continued, "It's true that we estimate with a high level of probability that the ship is smuggling weapons, but we still have no confirmation of this from the materials collected. And let's see when the ship finally actually leaves Dubai. Without knowing this, we can't do any kind of serious analysis about its expected progress and trajectory."

The best surprises, just as the worst ones, always came in packages, one after the next. A bunch of new pieces of information streamed in that afternoon of December 10. The most important piece of intelligence arrived late in the evening and predicted that the ship was leaving the next day. Kobi immediately updated the navy's Operations Division and Itamar, the navy seals' intelligence officer.

Ram was just returning from a counterterrorism operation in the West Bank. He was exhausted and looking to rest a bit. He took off his belt and started to settle down when Itamar came in to update him about the brand-new intelligence. Ram was buoyed and began envisioning an ambush and an exotic island from which his seals would take over the *Karine A.*

"Call Ori," he said to Itamar. "If he's sleeping, wake him up." A few minutes later, Ori, Ram's deputy, joined them.

"Ori," said Ram, turning to him, "tomorrow, the question of what to do about the ship will come up as part of the operations approval forum before the head of the Operations Command, Dudu Ben-Besht, at the base in Haifa. [Rear Adm. David "Dudu" Ben-Besht was also deputy commander of the navy.] As my seals' representative, you'll raise the possibility of the exotic island near Yemen. I know they'll laugh at you, but we need them to hear an out-of-the-box operational approach."

Ori's eyes went wide with astonishment, but Ram calmly continued: "Yedidya is coming back tonight from overseas. I'll speak to him. Maybe I'll even convince him. Don't worry about it."

On Tuesday, December 11, the navy's operations approval forum was held at the base in Haifa. Different views were aired, including the possibility of taking over the ship in the Gulf of Eilat or in the Red Sea. Ori emphasized that the navy seals had the capability to capture the ship in the Red Sea even without involving the missile boats. This point was important since no missile boats were stationed there. He also more hesitatingly raised the idea of taking over the ship by coming at it from an exotic island near Yemen. "We're in touch with the intelligence community, and we'll be sending a team to do a search." When shocked eyes descended on him, Ori had the feeling that if they could have, they would have thrown him out of the room for raising such a fanciful idea.

The summary of the meeting's minutes, which would be presented to Commander of the Navy Yedidya Yaari, said:

The goal is to use the navy to stop the *Karine A* based on the theory that it's a weapons-smuggling ship. The preferred venue for action would be the Mediterranean Sea, but there is also a naval operational capability in the Gulf of Eilat. Action in the Red Sea is viewed as problematic and only as a last resort. We need to be ready to provide information to our partners in other countries if we figure out that the ship is going to unload its cargo in an area where we cannot capture it.

After the forum, Yossi Meshita, the deputy for Avi, head of the Operations Division, hurried to update the IDF Operations Command, which directed operations beyond the navy. This would be the first time that the broader IDF would be informed of the *Karine A* threat.

"I am missing one key thing," he said to himself as he went into the high command's bunker, "when in the hell will the ship leave Dubai? Without knowing that, we can't calculate the timing of when it will arrive in the Red Sea or the Suez Canal or the Gulf of Eilat. Or maybe, the ship has already left, and the Mossad and our other intelligence agencies just missed it?!"

Had the ship left? Shimon meanwhile hurried to the section for receiving satellite photos in the satellite control station, cutting through the bureaucratic red tape. He looked over the new satellite photo from that afternoon, December 11. Most important, he checked whether the suspicious ship from the December 7 surveillance photos was still in Dubai.

It wasn't. Had that been the *Karine A*, and now it had left? The image's resolution was poor, and there was no scale. He reported his findings to the navy's integrated intelligence operations center and to Kobi.

"What do we do now when the ship has set sail, and there are no Israeli Navy ships in the Indian Ocean?" Shimon asked Kobi as he entered his office. Shimon's tone was one of despair.

Kobi was deep in thought. "Maybe we get help from the Americans?" popped out of his mouth. Then he added, "Anyway, maybe we'll use the ship's estimated course and speed to request satellite coverage of all of the ports that it might visit."

"We can do that," responded Shimon.

"Can we determine with certainty that the *Karine A* was the ship that left Dubai?" Meshita asked Gil.

"From yesterday afternoon until now, we have no additional information about the ship. Throughout the time that the ship was there, we were getting a lot of information. My conclusion is that it set sail."

The navy's intelligence dispatch alert said:

The *Karine A* ship left the port of Dubai around December 11–12. The ship has a capacity of around 4,000 tons, and it appears to have weapons as part of its cargo. Senior members of the Iranian Islamic Revolutionary Guard Corps are involved in the move. The ship is expected to come to the Mediterranean Sea. According to our calculations, based on time, speed and distance, the ship is expected to pass through the area of the Horn of Africa near Yemen sometime between December 15–18, to pass through the straits between the Red Sea and the Gulf of Suez sometime between December 19–24 and will arrive in the Mediterranean Sea sometime between December 20–25.

Meshita told Gil, "What's really disturbing me are the Palestinians' severe daily terrorist attacks, which seem to have spiked as if 'to honor' Zinni." The American general, Bush's envoy for the Israeli-Palestinian conflict, was still in the area trying to obtain a cease-fire. "Who knows what kinds of higher-quality weapons they are planning to smuggle in on the ship!"

That same day, Zinni had met with IDF high command officials at the King David Hotel in Jerusalem. Kuper, the head of the IDI's Research Department, was there and opened the meeting with a presentation about the general intelligence picture. He discussed the attacks and the warnings about impending attacks. Then he tossed in nonchalantly, "And right now they are preparing a major weapons-smuggling ship in the Persian Gulf."

Zinni didn't respond. Kuper felt as if he wasn't even listening.

"Yes, yes, I need to go now," muttered Zinni shortly after the meeting had begun. Suddenly, they heard a loud explosion outside the hotel that added a tinge of drama to the meeting even though it emanated from construction work on the building. For the first time, the Americans at a senior political level were given an update about the ship. But top-down from President Bush, the American administration still had a deep and abiding faith that Arafat was striving for peace and that he opposed the terrorist attacks. All of the efforts to explain to the American officials that Arafat was behind the attacks were impatiently rejected.

4

Enter the Americans

How Can the Ship Be Intercepted?

DECEMBER 12, 2001, MORNING

The rain soaked the navy seals' camp. The nearby mountains were covered in black clouds. Ram ate his breakfast speedily with his deputy, Ori.

"Come on," Ram said, "so tell me already about what happened at yesterday's meeting."

"They wanted to toss me out of the room," said Ori, smiling. "They're going to tell the commander of the navy, Yedidya, that the primary recommendation is to take action in the Mediterranean Sea. The missile boats in Haifa have already started planning. They left open the option of taking action in the Gulf of Eilat, but it's very unlikely."

"What do they mean when they say 'the Gulf of Eilat'? Where would they plan to commandeer the ship?" Ram thought out loud. "They spoke about the Gulf of Eilat, but it was empty talk because no one asked me to prepare."

After Ori left, Itamar entered and updated Ram about intelligence regarding the ship. Ram told him to get Yedidya for him on the secure line.

Yedidya Yaari grew up on a kibbutz in the middle of the country and had served in the full range of naval combat positions and in naval intelligence. He was quiet, modest, and struck just the right balance between being thoughtful and a man of action. He had seen tons of action leading commandos at sea, having started his military career in the navy seals and serving from 1965 to 1970. In one operation on the Green Island in the northern part of the Suez Canal, July 19–20, 1969, he was wounded in a battle with Egypt and was accidentally declared dead. Six Israelis were killed and eleven injured, while seventy to eighty Egyptians were killed during the battle.

This daring operation, five months into the War of Attrition, came after Egypt's multiple narrow incursions into Israeli-held areas that had led to losses on the Israeli side. Israeli intelligence viewed the Egyptian fortress on Green Island as a forward area with advanced radar that was assisting the Egyptian invasions. Israel attacked the installation to degrade Egyptian radar capabilities and to restore deterrence against additional incursions. The operation and its purpose became a permanent part of Yedidya. His experience would be influential later in convincing him of the importance of sending a clear deterrent message to the PA-Hezbollah-Iranian alliance with a daring operation by the Israeli Navy Seals, just as Yedidya had done with Egypt decades earlier.

He left the army in 1970 but returned during the 1973 Yom Kippur War. He graduated from the ship captain's course in the Israeli Navy as well as from the U.S. Naval War College and was the commander of the navy seals before eventually rising to become the chief of the navy in 2000.

On December 12 Yedidya had returned from an overseas tour and was exhausted. At midday, he was sitting in his office and facing a large stack of papers. All of them were urgent. "Hold all my calls," he told his bureau as he became engrossed in reading. He read the bulletin about the *Karine A* and thought about how to possibly locate it in the Indian Ocean as it made its way to the Bab el-Mandeb Strait between Yemen and the Horn of Africa. Suddenly, his door opened, and one of his female soldiers popped her head in.

"Ram is on the telephone. He said it's urgent and that he wants to speak to you," she said with slight hesitation.

Yedidya laughed and picked up the telephone. He might have been more into hierarchy than Ram was, and Ram was several ranks his junior, but Ram was special and got special treatment.

"Didi," Ram began, using Yedidya's nickname, "how was your trip? Did you relax a bit? We are working our butts off with our operations in the 'territories'—until now with no casualties."

Yedidya had not even begun to answer when Ram cut him off: "Have you had time to update yourself about the smuggling of weapons from the Persian Gulf—this ship the *Karine A*? Meshita and his staff did impressive work."

"Yes, I just finished reading right now. Soon they'll present to me all of the operational plans."

"Didi," Ram suddenly got enthusiastic, "I know what they'll tell you. They're going to present to you what they're used to doing—to capture the ship using missile boats in the Mediterranean Sea."

"You have a different idea?" Yedidya asked curiously.

"Yes, to capture the ship near an exotic island near Yemen. We'll be assisted by our good friends in the Mossad and other parts of the intelligence community." Ram was silent as Yedidya tried to digest what he was hearing, and then Ram continued: "I'm currently checking the feasibility and plan to send a patrol into the field already tomorrow to find a good spot for an ambush."

"Ram, have you lost your mind and gone crazy? Stop immediately, and I mean immediately before we even continue talking!" Yedidya yelled at him, fully animated.

A minute passed. Yedidya calmed down, glanced over at the papers, and then heard Ram's voice: "Okay, then I have another idea. I have a plan in my head. Instead of capturing the ship in the Mediterranean Sea, as currently planned, let's capture it in the Red Sea."

"Why specifically in the Red Sea and not in the Mediterranean Sea?" Yedidya asked.

"The ship cannot unload the weapons she is carrying in the Mediterranean Sea. Maybe it will not even travel to the Mediterranean Sea. The weapons could be unloaded in Sudan or anywhere off the Sinai Peninsula coast. Anyway, while the ship is in the Red Sea, the crew's guard will be down. The moment they enter the Mediterranean Sea, they'll be on high alert. The crew knows that's where we catch their ships."

A moment passed. Then Yedidya asked, "And how would you capture her in the Red Sea?"

"In high-speed [*Morena*-class] commando boats and maybe with some air cover," said Ram, knowing he might be getting through to Yedidya. He wanted to achieve something new, which the navy seals had been aspiring to do for years, and he knew Yedidya longed for this too. He was right. He only needed to say it, and Yedidya conjured up images in his head of making history.

Yedidya had been the commander of the navy seals during the hijacking of the Italian ship *Achille Lauro*. In October 1985, on its way to Alexandria, four Palestinian terrorists hijacked the ship and demanded the release of Palestinian prisoners from Israeli prisons. During the hijacking of the ship, the terrorists shot a disabled American Jew named Leon Klinghoffer while he was still strapped to his wheelchair and threw him into the water. This attack was a wake-up moment conceptually for both the Israeli and U.S. Navies. It was apparent that, as with the hijacking of airplanes, terrorists could hijack an Israeli ship (or a ship of a Western country), and the state of Israel did not have the capability to confront them. Developing a naval-commando operational capability to clandestinely recapture a hijacked ship while it was underway became a high priority.

The Israeli Navy, along with that of the United States, started to develop tactics and strategies for stealthily pulling up next to a ship and boarding it. The mission was given to the Israeli Navy Seals, which participated in training with the U.S. Navy. In addition to their capability of climbing onto a ship, they added the capability to fast rope down onto a ship from helicopters. This technique was noisy, but it enabled a larger volume of combat fighters to reach the deck of a ship in a short period. For this particular operation, the seals would need to synchronize the two approaches exactly: first they would have to surreptitiously climb aboard and take over the ship's bridge and other important points, and immediately afterward others would fast rope down from helicopters. The Americans already had developed a capability to slide down ropes from helicopters: they started at a tailor-made platform on the helicopters and used fast ropes to drop down to the ship's deck. The Israeli Navy had not yet developed this capability and had asked the Israeli Air Force to speedily develop a slide-down capability.

But for years the Israeli Navy's request had remained a pipe dream in the eyes of the air force. It did not have helicopters that fit the mission, and the air force dreaded the danger to the fast ropers, knowing a disaster had occurred with a highly skilled American commando. The Israeli Air Force's proposal of using a rope ladder from the Sikorsky CH-53 transportation helicopter or rappelling from the Heron helicopter, which only held up to six combat fighters, was inadequate.

The Israeli Navy pressed, and the Israeli Air Force hesitated until 1994 when it got the Black Hawk helicopter (its nickname in the Israeli Air Force was the Yanshuf, or "Owl") that provided a solid platform for sliding down. And in fact, the air force had acquired some fast ropes. But the program stalled. The air force was still concerned about accidents, which had hit the U.S. special forces. Meanwhile, in different parts of the world, the Israeli Navy Seals began training some of its fighters to slide down by fast ropes. Then, at the end of the year 2000, Lt. Col. Yoni Mann, the helicopter unit commander, was appointed head of the Israeli Air Force's special forces operations. He came to an agreement with naval operations that by the summer of 2003, the air force would train the navy seals in sliding down fast ropes from the new Owls. Moving from the agreement to action, the air force directed its flight simulators to install a platform in one of the helicopters that could be used for fast roping and even executed a first drill, with troops sliding down to the land during daylight hours. But the capability was still far from being operational.

Yedidya was quite fluent regarding this history. Ram maybe knew less. But inside both men a desire burned to successfully execute a test run of the climbing drill after the many exhausting training sessions. When you drill for years toward a potential operation but don't get to execute it, despondency can eat you up inside. And now, as if from the heavens, an opportunity had come. Sure, it was not a ship with hostages, but it was one with weapons aimed at igniting the Second Intifada. Yedidya was silent and became immersed in his thoughts.

Suddenly, he heard Ram yell enthusiastically, "Yedidya, only a short time ago, a group of my fighters returned from overseas fast-rope training."

Yedidya was torn. His emotions were with Ram, but his mind was against him. "Ram," he said, "I agree with your concept that we need to commandeer the ship in the Red Sea, but we have no backup. We have no missile boats there. Not only that, you don't know the Red Sea. I do know it. With the high waves that we'll have to grapple with there, your commando boats won't make it to the ship, and the combat fighters won't be able to make the climb. The danger in those stormy waters is real. I have bitter experience with it."

Yedidya was then silent. Disappointed, Ram was ready to hang up the telephone when Yedidya suddenly shot a question at him: "How would you propose getting the combat fighters from Eilat to the Red Sea in the commando boats? In the Straits of Tiran are Egyptian forces that check all ships coming through. Most important, all that sailing would exhaust the combat fighters."

"Let me think about it," Ram answered. "But you should know that I'm not letting up and that I'll try to convince our senior staff it is better operationally to capture the ship in the Red Sea as opposed to the Mediterranean Sea. I'll also try to convince them to go for a surprise and clandestine approach combining forces from the sea and forces sliding down using a fast rope."

Yedidya sank in his chair. He thought, "Ram and I are speaking about the Red Sea as if the *Karine A* ship is already there, but it needs to make its way through the Persian Gulf and from there through the Indian Ocean. How can we know where it is? And if suddenly we hear she has entered the Indian Ocean, how will we know confidently that she will travel through the Red Sea?"

This issue troubled him. As he drove north from Tel Aviv to chair an operations approval forum in Haifa, it was all he could think about.

Handoff to the Americans!

Meanwhile, in another part of naval headquarters, Kobi was planning to travel to Haifa and attend the forum that Yedidya would chair. He was engrossed, thinking through different operational ideas. Late into the previous night, he and Meshita had dissected the operational issues according to a range of possibilities: The ship might enter the Gulf of Eilat and unload the weapons at a Jordanian port; it might enter the Gulf of Suez and unload the weapons at one of the ports or harbors on the western coast of Sinai, and from there transfer them through the Rafah tunnels; it might enter the Suez Canal and transfer the weapons to another ship at the port of Suez; it might cross through the Suez Canal, travel through Egypt's territorial waters, and unload the weapons at an Egyptian port near the Gaza Strip; or it might travel to Lebanon. There were lots of possibilities from the Mediterranean Sea.

Meshita was annoyed that he couldn't be at the operations approval forum to present his view. He was due to leave that same night for a short overseas mission, so Kobi and Gil would attend on his behalf. "In theory, the best option would be to capture the ship in the Red Sea," was what Kobi absorbed from Meshita. But then Meshita had added that in the Red Sea, "the navy does not have established capabilities other than in the Gulf of Eilat. Also, it's unclear if the intelligence coverage will be adequate. In the Mediterranean Sea, the navy has the maximum capability and intelligence coverage." Kobi nodded his head in agreement. Some officers had sympathy for the Red Sea idea, but only Ram was ready to go to the mat for it.

Kobi returned to his office. Suddenly the telephone rang.

"Kobi, can you come by? I am in the last office on the top floor. It's a little messy but nice."

"Chiny!" Kobi yelled enthusiastically as he threw down some papers and shot up the stairs like a missile. He and Chiny went way back, and he had been his chief intelligence officer when Chiny led the forces that had captured the *Santorini* in May earlier that year. They hugged, a true embrace between a rear admiral and a captain.

Chiny's real name was Eliezer Marom. He was born in the village of Sde Eliezer. His father was born in Germany; his mother, Leah (born Chi-Li), was the daughter of a Chinese man who had converted and married a Jewish woman of Russian descent. From his mother and from his Chinese grandfather, Eliezer had the facial features of a Chinese person, especially his eyes. This was extremely rare in Israel. When he was studying in the naval officers' course in Acre, he got the nickname "Chiny," and it stuck. He was proud of the name and of his background. He had started his naval career at the bottom: a mechanical engineer, a navigation and communications officer, and then a missile boat commander. From there he became a commander of a squadron of missile boats and a commander of the missile boats flotilla. In 1999 he attained the rank of rear admiral and became the commander of the base in Haifa and of the northern maritime area that faced off against Hezbollah in Lebanon. He had also served in various positions within naval intelligence, including the position Kobi currently held.

Kobi sat and looked at Chiny's smiling face. The smile, the humor, and the rolling laughter were some of his distinct characteristics. Many naval officers were professionals, but Chiny had a unique cool headedness under pressure. He made clear and precise decisions and was ready to be daring to accomplish the mission. But Kobi also knew about his fiery temper when his orders were not properly carried out.

In June 2001, a short time after capturing the *Santorini* weapons ship, he had finished his position as the commander of the large Haifa base. Yedidya then sent Chiny to study at Harvard University and to visit with the U.S. Navy; he would return to Israel in November 2001 with the number 2 position in the navy, commander of Naval Operations Command and deputy commander of the navy. While Chiny was at Harvard studying in a senior management course, the September 11 attacks took place. Also, the Israeli Navy decided to separate the position of deputy commander of the navy into two roles, both with the rank of rear admiral: One would be responsible for all the naval forces' actions and day-to-day operations. The second would be the head of manpower and resources, and serve as the deputy to the commander of the navy with the responsibility of assembling and managing all its forces—that is, its purchases, equipment, and training. Rear Admiral Ben-Besht, who had been the commander of Naval Operations Command, was promoted to be the head of manpower and resources, as well as the deputy to the commander of the navy—the navy's number 2 position. Chiny would replace Ben-Besht as the commander of Naval Operations Command, the navy's number 3 position.

Toward the end of November 2001, Chiny came back to Israel. He saw that he would hold the position for one year and then replace David Ben-Besht as the head of headquarters. January 1, 2002, was the declared date that Chiny would be appointed the head of naval operations. Until then, he would give lectures and work out the division of responsibilities between himself and Ben-Besht. Chiny, with his battery fully charged and seriously missing the sea and operations, leaped into his new job like a tiger.

"Kobi," Chiny opened, "give me the main points of intelligence regarding this *Karine A* ship. I'm going to the operations approval forum, where we'll be delving into things with Yedidya. Essentially, starting tomorrow, I'll be handling all operational issues."

Kobi started to speak, and Chiny listened carefully and studied him. He knew Kobi well and appreciated his diverse experience not only in intelligence but also in understanding operational issues. Some intelligence analysts were interested in studying the other side but did not know as well as Kobi did about how to provide tailored intelligence for combat fighters. Kobi knew how to make their takeover of the *Karine A* more efficient.

Suddenly, Chiny asked Kobi if he was "fluent regarding the operational idea of capturing the ship in the Red Sea, simultaneously from the sea and from the air using the navy seals."

"Of course, I know," Kobi responded. "I am discussing this constantly with Ram and his officers. Meshita and I had many talks about this. Our joint view was to give priority to an operation in the Red Sea and press for a special navy seals–led operation from both the sea and the air."

Chiny, who also supported the Red Sea concept, sank into thought. "We'll see what Yedidya says," he said, and Kobi left.

That evening at the operations approval forum, Gil presented the ship's entire story, including pictures and calculations about the timing of its movements, for Yedidya. He explained all indications were that it was planning to smuggle weapons to the PA. Gil and Kobi then outlined the different options for unloading the weapons and emphasized the risk that the weapons might be unloaded before the ship arrived in the Mediterranean Sea.

Yedidya listened and looked at the map of the wide Indian Ocean and Red Sea before him. He thought about Israel's weak ability to perform surveillance in that area versus the Americans' impressive ability, which at that very moment was being employed to search for bin Laden. He also considered the Americans' tools for detection that undertook surveillance at all times over the Hindu Kush Mountains and the India Ocean.

And then, as Gil was speaking, Yedidya blurted out an idea he had been toying with internally: "Fine. Give this to the Americans!"

The U.S. government had been using every tool at its disposal to locate bin Laden since the horrific 9/11 attacks on the United States and conducted possibly the greatest global manhunt of all time. On September 17, 2001, President Bush had stated, "I want justice. There is an old poster out west, as I recall, that said, 'Wanted: Dead or alive.'" Thus, every satellite, aircraft surveillance tool, and spy network were dedicated to locating him.

Bin Laden retreated from public contact or appearances in a desperate attempt to avoid being located by the full force of the U.S. military, the CIA, the National Security Agency, and the intelligence agencies of U.S. allies. Numerous press reports speculated about his location or alleged death, but none were definitively proven.

On October 7, 2001, the U.S. military launched Operation Enduring Freedom, counterattacking Afghanistan, the Taliban, and al-Qaeda for the 9/11 attacks and to find bin Laden. By December

2001, the Taliban and their al-Qaeda allies were mostly defeated, but bin Laden was still nowhere to be found. The United States was still investing maximum resources in the search.

Israel lucked out in this context. Under any normal circumstances, the U.S. government would not have been assigning regular massive assets for surveillance of the India Ocean and Middle East area where the *Karine A* was docking and sailing, but on December 12, 2001, the CIA and all other U.S. resources were still in a full-fledged search. Thus, the U.S. administration was more likely to share specific aspects of the surveillance it was already undertaking while trying to find bin Laden (who was not found and killed by U.S. forces until May 2, 2011). Israel could benefit from the massive global surveillance project and receive help in finding the *Karine A*.

That was what Yedidya was thinking when he made his daring and controversial suggestion. But for most of the Israeli officials at the meeting, handing the search over to the CIA, U.S. naval intelligence, and other agencies was heresy.

The entire room was in shock. They were all thinking, "Was Yedidya also saying the Americans should capture the ship? Really? Were we going to let the Americans steal the operation from us?"

"Commander, this is not the *Santorini*. The Iranians are involved. This is huge!" Gil emphasized, hinting that it would be unwise for Israel to give up taking down this big fish itself.

"Give the Americans the information we have about the ship by the end of the day, and if they stop the ship, we'll have contributed to capturing it," Yedidya said decisively.

Yedidya concluded the meeting, saying that in any case the Israeli Navy would continue its own preparations. Despite Ram's urgings for a Red Sea operation and some moderate support he had from a minority of other officers, Yedidya ordered that *priority would be given to an operation in the Mediterranean Sea* and that the missile boats, not the navy seals, would take the lead. He also directed that they prepare for the option of acting in the Gulf of Eilat.

When the meeting was over, Yedidya called IDI director Maj. Gen. Amos Malka to update him. Amos was ready to move on his orders, and Yedidya emphasized, "I want to meet with the Americans by the end of the day to share our intelligence with them."

"It's not a problem from my perspective, but you know the bureaucracy. We need to get approvals from information security and from the Mossad. My people will get cracking at it," Amos responded. Then he added, "Who from your group will be the point person with the Americans?"

Without hesitation, Yedidya said, "My head of naval intelligence, Meshita, along with his senior staff."

"Fine," said Amos. "Organize the meeting. The lead intelligence body is naval intelligence, and the IDI will give all of the help it can to trap the *Karine A* ship."

Israeli intelligence went into high gear. But all of the senior American intelligence officials in Israel were accompanying General Zinni on a tour of the northern border. The earliest a meeting could be set with them was the next day, December 13.

The meeting needed to be organized, a presentation in English needed to be prepared, all approvals to share the intelligence had to be obtained, and an official request for U.S. assistance needed to be drafted. The intelligence establishment, meanwhile, was irritated and under pressure. A grave terrorist attack on a northern West Bank town had occurred in the middle of what was supposed to be the festive Chanukah period.

Despite feeling despondent, Lieutenant Anat was still knee-deep in documents relating to the *Karine A*. And the terrorist attack wasn't the only reason this daughter of a retired navy captain and former deputy commander of the Red Sea arena was so pissed off.

"Why are we working here?" she thought after she learned the IDF would ask the Americans to capture the ship in the Red Sea. "How come Israel isn't taking the lead in capturing the ship if there are weapons on it? It would be a huge intelligence coup. And if the top brass don't believe us that there are weapons on the ship, then why are they dropping it on the Americans? Why mislead them? If the commander of the navy is sure that there are weapons on the ship, then the Israeli Navy should act! What? They don't trust us?"

When she got home, she wanted to cry.

"Don't take it so personally," her husband, Shlomi, said while trying to calm her down. He added that the commander's decision was not about her work or even her unit's work and that the navy commander had a broader perspective.

Anat refused to be comforted. She had no interest in those broader considerations. Shlomi's kind, patient, and rationally focused words could do nothing to assuage this deep, personal betrayal. Anat felt stabbed in the back by the navy commander's decision. Stabbed in the back! Of course, she wanted Israeli security protected however necessary, but this mission had been her life and her naval intelligence unit's life for several months. They had put their very beings into it so that the Israeli Navy could catch the ship—not someone else.

"To hell with broader concerns!" thought the generally calm Anat.

The Americans Arrive

DECEMBER 13, 2001, EVENING

In Meshita's bureau, the secretary prepared refreshments of seasonal fruits, cookies, and drinks, while the cool-headed Meshita awaited the meeting with the Americans. Earlier that year in July, he had visited U.S. naval intelligence and established a deep and personal connection with the director of U.S. Naval Intelligence. Since September 11, he had felt his working relationship with the Americans had only grown tighter.

"They are here!" his bureau chief called to him.

At the entrance to his office, Meshita greeted the U.S. Defense Intelligence Agency representative, the CIA representative, and the U.S. Naval Intelligence attaché, Ms. Stephanie, who was noticeably pregnant. Stephanie had worked many times with Meshita and knew him, and the conference room where they were meeting, quite well. Thus, Meshita was not surprised to see that she was pregnant. He knew that whatever was going on in her personal life, he could count on her.

After exchanging relatively short pleasantries, Meshita cut to the chase and opened with a general survey regarding the *Karine A* and all of the players involved with the ship. Then Yaron took over and led a PowerPoint presentation that included a detailed survey regarding the ship, all of its schematics, the reasons why there was a high probability that it was a weapons-smuggling ship, its expected course, and more in-depth information about the players involved.

Yaron said, "The estimated course of the ship takes it through the Red Sea and through the Suez Canal." He estimated that at a speed of nine knots, the ship was expected to reach a northeastern Egyptian port around December 25. "Meaning in another *twelve days*," Yaron emphasized.

The CIA official was impressed but also shocked. He interrupted Meshita and Yaron at different points to ask about the sources and methods by which they had acquired the intelligence. How were the Israelis sure that this ship was smuggling weapons and where it was headed? Were they sure the Iranians were involved?

Meshita calmly and politely declined to reveal his group's sources and methods, but he noted that this detailed sharing of intelligence with a foreign agency, even for an ally such as the United States, was extraordinary and that the intelligence had been carefully built up from many sources over time. He added that he had more information that was less certain that they were not presenting, but what they had shared with the U.S. intelligence delegation was hard and proven information.

The CIA official's surprise might have reflected the position of CIA director George Tenet, who at the time backed dealing with Arafat as part of the broader strategy for a negotiated settlement between Israel and the Palestinians. The Israelis who were present also had the impression that the CIA official was trying to exercise some measure of control or prominence even though they all knew that Stephanie was the real American expert when it came to naval intelligence. She made it clear that despite the CIA official's interjections, she would be the point person for U.S. intelligence.

Then Meshita raised his soft voice: "We are requesting two things from you—all possible intelligence support regarding the ship and operational support. Will you be able to carry out an operation to stop the ship? The Israeli Navy's ability to act in the Red Sea is limited. In my opinion, the ideal spot to stop the ship is after it leaves Yemen. To assist you, we'll provide you with all of our intelligence, and we'll send you updates as needed."

The office fell silent. Stephanie quickly took notes and looked at Meshita. "We'll check and get back to you," she responded, glancing at her American colleagues. They nodded their heads in agreement. As they left the room, the Israelis gave them printouts in English of Yaron's presentation.

It was Thursday, December 13. When would the Americans answer? It was not every day that the Israelis made a request such as this one of the Americans, whose answer would require decisions at the highest levels. What would they decide? Would the request get stuck in the American bureaucratic labyrinth? What would the response be from U.S. Central Command's military commanders in the field?

Until the answers arrived, a black cloud hovered over Israel's naval intelligence staff members. Had they made a mistake? Were they even pointed in the right direction?

5

A Moment of Doubt

Is the Intelligence Wrong?

DECEMBER 15–16, 2001

In the early hours of the morning of December 15, Gil received a jarring call from the intelligence operations center. "As of last night, intelligence information started to come in that the 'singer' of 'Milk and Honey' didn't leave."

Gil's world suddenly went dark. The "singer" was the *Karine A*. His brain tried to work through the shock to absorb the new information. He thought, "Maybe we're just dealing with a mistake about the timing of the ship's plans to set sail from Dubai. That's just a technical issue. If it didn't leave on December 11, so what? It'll leave a little later. And we'll have lost nothing. On the other hand, the second possibility is much worse."

His brain entertained the dark consequences of the second possibility. "Maybe there are two ships! The ship that left Dubai on December 11 with weapons and Iranian assistance is a ship we know nothing about. And the second ship, the *Karine A*—Adel's ship and 'our ship' since October—is just a legitimate commercial ship?!"

Suddenly he saw all their months of research collapse like a house of cards. He called the operations center back. "Call Gal, and tell him to look over the intelligence information!"

"We can't have made a mistake this large! It can't be!" he actually yelled out loud after he hung up. He also updated Yaron.

"*According to the latest information items, the ship was still in*

Dubai." Upon hearing this news, Gal tried to gather his thoughts. His first reaction was that maybe the information was wrong. "But why?" he asked himself. "Could it be a false trail?"

Then he started to question his own assumptions. "But it would make no sense to sail a ship from Sudan to the Persian Gulf, as one piece of information said, and then to load it up with thousands of tons of processed iron in order to bring it to Bulgaria?!" Suddenly he envisioned Capt. Hanania Peretz telling the team that "even if the cargo . . . was gold," the proposed course of the ship didn't make sense economically.

When Gil arrived at the office, he started to read the initial intelligence materials. His heart was beating rapidly. He took a break to listen to the latest news about a grave recent terrorist attack. Prime Minister Ariel Sharon had taken the dramatic step of responding by ordering the IDF to surround Yasir Arafat's office. Their rivalry and mutual hatred and distrust bred twenty years before in Beirut was in full swing. Israel had cut all ties with Arafat and had declared him irrelevant. But the U.S. administration was still standing by Arafat.

On Sunday, December 16, Anat arrived at work early. She picked up the telephone to call the intelligence collection agencies. "What's new?" she asked.

"What, you didn't see it? The ship has not left the port! We have unambiguous new intelligence about this."

"How can that be? The whole time we've had good intelligence about the ship leaving. This doesn't sound too convenient to you, maybe even a false lead?" She was both embarrassed and completely absorbed in the moment. She started to review all of the intelligence connected to Mughrabi.

Later, Yaron also delved into the issue. In a meeting with Anat and Gal, he told them, "We need to check two interconnected issues: One, are there two ships? Meaning, there is a ship that is carrying weapons, it's connected to the Iranians, and we think it left Dubai on December 11. But it's *not* the *Karine A*; rather, it's a different ship that we are clueless about. And the second ship then would be the *Karine A*, which used to be *RIM K* and is a legitimate commercial ship still anchored in Dubai, and—"

A Moment of Doubt

"No, no!" Anat burst in.

"Anat!" Yaron said stridently and calmed her down. "We need to look into this. That's why we are meeting—to read through all of the intelligence information together and try to identify what might be false."

At this, Anat was the best and wise beyond her years. She went through all of the information and highlighted aspects in each item of information that were false. Anat concluded that intelligence information coming out of the Bulgarian shipyard was wrong, that there was still only one ship, and that Mughrabi's people were lying to the civilian authorities.

Eventually, Anat's conclusions reached Gil, who made a fateful decision and supported the narrative that only Anat had been 100 percent confident about. "We need to completely ignore the conclusions of the intelligence information that came in on Saturday, December 15," he decided. At a meeting that night, Meshita agreed, having been convinced by the enthusiastic and self-assured know-it-all Anat.

The truth was that Arafat had instructed Mughrabi to run two separate parallel operations regarding the *Karine A*—a legitimate commercial operation as a cover and the secret weapons-smuggling operation. Every single step of the way, Mughrabi systematically and meticulously not only made sure that Akawi was maintaining a ship's log of legitimate port stops and carrying legitimate cargo but also spoke on the telephone with ports, insurance companies, and other authorities relating to the camouflaged version of the *Karine A*'s voyages.

Anyone listening to Mughrabi's calls or tracking the actually filed insurance and port documents would be confused or unable to discern the *Karine A*'s true purposes due to an extensive and consistent trail of misinformation. He might discuss scheduling future repair work with a company in Bulgaria and provide a fake current location for the ship, when it was clear that the ship was elsewhere. He might place additional orders for legitimate products, which would require additional stops and delays to pick them up. But at the same time, the Iranians were yelling at him on the secret channels for moving too slowly to the Iranian island of Kish to get the weapons, thus making it clear that the additional stops were fantasy.

The only way to know where the ship was actually moving and what it was doing at all times would be to follow Mughrabi's calls and communications with Mughniyeh's Hezbollah representatives and Khamenei's Iranian IRGC representatives. Israeli intelligence had not sufficiently cracked Mughrabi's communications in this area, but Anat and the rest of the team used their human intuition and painstaking analysis of the intelligence to help them avoid coming to the wrong conclusion and being duped, as some of the others in Israeli intelligence had been.

What really convinced Meshita to go with his team and Anat's conclusions over those of the other Israeli intelligence agencies? No matter how many ways he tried to pick her apart with questions to find holes in her explanations, Anat maintained her calm and quiet confidence. When he asked a hard question, her eyes narrowed and zoned in on him. Her expression was unflinching.

She, a junior officer, could stare him straight in the eyes and assure him that they were on the right track. Although subsequently Anat found that not every analytical point she made related to the *Karine A* was always right, on the broad issues she was dead-on and reached the right answers faster than everyone else.

In the meantime, their operational concept going forward was to ignore all the collected information that claimed the ship had not left its port. Still, they remained troubled as they had no idea where the ship had disappeared to and whether they would find it.

The Moment the *Karine A* Is Located

DECEMBER 17, 2001

It was the Muslim holiday of Eid al-Fitr. Just as he did every morning at 5:45, Major Tamir, who was responsible for intelligence in the bureau of the IDF chief, came to the bureau, went over the gathered recent intelligence materials, and highlighted the important sections in yellow magic marker. He then prepared a black folder, opened the office door of the chief of staff, and put the folder on Lt. Gen. Shaul Mofaz's desk. The folder included multiple items including the daily briefs from the IDI, the Shin Bet, and the IDF Operations Planning Command that summarized key events. The items listed covered both events that had occurred and those that were expected to occur, with an emphasis on various warnings; and original versions of the latest major pieces of intelligence information.

Mofaz was looking over the newspapers. They all covered Arafat's speech the day before on Palestinian television. It was the first time Arafat had appeared since September 2000, and he had called for a cease-fire. Israel and the United States said they would judge his actions, not just his words, while the EU and the Arab states praised him without qualification.

"Is the IDI's analysis of the speech here?" Mofaz asked as he raised his eyes away from the newspapers and looked at Tamir's folder.

"Yes."

Mofaz took the file, searched through it, and took out the IDI's analysis. His mind was flooded with thoughts. For fifteen months he had commanded the IDF under the cloud of war. Before that, he had prepared the IDF for just such a war. He hadn't known even a moment of peace. But for every small tactical development in the field, sometimes there were major strategic implications. He didn't believe a word that came out of Arafat's mouth about preventing terrorist attacks.

"At the upcoming status update meeting, I want to hold a special discussion about the impact of Arafat's speech," he said to Tamir. Then he added, "And take this too." He gave Tamir the intelligence dispatch alert from naval intelligence about the *Karine A*'s having left Dubai a few days earlier. In the top margin of the document, Mofaz had handwritten a note: "For the status update with the navy: What are we doing about this?"

He watched Tamir leave. For some reason, the ship was intertwined with the greater strategic picture of Palestinian violence. The situation with this ship was still off in the distance, but the document's mentioning of the Iranians caught his attention.

Mofaz was fifty-four, married with four kids, and the perfect enemy for Iran. Born in Iran's capital of Tehran with the name Shahrām Mofazzazkār only a few months after the state of Israel was founded, he moved to Israel at the age of nine and Hebraized his named to Shaul Mofaz. From his Iranian background, he always had a deeper instinctive understanding than most Israelis of one of Jerusalem's most dynamic adversaries.

Was it fate or irony that a Persian Jew happened to be the IDF's chief at the key moment when his intelligence officers uncovered Iranian attempts to gain new footholds in the Middle East region? When he had the power to block Iran from providing the Palestinians with advanced weapons to attack Israel?

Mofaz's military career started with Israel's elite paratrooper unit in the late 1960s. He was eventually promoted and became an officer in a special operations unit that routinely carried out operations behind enemy lines. Some of the high-stakes operations he was involved in early in his career helped shape his worldview, which influenced some of the critical decisions he would make during the *Karine A* saga.

On October 11–12, 1973, during the Yom Kippur War, then major Mofaz and a few dozen of his troops carried out two very different operations. The first day, they pulled off a daring raid behind the Syrian front lines. They intercepted and took out a column of various Iraqi military units that had planned to cross into Syria to provide support in fighting Israel. The element of surprise was key as Mofaz caught the Iraqi forces in a place they thought was still safe, and they had no idea the Israelis were coming.

However, on the second day, when he and his elite commandos tried a similar trick again, they were surrounded and ambushed near Damascus in Syria. At one point, they were retreating to a rescue point under heavy fire, but their rescue aircraft was flying away from them and unable to return until refueling. The entire operation had been thrown together quickly without even standing orders to guide them. Mofaz and his troops did not believe they would make it out alive.

When making the critical decisions during the *Karine A* saga,

Mofaz relied on two major lessons from these two wartime operations that had such different outcomes. First, timing and the element of surprise are crucial. Choosing the right one of two different potential moments to attack the exact same enemy could be the difference between success and failure—that is, death for the troops sent into battle. Second, he would expend extraordinary resources for training and gathering intelligence and would take major risks earlier in the game to ensure his special forces were not sent into an ambush or a situation from which they could not escape.

"We'll wait for the status update in three days," he muttered to himself, "but we need to keep an eye on this. I'll see if the IDI says anything about it at the IDF high command meeting today."

An endless number of issues were on his table for that meeting. But now, he added one more. Iran's involvement set off all his alarm bells; this ship was not on just another smuggling run. From that moment, the *Karine A* became an issue that the IDF chief himself dealt with personally. His personal involvement would change the course of the mission at multiple critical junctures. But no one knew that yet.

Meshita picked up the telephone. It was Stephanie on the line. "I'm coming to you," she said.

Meshita looked at his watch and at his calendar. It was around noon. All of his meetings could be postponed. Who knew what she might have to say? Since their meeting on December 13, four days had passed, and he had not heard a peep from the Americans.

In less than twenty minutes, she had arrived. When she came in, she was breathing hard and looked exhausted. She had worked much of the night in Israel so she could coordinate with officials in Washington DC during their work hours.

"I have an answer for you," she said, "And later it will be sent to your IDI foreign relations coordinator officially." Meshita tensed up as Stephanie got ready to read the answer. The main points were that "the *Karine A* was located on the morning of December 17 near the city of Aden in Yemen. The United States will maintain surveillance of the ship."

"You are sure that it's the *Karine A*?" Meshita pressed her.

"We're sure," Stephanie responded.

"Why are you so sure? How do you know?"

Stephanie straightened her shoulders. After a short silent moment, she said, "U.S. Naval Intelligence will forward to me all the most updated surveillance intelligence of the ship, and I will pass it on to Israel. I'm your point of contact for this issue."

Meshita thanked her warmly. He preferred not to ask yet about whether the United States would agree to capture the ship. "Captain Gil will be your Israeli point of contact. His door is open to you at all times for updates. I expect to hear more things about the ship very soon," Meshita said, concluding the meeting.

"I promise," said Stephanie.

Meshita had been tough on her, but in the back of his mind, he was thinking they might finally have a breakthrough.

In a meeting with Kobi and Gil, Meshita shared Stephanie's information and said excitedly, "We need to quickly update our operations people and the intelligence officers. As of now, we finally have an excellent starting point to calculate the ship's course. Based on that, we have a way to calculate the time frame more definitively."

Gil was beside himself. "Hezi, we were right! We were right to ignore that whole set of questionable intelligence information that came in. We have one ship, and it's the *Karine A*. That's it!

"Of course, we still don't know for sure that it's carrying weapons, but now our estimate is close to 100 percent," Gil continued.

"The question is: Why didn't Stephanie mention an American operation to capture the ship? We had requested that they capture it in the Red Sea," Kobi interjected.

"The fact that they are tracking the ship shows that they are interested in it, and they'll for sure capture it in the Red Sea," said Meshita, as he started to think.

"Stephanie's report shows that the issue is now under American control," Kobi commented. "I suggest that we wait for an answer from them. If suddenly we hear that they have already captured it, that is another thing entirely, obviously."

"I agree," said Meshita, "but as an operations man, I know our operations people will assume that if the Americans are collecting intelligence about the ship, they are planning on capturing it soon."

Anat and Gal hugged when they heard about the report from Stephanie. Though Anat generally evinced a sense of calm, while waiting to find out whether they were on the right track, she had sometimes felt her body practically trembling. In hugging Gal, she released all that energy and freed herself from doubt. While doubt plagued regular people and usually did not bother her, Anat had gone through a roller coaster of inner terror that she had caused a national failure that could cost innumerable lives and shift the balance of power between Israel and the axis of the PA, Hezbollah, and Iran. In many ways, the fate of the nation had not been solely on the broad shoulders of top leaders such as Prime Minister Sharon and IDF chief Mofaz but also very much on the smaller shoulders of junior officers such as Anat, those who had to dive deeper into the intelligence and on whose judgment the final decision makers had to rely.

In real time and in her first true mega operation, Anat was learning a point about being an intelligence officer that outsiders would never fully grasp: The stakes were life and death, and the senior officials, whose attention was spread out on a variety of issues, could not really delve into the details to unmask what intelligence was true and what was part of Mughrabi's meticulous disinformation campaign. Anat knew that she had no room for error in putting together a mystifying puzzle whose pieces had misled some other Israeli intelligence analysts. But she had gotten it right. She had cut through the noise and the falsehoods, and given the crucial and correct information to the higher echelons. They still had a chance to catch and stop the *Karine A* and the PA-Hezbollah-Iran plot.

An Israeli naval intelligence dispatch that went out on the following morning, December 18, with a map showing the *Karine A*'s movements had the feel of being issued for a capture operation. Its gist included several details:

The *Karine A* ship, which is carrying a cargo suspected of being weapons, was located on December 17 traveling near the city of Aden in Yemen. Based on calculations of time and distance, the ship will get to the straits between the Red Sea and the Gulf of Suez around December 24 and will enter the Mediterranean Sea on December 25.

United States Drops Out of Capture Operation

DECEMBER 18, 2001

Stephanie telephoned Meshita's bureau. She wanted to come by and relay an important message. Meshita was due in Haifa almost all day, so she reached him on his cellphone as he was driving there. She spoke in half code. Meshita thought she was saying the U.S. military would not lead a capture operation because it didn't have enough forces to spare from their fighting in Afghanistan. But he was not sure if that was the message. A round of broken telephone calls ensued to determine whether the United States was leaving Israel to capture the ship.

The point was crucial. The underlying assumption of the morning operations approval meeting was going to be "let the Americans take care of it." Now, at 1:00 p.m., as Chiny was about to preside over his first meeting, would the intelligence staff tell him that the Americans were ready to capture the ship or that they weren't?

Yoki, the head of the navy's intelligence collection branch, stood in the entrance to the conference room. He would present the intelligence at the meeting. As everyone sat in the room waiting for Chiny to enter, a tense and irritated Yoki was waiting for a call from Tel Aviv that would solve the mystery. But when Chiny entered the room, there still was no answer from Tel Aviv. Yoki entered, running after him.

"The intelligence staff is late?!" Chiny growled at Yoki and asked him to open with a survey of the intelligence status.

Yoki started his survey. Chiny listened intently. Then he heard the sentence, "It's possible that the Americans will give us a negative answer regarding our request that they capture the ship."

"What do you mean, 'it's possible?'" Chiny shot off in surprise.

"This was the reason I was late. I wanted to try to clarify this," Yoki responded.

"Then clarify it, so we'll know whether it's yes or no!"

"I'm waiting for a telephone call," Yoki answered. He surveyed the room. Everyone was taken by surprise. Suddenly, they were all under more intense pressure. The reigning plan had just collapsed. Now an operational plan that had once seemed a half-theoretical, unlikely scenario had changed to being imminent. The Americans had been expected to stop the ship in the Red Sea. Now did Israel need to figure out how it could capture the ship in the Red Sea?

Then Yoki was called outside. Tel Aviv was on the line: "It's what we feared."

"What is?" asked Yoki.

"There will be no U.S. capture operation."

"You're sure?"

"Sure!"

Chiny's summary of the meeting was as follows:

Naval intelligence and operations needed to check the procedures for a ship passing through the Suez Canal with an emphasis on ships that are passing through for the first time.

Naval intelligence would start the ball rolling to get Shin Bet interrogators on the operational team.

The operation could take place in two areas—the Mediterranean Sea or the Red Sea. Combat readiness of the relevant forces would need to track those two scenarios.

The navy seals and the Eilat Base's operations staff would analyze where the takeover should occur.

Naval intelligence operations would liaison with the broader IDF Operations Command to get approval for the navy seals to carry out a fast-rope drop.

Ram was at the meeting and talked with Chiny extensively. Finally, the words "Red Sea" had been heard in an operations planning meeting, but part of the attendees still felt that taking over the ship in the Mediterranean Sea was the preferred option. Anyway, Yedidya would make the final determination. Ram and Chiny both knew that Yedidya preferred the Mediterranean Sea scenario. He would give his opinion the next day.

That same afternoon, the missile boat commanders in Haifa held a meeting. They focused on how to capture the ship in the Mediterranean Sea instead of the navy seals' taking the lead in the Red Sea.

Meanwhile, Ram returned to the navy seals' base near Haifa. From there he went out for another counterterrorism operation in the West Bank along with the paratroopers' brigade under Aviv Kochavi's command. (Kochavi would later go on to climb the highest echelons of the IDF, being sworn in as the IDF chief of the general staff on January 15, 2019.) The forward command group was on Mount Gerizim. There, sometime during a strange hour of the night and far away from anything having to do with the sea, let alone the Red Sea, an idea started to germinate in Ram's mind about how and where the navy would capture the *Karine A*.

Chiny, whose operations-focused mind was continually preoccupied with the fast-rope scenario, decided that time could not be wasted. He understood from Ram that just one month before, a portion of his seals had undergone fast-rope training overseas. He also understood they needed to get an approval from the air force, which had authority over the issue, to move forward with any action. He would get the ball rolling with the head of the air force's helicopters operations, Brig. Gen. Shlomo Mashiach.

That same day, Lt. Col. Yoni Mann was called to a meeting with Yossi Meshita, the deputy of the Naval Operations Division. Yoni was the head of Joint Special Operations of the air force that coordinated with other special forces. His experience included being a computer engineer, a pilot, and a commander of a helicopter squadron.

"There's something unusual," Yossi revealed to him. "There's a ship called the *Karine A* that is smuggling weapons. In a few days, the ship is due to pass through the Suez Canal on the way to Bulgaria. It's expected to turn toward Gaza and drop off barrels with weapons."

"So what do you want from us, from the air force?"

"Assistance, like with the *Santorini* captured near the Lebanese coast," Yossi responded. "Helicopters should be ready to assist with the operation in both an attack and a rescue capacity."

"No problem," Yoni answered. He returned to his office and ordered his staff officers to review the *Karine A* issue and prepare for the air force operations approval forum the next morning on Wednesday, December 19.

6

Operational Preparations in High Gear

Ready for Anything

DECEMBER 18–19, 2001

Where would the Israelis capture the ship? In the Mediterranean Sea or in the areas of the Gulf of Aqaba (at Eilat) and the Red Sea? Although naval intelligence preferred the Mediterranean Sea, it had to be prepared for both scenarios, so it had to develop and send out an intelligence collection plan for both arenas. Kobi, the point man on the issue, knew time was running out. He needed to get the intelligence collection apparatus moving and to present a plan to the IDI's Collection Division the next morning. The IDI would then put the Mossad, Unit 8200, and all the other intelligence collection agencies to work.

Kobi and his team started preparing a document to present all of the expected collection needs; it would delve deeply into the smallest details. The team also reviewed with all the relevant authorities what the different surveillance options were. Those intelligence officers who were married called their spouses to tell them not to worry and that they would be working through the night.

Meanwhile, after a counterterrorism operation in the West Bank, IDF chief of staff Mofaz visited the forward command group on Mount Gerizim. He shook hands with Aviv Kochavi and with Ram. Kochavi gave him a status update. Mofaz was satisfied with the operation, but inside he knew that the general strategic status quo could not continue. They needed to strike a major blow against the terrorists. He had a broad plan for taking control over most of the terrorists' centers in the territories and for taking out their associated cells based there. He believed in the IDF's power. Every time he saw Ram's seals and Aviv's paratroopers, he felt more confident that the IDF would overcome the terror challenge. He knew Ram well, dating to when Mofaz was the IDF commander for the West Bank and Ram was the commander of the undercover Duvdevan Unit's special forces that operate in the West Bank and Gaza.

Ram realized he had an opening. "Can I talk to you privately?" Ram asked Mofaz.

"No problem," Mofaz said immediately.

The two of them went off to a corner, and Ram started to tell him about the *Karine A*.

"I'm familiar with the issue," Mofaz responded. "A day or two ago, I read that the ship left the port of Dubai. It appears that the ship is carrying a large volume of weapons and that the Iranians and Hezbollah are mixed up in this somehow. This bothers me. I'll see what the navy presents me with at the operations approval forum on Thursday, December 20."

"I'll tell you what they're going to tell you," whispered Ram. "They're going to present you with the plan to capture the ship in the Mediterranean Sea while using the missile boats. The navy is used to this scenario and regularly trains for it."

Mofaz gave him a fatherly glance and asked, "Ram, do you have a different plan?"

Though a captain and head of the navy seals, Ram was still a junior-ranking officer to Mofaz and years away from any chance at a promotion to the high command. In all militaries, including Israel's, mid-level officers rarely got to speak directly to the chief. Rather, any concerns they had would be communicated first to their rear admiral, who would communicate them to the admiral on the high command, and that officer would choose whether to raise them with the chief or not. By taking advantage of the chance moment in which Mofaz was physically nearby and without intermediaries present, Ram was very clearly breaking with the standard procedures for the chain of command.

Even more controversial, Ram was not just discussing the details of the operation Mofaz had come to watch that day; rather, Ram was advocating to Mofaz a way to run the *Karine A* operation, which carried major strategic consequences that were over his pay grade. What was more, his staff already had lost two rounds in pitching his ideas to his direct superiors at the naval operations meeting on December 11, and he himself had failed to convince the commander of the navy, Yedidya, on a December 12 telephone call. He was now leapfrogging through the ranks to wage a guerrilla-style war to get his ideas accepted by the chief.

Ram was launching a preemptive strike against the near-consensus his superiors had reached about how to run the *Karine A* operation. This was no normal off-the-cuff conversation, and it would have a fateful and massive impact. Speaking to Mofaz about the *Karine A* operation before the issue had even been seriously raised with the IDF chief for discussion in high command meetings, Ram pushed hard for the operation to take place in the Red Sea, the location farthest from the Israeli coast.

"Yes," said Ram enthusiastically, "we need to capture the ship in the Red Sea at a point that we'll designate. We'll take it clandestinely and by surprise. We'll capture it with forces coming from commando boats that will climb up the ship, and another group of commandos will drop down onto the ship from a helicopter using a fast rope."

Virtually the entire high command except Chiny and Meshita were opposed to this idea. It was without recent precedent as essentially all Israeli naval operations at that time were conducted in the much less choppy, less dangerous, and closer Mediterranean Sea. The Israeli high command, including Yedidya, all dreaded the Red Sea as a horrible risk to avoid. They viewed their soldiers as totally untrained for it and their boats as unable to withstand the harsh waves.

"Tell me a little bit more about this," Mofaz asked, showing some strong interest in the idea. Ram started to tell him how, in a short time, twelve seals could fast rope down to the ship from two spots on a Black Hawk helicopter. Suddenly, Kochavi needed Mofaz, cutting their conversation short.

But when the location for capturing the *Karine A* came up days later before the high command, Mofaz would remember what Ram had told him.

A Capture in the Mediterranean

DECEMBER 19, 2001

"So, what am I always saying? He's glorifying terrorism," Mofaz muttered to himself as he read reports of Arafat's speech for the Eid al-Fitr Muslim holiday in which he had declared that "one Palestinian martyr in Jerusalem is worth seventy martyrs elsewhere." In the field, violence had dropped slightly, but Mofaz clearly saw it was only temporary. He was going to spend most of his time that day with combat fighters in the field. He had requested that Major Tamir, his bureau chief for intelligence, accompany him. When Tamir entered the chief's office, Mofaz offered him the two intelligence dispatch alerts from the day before regarding the *Karine A*. The last paragraph of the dispatch from the IDI's Counterterrorism Division said that the joint purpose of the PA-Hezbollah-Iranian operation was to influence the broader strategic picture in the region and to introduce force-multiplying weapons into the Second Intifada to further ignite it. Mofaz took the dispatch from naval intelligence and looked over the estimated time frame again. Then his view was settled. This situation was nothing like the *Santorini* operation. The *Karine A* was an issue of strategic value. He wrote in the margins of the naval intelligence dispatch: "I want to hold a discussion on this issue today, without delay!" Then he recalled the discussion he had with Ram at Mount Gerizim.

Later, Tamir called Lieutenant Commander Ido, the bureau chief for the navy commander: "The IDF chief wants to hold a discussion today about this ship, the *Karine A*. You're familiar with the issue?"

"Of course. The operations approval forum is currently discussing the issue. The operation's code name is Noah's Ark."

Preparations in High Gear

"Good name!"

"So why do we need to present this already tonight? The issue can be discussed tomorrow in the regular framework of the operations approval forum."

"He knows, but he wants it to happen *today!*" Tamir said for emphasis.

"When?"

"At 9:15 p.m. It will be a smaller meeting. You, the IDF Operations Command, the air force, and the IDI."

Earlier that morning Yoni Mann arrived at his air force special operations office at air force headquarters. Suddenly he saw the intercom light flashing for the head of helicopter operations, Brigadier General Mashiach. "Are you looking for me?" Yoni asked.

"Yes, I need you to pop over here immediately," came the curt answer. It was 7:45 a.m.

Yoni, both surprised and curious, went up the four floors to Mashiach's office. He was shocked for a second. He saw a man with Chinese features in an Israeli uniform—once again, a very uncommon sight. Embarrassed, Yoni laughed. Then Rear Admiral Chiny stood up, shook his hand, and said, "Nice to meet you. I'm Chiny. I'm replacing Dudu Ben-Besht as the head of the navy's Operations Command."

Yoni introduced himself and understood that he had entered the office in the middle of Chiny and Mashiach's discussion.

"Yoni," Chiny said, "you met yesterday with Yossi Meshita in the navy's Operations Division. He did not sufficiently emphasize the situation's significance. We're not talking about another *Santorini* here. We're talking about a ship with a length of three hundred feet that can transport dozens of tons of weapons. Did you hear me? Dozens of tons of weapons.

"This mission has national importance. Part of our plan for capturing it must include fast roping down from helicopters. We need this to be ready to go by Saturday, December 22, at the latest." Chiny finished and rotated his gaze over to Mashiach.

"On Saturday night, you'll have a fast-roping capability," said Mashiach firmly.

Yoni practically fell out of his chair. He had been sure that Mashiach would forcefully blow Chiny off, and the exact opposite had happened.

"We have nothing in place," Yoni spat out, raising his voice.

"Just stop, Yoni. I'll talk with you about this later," Mashiach said to calm him.

Chiny didn't waste a moment. He immediately got up, shook Mashiach's hand hard, and left the room—thrilled with his success. Yoni even imagined that when Chiny closed the door that he roared, "I did it!"

Outside, it was pouring rain. Chiny got soaked, but he didn't care as he jogged over to the navy operations approval forum.

Yoni stayed behind, still seated and still beside himself. "Mashiach, you know that the navy seals know how to slide down the fast ropes, but nothing beyond that! You know that our understanding with the navy is that all of the preparations for making this capability operational are set to be finished by August 2003. You know that we don't have helicopters with the platform for the fast ropes. There is only one helicopter with a platform, and it's not operational. You know that we don't have any pilots trained for this. You know that the seals haven't trained with our pilots. Do we even have enough fast ropes? And will the ropes meet international standards?"

Mashiach knew that Yoni was right. He answered curtly, "Yoni, this is an order from above. We have no choice. You need to make sure that everything you've said that we don't have and isn't ready will be ready by Saturday night. Get working."

As Yoni descended the four floors to his office, all he could think about was that he would need a miracle to pull this off. He didn't know about the meeting that morning between Mashiach and Israeli Air Force commander Dan Halutz. Halutz had immediately understood that with the air force involved in the operation, he needed to contribute everything he could to make it a success. He had faith that his operations officers could create something from nothing and develop a new capability for carrying out fast roping in only three to four days.

When Yoni arrived at his office, he called Maj. Reuven Ben-Shalom, head of the helicopters desk in the special operations branch. Originally from the United States, Ben-Shalom was a helicopter pilot and an operations man. Together they quickly formulated a plan and a time frame:

Today, Wednesday, we'll set up the fast-rope platforms on three helicopters. We need to find at least four usable ropes for two helicopters.

Thursday, December 20, the helicopters will fly to the seals' base near Haifa, and they'll formulate their tactics, carry out drills, and achieve operational readiness. First, they'll fast rope down to the land in broad daylight, then onto a ship during daylight, then onto a ship—one similar to the *Karine A*—at night.

Friday, December 21, we'll do a formal inspection and write up the finalized tactics and directives.

Saturday, December 22, we'll train on an operational model. The same day, if necessary, we'll take over the ship in the Mediterranean Sea after the missile boats stop it.

Ben-Shalom and Yoni started to work with the relevant air force officials on the plans, leading with the Black Hawk pilots. The air force went into high gear. But even pushing the envelope, would they be ready in time?

Gil and Kobi presented to Yedidya the different intelligence and operational issues for taking the *Karine A* in either the Mediterranean Sea or the Red Sea. Kobi said, "In our opinion, the chances that the weapons will be transported all the way to the Mediterranean Sea are low. On the way there, the crew can unload the weapons at any port or harbor on the Sinai Peninsula's west coast."

"What about the Port of Aqaba?" someone asked.

"That's a possibility, but our estimate is that it's unlikely. We already have some early signs that the ship's course will take it through the Suez Canal," Gal interjected.

"Do we know where the ship is now?" someone called out.

"No. For us to know where it is, we'll need to activate our long-range surveillance abilities for the Red Sea. We're also waiting for updated information from the Americans."

Yedidya, who was listening carefully, took some notes.

Kobi continued, "Therefore, we think that the best place to capture the ship is in the Red Sea, south of the Straits of Tiran." He felt as though the others disagreed.

Meshita got up to summarize the situation and reiterated the importance of capturing the ship in the Red Sea. He also emphasized the possibility that the ship might enter the Mediterranean Sea while hugging the Egyptian coast and might drop off the weapons to fishing boats.

As he was speaking, Kobi passed a note to Chiny. The note said, "We need to take the ship south of the straits, outside of Egypt's territorial waters. If there are operational limitations for deploying the navy seals that far out, we can carry out our takeover without being quiet about it, using the fast patrol boats and the combat helicopters."

Chiny read it, nodded his head, and tore the note into tiny pieces, as was his way.

For Yedidya, a former head of naval intelligence, though there was no 100 percent proof, he knew the ship was "dirty." Even a week earlier when he heard who was involved in the saga—Hezbollah, Iran, and the PA's smuggling network—he understood that the Israelis would need to seize it. He thought, "Let our mistake be to withdraw after stopping an innocent ship. We stop it and inspect. If we don't find weapons, then we say, 'Sorry, we were mistaken,' and we let the ship go on its way. Better that than to let a major weapons-smuggling ship through."

But his first preference was still an operation in the Mediterranean Sea because of the established and set military capabilities he had there. In the Red Sea, his military abilities from the closest base, which was located in the resort town of Eilat on Israel's southern tip, were insufficient—with only a few fast patrol boats, which were basically guard-duty boats, and not a single larger missile boat. At the same time, he clearly saw that he had to prepare an option for acting in the Red Sea, but this would require locating the ship in the Red Sea at an earlier date and obtaining intelligence information from the Americans. He ordered the emphasis to remain on the Mediterranean Sea.

Lieutenant Commander Ido, Yedidya's bureau chief, then updated him about Mofaz's order to hold a meeting about the ship that evening. Meanwhile, Chiny left and flew to Eilat for a multiyear planning meeting with the Eilat Naval Base commanders.

But where was the ship? The estimate was that around December 21–22, it would arrive at the area between the Straits of Tiran and the entrance to the Gulf of Suez. But what if this estimate was mistaken? The Atara surveillance airplane could provide the answer.

The navy had three maritime patrol aircraft, nicknamed Sea Scans, that were modified from the Westwind civilian aircraft. They were operated by the air force but managed by the Missile Boats Command. The Sea Scans increased the range of the aerial surveillance scopes and the color scopes of the missile boats. But the planes were unable to do long-range surveillance, and one of them was getting fixed. How would the navy perform the long-range surveillance?

Rear Adm. Dudu Ben-Besht, a sailor even in his youth, had served as Israel's military attaché to Singapore. During his vacation time in Israel, he visited the ELTA Factory, where he saw a Boeing 737 aircraft that Israel Aerospace Industries had purchased and used mostly for testing for the advanced military systems ELTA was developing. Dudu was blown away and wrote to Yedidya while he was on the aircraft. When he returned to Israel in 2000, he cut a deal with the ELTA Company so that in times of war, the ELTA-equipped aircraft could be drafted into the service of the navy. From time to time, the Sea Scans would train alongside the aircraft, which was given the name "Atara." Its pilot would always be an Israel Aerospace Industries employee, while the central operational commander of the aircraft (controlling everything related to its surveillance capabilities) would be an IDF pilot from the Sea Scan unit. The aircraft could also be equipped with special surveillance scopes to take high-resolution photographs.

The afternoon of Wednesday, December 19, Zvi Tiron was sitting in his office at the ELTA Company's building in the southwest coastal city of Ashdod. A former pilot, the retired IDF lieutenant colonel had been with ELTA for twelve years and headed its long-range aerial surveillance radar program relating to the Israeli Navy's needs. He was also responsible for the Atara.

The navy's Weapons Division, which he regularly worked with, called him: "Zvi, we need the aircraft to fly Friday, and far."

"What's going on?"

"There's a threat to the state of Israel, and we need to locate it."

Later that day, Zvi met with naval intelligence personnel and moved up the flight to Thursday afternoon. On that morning, Zvi and his staff would prepare the Atara and its new aerial surveillance radar developed especially for the navy. It had very long-range surveillance capabilities that enabled the viewing of the exact shape and image of a target and its movements. The staff also would work practically without a break on readying the new scope, which had a color photo capability both during daylight and nighttime hours.

Meanwhile, Kobi and Commander Yoki told the IDI's collection unit officials at a preparatory meeting that they would need prisoner interrogators who could keep up with the naval combat forces. When the officials said IDF interrogators did not operate at sea, Yoki got mad: "Do you understand what you're saying? If the operation is in the Red Sea, even if the current focus is on the Mediterranean Sea, it would mean the *Karine A*'s crew members couldn't be interrogated until they sailed to Eilat. The interrogations need to be carried out on the ship, in real time, when they are caught, and things are fresh!"

The IDI officials made a noncommittal statement about looking into it, but Yoki understood they would just come back and say it was impossible. What would he do? If the operation ended up being in the Gulf of Eilat, or worse in the Red Sea, where the main force would be the seals, having interrogators for the crew as soon as the seals took over the ship would be imperative.

Captain Hanania, the external civilian adviser to naval intelligence, continued to contribute his rich knowledge and experience to the navy on a voluntary basis. He had searched in different databases for authentic diagrams of ships similar to the *Karine A* but had come up empty. The website information of Spain's city of Vigo regarding the ships built there in 1978 was not relevant. He sketched a blowup of the internal structure of the ship that fit the *Karine A*'s description, "based on certain standards, technical issues, the year the ship was manufactured and my experience." He also asked sailors he knew to try and find sketches of ships similar to the *Karine A*. Hanania's sketches and the sketches prepared by the naval engineering unit from the Naval Logistics Command were transferred to the special imaging unit, which would convert them into three-dimensional computer models. The indefatigable intelligence officer Itamar sped to Tel Aviv to meet with the imaging unit and explain what models he wanted regarding the points of view, the different sections of the ship, and so on.

On his way back to the seals' base near Haifa, he called Hanania: "Hanania, I need to come to you. How about 5:00 p.m.?"

"Itamar, come whenever you want. How many years have we known each other—ten? I'm here for you!"

Immediately, Itamar called Dror, the commander of the navy seals' combat fighters: "I'm going to see Hanania Peretz. I want you to meet with a professional expert."

"Fine. When are we meeting?"

"At around 5:00 p.m. I may be a bit late because of the rain."

The rain stopped. Hanania greeted Itamar and Dror upon their arrival at his office and offered them coffee. Following coffee he presented them with his sketches and provided his analysis. They were interested in the height of the ship's sides and if anything could lower the sides in relation to the water. "Every ten tons loaded on the ship lowers it in the water by a centimeter and slightly reduces its height," Hanania explained to them in his comforting and quiet voice. They also were interested in the angles of the ship's sides, how much the ship's compressor would stick out of the water, and other issues. Then they would utilize the key intelligence in forming the operational plan.

They left his office with positive vibes and traveled with Hanania to the port of Haifa. Darkness had already fallen.

"I want to show you ships that are at least a little bit similar to your ship," Hanania said to them. They toured the port, boarded a similar ship, saw where the "dead spaces" were on the different parts of the ship, and viewed the bridge. Itamar wrote down everything he observed and sent it to naval intelligence. Most important, he added it to the intelligence briefing he was planning with the seals. At the exact same time, there was a Noah's Ark meeting at the office of the Haifa Base commander to determine directives for the operation.

The next day, December 20, all of them would go before the navy commander at 7:00 a.m. for a commander's briefing. The operation was scheduled for December 21, and the Mediterranean Sea was still the preferred arena for the operation.

In the evening, the IDI's Collection Division sent out an intelligence collection order addressing both the Mediterranean Sea and Red Sea arenas, leaving out the idea of including IDI interrogators. As Kobi and Gil were busy meeting with Meshita to prepare for the evening meeting with the IDF chief, they delegated to Yoki the task of finding interrogators for the prisoners. But from where? Suddenly, he had the idea that the Shin Bet could provide the answer. Yoki knew two interrogators with navy seal backgrounds. He started making calls to his Shin Bet connections and worked through the issue.

Later that night, he was able to speak in person to the Shin Bet's deputy head of interrogations. Yoki concisely presented the story of the ship and the operational plan to him.

"So what do you want from us?" he asked.

"Two interrogators," Yoki answered, and he provided their names.

Those present in the meeting smiled. "When do you want them?"

"Tomorrow!" Yoki saw that they were ready to fall out of their chairs.

"We can't give you an answer. Give me your cell phone number."

When Yoki started heading home, he felt despair. Suddenly his cell phone rang. "Tomorrow at 10:00 a.m., you have a meeting with Shin Bet deputy director Yuval Diskin."

Yoki let out a sigh of relief. Now he knew. The Shin Bet would give him the two interrogators. They would set certain conditions, but they would give him the interrogators, who would later become critical.

"Way to go, Shin Bet!" muttered Yoki. He didn't know—neither did the Shin Bet—about the drama happening in Mofaz's office.

Daring Shift to Red Sea Op

DECEMBER 19–20, 2001

Tamir sat next to the IDF chief of staff and peered around at the impressive gathering of officials from the IDF high command. The seals' chief, Ram, was not present; only the most senior officers appeared at high command meetings with the IDF chief.

When Yedidya told Ram about the meeting beforehand, Ram had said, "Yedidya, give us the green light to do this in the Red Sea. That's the only place where we can do what we have been training all these years for—to climb on and infiltrate a moving ship from the commando boats."

Yedidya had laughed but promised, "Ram, you'll be the first one to know what happens at the meeting and what Mofaz decides."

Tamir looked at Mofaz, who was totally focused and serious. It was 9:15 p.m. "There's no way he'll spend more than thirty minutes on this," Tamir thought. It seemed to him that a majority of the attendees thought the same way.

After a short silence, Mofaz opened the meeting, saying, "Okay, who's going to start?"

Yedidya looked over at Meshita, who stood up and placed a map of the Middle East on the conference table. He marked the course of the *Karine A* from Sudan to Dubai. Then he marked the returning course, the place where the Americans had located it two days ago, its expected circular path through the Red Sea to the Mediterranean Sea, and the expected timing. Everything was bolded with a clear color scheme.

"Commander, I'll present the intelligence regarding the ship," Meshita opened. "We suspect that it is a dirty ship. In a moment I'll explain why. This ship was purchased by Adel Mughrabi. He is a man who is known to have exploited his past smuggling operations to the fullest, including the *Santorini* . . ."

Mofaz bent forward and studied the map. Meshita stopped for a moment and then started to describe the ship's entire story, the coordination with the Americans, and the reasons the ship was viewed as suspicious.

"Maybe we won't find anything on it, but the ship is 'dirty,'" Meshita emphasized. "It's similar to a situation where we would gun down a suicide attacker before he gets to put on his suicide suit. That is what this ship is—dirty."

"You agree with this opinion?" Mofaz said turning toward Kuper, the head of the IDI Research Department.

"Absolutely," said "Kuper."

"Where is the ship now?" Mofaz asked Meshita with a look of interest.

"The Americans told us that on December 17 it was located in the Indian Ocean near the port of Aden, Yemen, close to the entrance to the Red Sea."

"When will the ship arrive at the Straits of Tiran?" pressed Mofaz.

"On the twenty-first of the month, which is Friday, if the ship is traveling at a speed of twelve knots—meaning, traveling quickly."

"This Friday?" Mofaz said with a bit of shock.

"Yes," Meshita responded.

Mofaz leaned forward again with a more serious look on his face. He marked a point forty-six miles from the Straits of Tiran in the Red Sea where there were markings for a "fork in the road," with one course toward the Gulf of Eilat and one course toward the Suez Canal. "Is this part of Egyptian territorial waters?" he asked.

"That is international waters," responded Yedidya. He added, "It's outside Egyptian territorial waters, but we don't have a capability there for capturing the ship."

"Why?" Mofaz shot back at him.

Tamir focused on Mofaz and Yedidya. Both of them looked animated. Clearly now the meeting would go on longer than he had anticipated, and he started to follow the exchange more carefully.

Yedidya explained, "Because we don't have the tools for it. This is a body of water that our fast [*Dvora*-class] patrol boats would at best struggle to cope with, and the navy seals wouldn't be able to take over a moving ship in these kinds of waters. The waves are too strong. We can only take it over once it enters the Gulf of Eilat on its way to a Jordanian port or in the Mediterranean Sea if it goes through the Suez Canal. Obviously, it would be best if the ship went toward the Jordanian port."

Mofaz asked for further explanations regarding why it would be impossible to take over the ship in the Red Sea in international waters and before the fork in the road.

"There the water is up to the sky. That operation would require a lot more, and the fast patrol boats would only survive with difficulty. The waves can be two and a half meters high and, with winds of thirty knots, can sometimes even reach four meters or higher. Our tools and capabilities are not set up for this—this is a wholly different animal. What I'm saying is, in order to capture the ship, we'd need to take control of it and bring it into the Gulf of Eilat. This is not a strategy I would recommend under any circumstances," said Yedidya assertively.

Mofaz sank into deep thought. Then he started to push Yedidya, asking, "And a fast patrol boat could not stop the ship?"

"Even two fast patrol boats could not. These are really difficult waters . . . We need forces that can take over the ship and sail it. For this I need the navy seals. I need to bring them south 115 miles from Eilat into the Red Sea, and I don't know how it will all come out."

"In commando boats, 115 miles is not doable?" said Mofaz, interrogating Yedidya.

"It's possible," Yedidya said in his typical low tone, "but it would be under pressure. We would need to refuel here, and currently that kind of operation would be impossible logistically. What I am saying is, it will be very hard to move all the forces south in time for such an operation, and even if that were possible, these waters would be really rough for the commando boats."

Then in the midst of the Mofaz-Yedidya back-and-forth that the others were starting to join, Yedidya added, "Maybe we'll get lucky with a situation where the ship arrives and the Red Sea waters are calmer; and if the waters are calmer, we can move. Let's say we go full speed with the commando boats and the fast patrol boats, we organize a place to refuel, and we try it. It's an option."

Tamir glanced at Mofaz. It seemed that Yedidya's words had been lost in the sea of words that had engulfed the meeting. Tamir then saw a spark in Mofaz's serious eyes. And just like that, the debate over whether the ship would unload its weapons in Sudan was tossed to the winds.

As a result, there was no reason to even debate whether it was possible to capture the ship in the Red Sea around southern Egypt. Tamir tried to recall if a report or a hint in a report supported this idea, but he could not think of one. He had seen reports about the smuggling network's establishing an infrastructure to smuggle weapons from Sudan, but not even a small report mentioned unloading weapons in Sudan. "This just seems like simple pig-headed daring," he said to himself.

But that daring had become the focal point of the meeting. Yedidya really did not see it as viable. He presented his analysis of the possibilities, and Mofaz took notes in his yellow notebook:

The ship enters the Gulf of Eilat. "The scenario we are all praying for," but everyone agreed this was unlikely.

The ship enters the Gulf of Suez and unloads the weapons in one of three Egyptian ports on the western Sinai Peninsula. If the weapons were unloaded already, we would be able to know from the timing when the ship would enter the canal.

If the ship passed by the western Sinai Peninsula and entered the canal without having unloaded the weapons, it was expected that its next destination would be a port on the northern Sinai Peninsula where it would unload them.

Based on all of this, Yedidya listed his various options for action in order of priority:

To notify the Egyptians generally, but without specifics, that a ship with weapons was getting ready to unload them in one of the ports in western Sinai.

If the ship actually did unload the weapons there and the Egyptians discovered the weapons, all the better.

If the ship did not unload the weapons at a western Sinai port and passed through the canal, Israel would capture it in the Mediterranean Sea.

Many in the room supported the navy chief's recommendations, but Mofaz continued to search for other options.

"There is another option from the air," the head of the Operations Department of the Operations Command suggested, "but it's problematic because to date there's been insufficient training. We could start to work on training for a fast-rope capability, but that would only be as of Sunday—and that's too late."

"We need to take all necessary efforts to ensure that the ship does not get to the Mediterranean Sea. What good is the ship to me if it enters the Mediterranean Sea with no weapons?" Mofaz thought to himself. "I cannot give the ship a chance to enter the Gulf of Suez," he kept repeating to himself.

Having heard different opinions around the conference table about the Egyptian option, Mofaz continued to push: "Let's think for a moment about a practical option." He leaned over the map again, pointed at the "fork" in the Red Sea, and said, "Imagine that the ship has long-range Katyusha rockets. Then there will be Katyushas falling on the large southwest coastal city of Ashkelon, and suddenly the very strategic balance of the Second Intifada will be altered. Let's find out what's on the ship. . . ."

"We shouldn't be giving up on the option of an operation in the Red Sea. Remind me again, why can't we come up with an option for capturing the ship there?"

The Red Sea option had taken hold of Mofaz. In those moments, he was recalling what Ram had told him: While the ship was in the Red Sea, the crew's guard would be down and easier to take by surprise. The moment they entered the Mediterranean Sea, the crew would be on high alert as the crew knew the Mediterranean was the area where Israel caught ships. Also, Ram had reminded Mofaz of the risk that the weapons could be dropped off before the ship arrived in the Mediterranean Sea and that catching the ship with no weapons would be a colossal failure.

Ram had sold Mofaz. Again, though Ram was a lower-ranking officer, Mofaz knew him well as a talented commander in charge of the West Bank's undercover Duvdevan Unit who had worked directly for him some years earlier. Mofaz also considered his lessons learned in the Yom Kippur War in Syria and the importance of surprise in special operations. He was ready to shock and bulldoze Yedidya and the rest of the high command into taking the risky option of capturing the *Karine A* in the Red Sea to maximize the element of surprise.

Silence fell over the room. Tamir surveyed those present. "Everyone understands now that Mofaz is dead set on the Red Sea option. He keeps coming back to it over and over again. That means either all of the explanations against it have not convinced him or he isn't taking them in," thought Tamir, mentally distancing himself from the situation for a moment. "The chief's main contribution has been to inject into the debate the concept of 'anticipated damage' regarding the scenario where we don't take over the ship in time and long-range Katyushas start falling on Ashkelon."

"We don't have an option right now for taking over the ship in the Red Sea because that kind of a capture operation would require a large number of forces operating for a substantial number of hours in those stormy waters," the navy commander said, doubling down on his position and again explaining the specific tactical problems.

Mofaz looked straight into Yedidya's eyes and then surveyed the others sitting around the conference table. The disappointment that had been troubling him for some time pained him like a wound deep in his chest. His frustration stemmed from different sources: the continued failure to convince the Americans that Arafat was the provocateur for the terrorist attacks, the failure to decisively defeat the wave of ongoing terrorist attacks, and the failure to block the Palestinians' arms buildup.

Mofaz selected his words carefully and gave them special emphasis: "This is a crucial matter, so I'm not giving up on the option of an operation in the Red Sea. I'm ready to take risks here. If we can clandestinely bring this ship to Eilat—with the smugglers arrested and with all the captured weapons laid out on the deck—that would be an incredible achievement!"

"How will the navy commander answer?" Tamir asked himself. "He is the highest authority when it comes to professional issues related to the navy. He understands the immensity of both the responsibility and the opportunities at stake. If he says 'no,' then the chief will need to drop the Red Sea option. How will Yedidya respond?"

Everyone waited for his answer. Mofaz was tense, but when Yedidya finally spoke, he did so without hesitation. It was unambiguously clear to him that he had received a directive from the chief. Yedidya said, "There is only one real chance to pull this off, and this would be with the fast patrol boat, which leaves tomorrow afternoon from Eilat. It can take a position in the Red Sea [about forty-six miles south of the Straits of Tiran and around the fork] and check the area. If the water is calmer, we can carry out an operation, and we can bring down the navy seals. After that we can refuel and take care of other logistical issues. Then there would be a chance that we could pull this off—if all the stars align. But I don't want to be counting on and basing our plans on assuming such a best-case scenario."

"Fine. Okay. But it's important to prepare for it," Mofaz answered.

"We will make sure there are plans for that scenario."

"So tell me!"

Yedidya briefly explained how the navy seals would use the commando boats to take over the ship. Then the question of fast roping came up. He said, "The navy seals are ready for this. Just less than a month ago they finished training for it overseas in an allied country. The problem is with the air force."

From that moment, the idea for training on sliding down a fast rope had taken hold of Mofaz, and it seemed that he really supported it. "I approve putting together a program to achieve the mission's goals."

The head of air force operations updated him next. Mashiach, the head of helicopter operations, had raised the training issue in internal discussions earlier that day with the commander of the air force. He estimated that the earliest date for getting to operational readiness would be Saturday. Also, he was lacking important details without which he did not want to commit to a specific date given there were technical problems, problems relating to the pilots, problems with the security of those sliding down the rope, and problems with the fast ropers being vulnerable to gunfire by the ship's crew if the men were armed.

Mofaz heard the issues and pushed to move forward on the issue the next day. By the next afternoon, he already wanted to see a "dry" plan for sliding down fast ropes and wanted preparations for doing it on Israeli Navy ships later that same day. "I'm telling you that this is extremely valuable. We can't miss this opportunity," Mofaz hammered home.

Tamir saw how Mofaz's face had lit up optimistically.

"Sir, tomorrow we will present everything to you!" the head of air force operations said while still hoping to cool Mofaz's enthusiasm for the idea.

"Tough for them," Tamir thought. "Now they'll be working an all-nighter like the navy."

Yedidya raised another issue—namely, the need to access the Boeing jet called the Atara. As noted previously, ELTA Systems, a subsidiary of the Israel Aerospace Industries, had developed a new radar system for the navy that could be mounted on the Atara for trying to find and track the *Karine A*. The navy first, however, required approval from the defense minister to have access to and use the Atara. The commander of the navy's plan was for the aircraft to start patrolling the next day at 2:00 p.m. to try to surveil the ship on its way north of the Saudi Arabian port of Jeddah in the Red Sea.

Eventually, Mofaz summarized the spectrum of options for the operation:

First Option: If the waters are calm—a clandestine naval commando sea-based capture operation of the ship in the Red Sea along with commandos sliding down from a fast rope from a helicopter.

Second Option: If the waters are not calm—capturing the ship mainly using commandos sliding down from a fast rope.

Third Option: "The Egyptian Option"—informing Egypt with the hope that the ship won't unload its weapons in Egypt but instead would head on a course toward the northern Sinai, during which the navy would capture it.

It was 11:00 p.m., but before the meeting concluded, the navy commander passed on the update that the necessary forces would travel down to Eilat the next day. Mofaz then turned to Yedidya to discuss the issue of who would be the lead commander in the field: "You need to have someone senior in the fast patrol boat. Someone serious who can tell you, 'Listen, under these circumstances, I don't recommend carrying out the takeover from either the air or the sea,' or who will say to you, 'It's a go,' and then you start to run with it."

Before he left the room, Mofaz took Yedidya aside and said, "Like I say before every forum, it is very important that there be a senior and experienced commander in the field who can give us a full picture—Chiny or someone like him."

Yedidya nodded his head, feeling the burdensome weight of authority hanging over him. To start planning an operation just now for the wavy and traitorous Red Sea with limited capabilities, with complex coordination required with the air force, with plans for sliding down fast ropes that still were not ready, and with everything happening at a breakneck pace but without even knowing where the ship was—it was an enormous task. And suddenly the state of the water, whether it was calm or stormy, became an Archimedean point.

From the IDF chief's bureau, Yedidya used the red phone to call Ram at the navy seals' base. Ram had sat in his office with his top aides, remaining cool headed while waiting for the drawn-out meeting to conclude.

"The chief has decided on the Red Sea," Yedidya told Ram.

"All right!" Ram called out with unabashed satisfaction.

"Settle down, settle down," said Yedidya, almost yelling. He updated him that the senior officer in the field, as was customary in the navy, would be Chiny, the navy's head of operations.

"You know that I have a plan ready for the Red Sea," Ram interjected, cutting him off.

"That is all very well and good, but how do we bring the commandos, those sailing in the commando boats, down to the Red Sea? How can we conceal them from the Egyptian lookout on the Straits of Tiran?" Yedidya questioned him roughly.

"I have an idea," Ram said suddenly.

"What's your idea?" asked Yedidya curiously.

Instead of having the commandos using up their energy by sailing in commando boats, Ram proposed that they travel aboard a civilian ship from Eilat up until the capture point in the Red Sea (the distance from Eilat to the capture point was 170 miles). Meanwhile, the commando boats would travel from Eilat with only a pilot and a navigator.

Yedidya was shocked for a moment. Then he said, "That's a brilliant idea, Ram! Very smart."

"You'll make sure that it is carried out?" Ram called out, raising his voice.

"Yes," said Yedidya and finished their conversation.

As Yedidya left the IDF chief's bureau, Ram's staff started to call up the navy seals, who had been in the West Bank city of Nablus to return to their home base at Atalit near the northern city of Haifa. With tremendous zeal, the navy seals started preparing.

Chiny, meanwhile, had spent the day in Eilat. He returned to Tel Aviv late in the evening and went to sleep at the Tal Hotel, where many naval officers slept when they worked late nights. "Let's see what the morning meeting with the commander of the navy brings," he thought a moment before trailing off to sleep around 11:00 p.m. Then the telephone rang.

Yedidya's bureau chief was on the line: "Come to the commander of the navy's office!"

"Why? What's happened? Isn't there a meeting tomorrow?"

"The commander wants you to come right now!"

"Come on, I'm dying to go to sleep. Today in Eilat was insane."

"No! The commander wants you to come now!"

"Okay, I'll come," said Chiny, who was now both surprised and very curious. Then he thought, "Why is the commander summoning me around midnight? Is a war breaking out?"

When Chiny arrived, Yedidya cut to the chase. "Listen," Yedidya started, turning to Chiny. His tone was serious; clearly something was bugging him. "I just came back from a meeting with the chief, and his orders were to carry out the operation in the Red Sea. The forces carrying out the operation will be Ram's navy seals, including sliding down from a fast rope. You're going to be the senior commander in the field. The plan, in general terms, is the navy seals' plan, which you are familiar with. You need to work through any remaining kinks, update it, and present it to me in the morning."

"The plan will be ready tomorrow morning, sir!" Chiny responded.

The streets of Tel Aviv were abandoned after a day of violent rain. On his way back to the hotel, Chiny envisioned all of the intelligence he had seen to date and noted that he needed to speak with Meshita. No less important, he also need to speak with Beni "the Weather Man" Ben-Porat, the head of the IDF Center for Meteorological Forecasts, and, of course, with Ram.

Even though he was not actually asleep yet, the eyes of Yoni Mann, the head of the Special Operations Branch in the Air Force, were already sealed shut after a long and hard day. His body felt beaten and worn out, his legs like jelly. Suddenly the telephone rang. Chiny was not the only one whose beauty sleep would be delayed.

It was the bureau chief of the head of air force operations: "Yoni, you need to come back to the base!"

Yoni was in shock. Just as Chiny did, he futilely pleaded, "I'm not coming back. It's almost midnight!"

He wanted to hang up, but then he heard the voice of Eliezer Shkedi, the head of air force operations himself: "Yoni, come! Your boss, the head of the Operations Division, is also coming."

"Okay, I'm coming," said Yoni. In only a few minutes, he was in his car, driving through wintery conditions back to Israeli Air Force Headquarters in Tel Aviv.

When Yoni arrived at Shkedi's office, other top officials dealing with helicopters and special forces were already seated. Yoni felt as if he had been hit by a tidal wave. He wondered what was going on.

Then Shkedi started talking. "I just came back from a meeting with the chief. I'm not going to go into all the details. The main thing is, Mofaz is very concerned that the smuggling ship may unload its weapons before it gets to the Mediterranean Sea. That means the plan of capturing the ship in the Mediterranean Sea is no longer the lead option. Mofaz wants to capture the ship in the Red Sea at a distance of forty-six miles south from the Straits of Tiran—outside of Egyptian territorial waters.

"This changes all of the navy's timing calculations. Based on its expected speed, the ship is expected to pass through there already on Friday, December 21. This leaves us only twenty-four hours to prepare a sliding fast-rope capability."

It was already midnight. Tomorrow, on December 20, Thursday, at 6:30 a.m., Yoni would need to present a plan before Commander of the Air Force Dan Halutz and the other air force brass. Yoni summoned his entire officer complement—more than forty people—to come to an emergency meeting at 2:00 a.m.

The room couldn't hold all of them. Choices needed to be made about who would get into the room. Most of those present were learning about the issue of the *Karine A* for the first time.

The Black Hawk helicopters would be in Atalit early that morning. Reuven Ben-Shalom, head of the helicopters desk, would fly there and be in one of the helicopters to better configure the tac-

Preparations in High Gear

tical plan. Ben-Shalom would check a range of issues: What was the distance from which a ship could hear the helicopter? How much time would it take for the helicopters to reach the ship and for the onboard commandos to slide down to the deck and take over the ship? How much time did it really take for the commandos to be transferred from the helicopters to the ship? How would they synchronize the arrival of the navy seals from the sea versus the commandos from the air? How would the two helicopters coordinate with each other?

Ben-Shalom would then fly to Eilat and be the air force's man in Chiny's forward command center. They would have to make other plans such as coordinating bringing the Atara into the service of the navy. According to the plan, the Atara was due to take off toward the Red Sea that day with the goal of locating the *Karine A*.

At 6:30 a.m., December 20, Yoni presented the plan to Halutz, who approved it.

7

Mission Ready—Overnight

The Crazy Day Begins

DECEMBER 20, 2001

At 6:30 a.m., Chiny met with Avi, the head of the navy's Operations Division, and with Ram. First, Avi told them that a fast-rope capability would be available.

"The air force," he said to Chiny, "already started to work on the issue yesterday after the air force commander issued an order. They have four usable ropes. So the operation can utilize two helicopters with two ropes each." None of them knew yet how many things were still unresolved, but they knew that the air force would still face serious logistical issues.

Then Ram presented the navy seals' plan to Chiny. The operational idea was to clandestinely take over the ship in the early hours of the morning while it was in motion and before a changeover of the ship's lookouts. At that time, fewer crew members would be on the bridge. The takeover would be carried out simultaneously by two sets of two commando boats converging on each side of the ship. The idea was to rush, surprise, and take over as much of the ship as possible while most crew members were still in their beds. Ram emphasized that the fast-roping forces would drop down on board according to developments, and those forces were prepared to assist in taking over the central positions.

Yedidya opened the next meeting but quickly handed it over to Chiny. Everyone who had expected the Mediterranean Sea would still be the operation's focus was very surprised to learn it was the Red Sea. Chiny emphasized that everything depended on the ability of the "Blue and White" (the Atara) to locate the ship and give enough advanced warning to the sea-based combat forces. So the idea was to use time and distance calculations of the ship's northern trajectory to carry out long-range surveillance overflights in the Red Sea during the time and in the area where it was expected to arrive. The Atara, with its long-range capabilities, long-range radar, and ability to hover in an area for six hours, was the expected answer to the surveillance issue. In parallel to the Atara's efforts, they would use a group of patrol aircraft with shorter ranges.

The intelligence, general operations, and navy seals' staffs all held meetings to make final preparations. Chiny met with Kobi to get the latest intelligence updates and continued to build up his staff for the operation, including appointing Shimon to be his personal intelligence liaison. All the pieces were sliding into place.

Then several things started to fall apart.

At 7:30 a.m. Yoni Mann received a telephone call from one of his desk chiefs. "We only have three fast ropes, but they don't meet international standards, and one of them is completely unusable."

The report made him stop breathing. The shocked Yoni could not even answer as the news had paralyzed him. He thought, "Could it be that the whole plan would fall apart because of ropes? Because of such minutia?"

Then the desk chief continued, "I delved into the issue, and I learned there are ropes in the upkeep inventory storage at the Tel Hashomer Logistics Base near Tel Aviv. But I can't get them."

"What do you mean? Why can't you get them?!" Yoni screamed.

"The sergeant major in charge of storage refused to give us the ropes without an approval from his superiors in the IDF Upkeep Command," his desk chief answered in a low voice.

"What do we do?" Yoni asked himself. "We have a major information security issue." He told the desk chief, "Get him on the telephone for me." Yoni hoped he would be able to convince the sergeant major.

When the desk chief got him on the line, Yoni said, "Hi, this is Lieutenant Colonel Yoni Mann from the air force. I'm in charge of all special operations for the air force. Tomorrow, we are carrying out special operations. You'll hear about it in the morning and be proud that you helped with it. So I need two ropes. You'll be helping with our operations."

Yoni was sure he had convinced him, but then the sergeant major responded, "Without a form from my superiors, I can't give you the ropes."

Yoni was beside himself. "Stay on hold," he told him. Yoni then called the air force control officer, who needed to check with Yoni to approve the three Black Hawk helicopters' leaving for operational training at the navy seals' base near Haifa.

"They are about to leave, and there aren't enough ropes," despaired Yoni, who was having trouble digesting the situation. And then a wild, mischievous but ingenious idea popped into his head. "Tell two of the Black Hawks they can take off, but tell the third to wait," he instructed the control officer.

He went back on the line with the sergeant major at Tel Hashomer. Yoni said, "If in about ten minutes, a helicopter flies over you, flashes its lights, and circles over the storage area, then will you believe me about who I am?"

After a short hesitation, the sergeant major answered, "So that might change things."

"Stay next to your telephone," Yoni said to him. He then called the control officer and gave him special instructions: "The third helicopter will first fly to Tel Hashomer, flash its lights, and do a circle pattern over the storage areas."

The confused control officer carried out the order, and the helicopter took off for Tel Hashomer. After ten minutes, Yoni was on the line again with the sergeant major. "So, do you hear something?"

"Yes, there's a noise from a helicopter over the base. He's a bit of a distance from my storage area. Wait, wait! He's actually circling now directly over my storage area. Wow! My facility is shaking—and it's an awful noise. Okay, okay! What do you want?" he asked Yoni.

With a smug smile, Yoni answered, "I want the two ropes. Go right now to the Tel Hashomer landing pad. A military helicopter will be waiting for you. Give the pilot the two ropes, and the air force will owe you one."

And that was how it went down. The three helicopters flew off with five ropes and landed at the navy seals' base near Haifa. Incidentally, one of the ropes was not usable, but the four usable ones they had could save the operation.

The Crazy Day Continues

DECEMBER 20, 2001

Mofaz finished his regular situation update, and Chiny entered to join the majority of the high command. A large picture of the *Karine A*'s sister ship was set on Mofaz's conference table along with a map.

"What are you calling the operation?" Mofaz asked with interest.

"Noah's Ark," Amitai, head of the IDF's Operations Command, answered him.

Halutz opened with the good news about the fast-roping developments. Then he and Amitai moved on to describing how they would employ the Atara and the other aircraft that would accompany it.

Chiny then started his presentation, emphasizing that the primary problem would be finding the ship. "Sir, everything here is built on the assumption that we find the ship. The moment we find her, the rest will become a rolling time line of specific mission goals." Then he described a range of tactical operational issues and different scenarios based on whether the weather was clear or stormy.

When Chiny finished, the IDF chief bombarded him with questions: "You'll be on one of the fast patrol boats?"

"Yes."

"You'll be able to receive and have access to all of the information and intelligence regarding the ship?"

"Yes."

"You'll be able to get a description of the ship and what cargo it's bearing and in which areas?"

"Yes."

"You'll be able to weigh the impact of the weather on the operation and pick among the options for action accordingly?"

"Yes."

"You already captured the *Santorini*?"

"Yes."

"You've been to the Straits of Tiran?"

"Many times."

During a short break, the head of the IDF's Operations Command went down to his office to meet with U.S. defense attaché Clark. Mofaz had instructed him, "If he has new intelligence, then update us. And under no circumstances can you tell them that we are about to carry out capturing the ship!"

Then Mofaz glanced over at Chiny. They stared at each other for a few seconds, and the room went silent.

"You are there," said Mofaz, bending forward a bit as he continued to stare into Chiny's eyes, "to make the tough judgment calls in the field. I'm not willing to risk a failed operation. If the weather is so bad that there is no way they can stop the ship, neither with the fast-roping commandos nor by climbing onto the ship from commando boats, then you say, 'Abort.' Then we start to recalibrate."

It was a moment Chiny would never forget. In that moment, they had formed a pact, a brotherhood of sorts. In Chiny's mind, it was now crystal clear to him that the IDF chief trusted him with this complex operation, which carried with it strategic consequences at a diplomatic level. And, in turn, both he and Mofaz implicitly trusted Ram to lead any group of forces in any scenario—even through the fires of hell. It really was a dream team.

Then one last question fell on him. Mofaz asked, "Would you prefer a daytime or nighttime operation?"

"Nighttime. I'm not sure that we'll have the freedom to choose between day and night. It depends on when the ship arrives in the zone of the capture operation."

Mofaz was about to fly to the navy seals' base near Haifa, where he would brief them about going to Eilat in the afternoon and would follow the fast-rope drills. Before he left, he turned to those attending the meeting and said, "We need to keep the Mediterranean Sea option ready to go. We still have time. I'll issue an additional approval of a potential operation in the Mediterranean Sea."

Even with the switch to the Red Sea, the stakes were too high. They needed to be ready for all eventualities.

As planning for the operation continued, Kobi's secretary called out, "Kobi, Yoki wants you on the telephone."

"Transfer the call to here!"

"Kobi," Yoki said, "just now I finished my meeting with the deputy Shin Bet director. He was furious that the request was only relayed at the last minute."

"Cut to the chase—did he grant our request?"

"He's giving us the two interrogators we requested. He has conditions: One is that they'll only be used once the capture of the ship is completed. The second is that they'll work together on the interrogations."

"Fine. They should come here with all of their gear at around 3:00 p.m. Give them a debriefing. In the evening, they'll fly to Eilat."

Later, Meshita presented the plan to the defense minister both to update him and to get his approvals. Then he was passed a note: he needed to be "at a meeting with the prime minister at his house in Jerusalem to present him with Operation Noah's Ark, including both intelligence and operational aspects."

Meshita apologized, ran to his office, grabbed his aides, and said to his driver, "Fly!" It was 1:30 p.m., and he didn't even know where the prime minister's house was in Jerusalem.

When Mofaz landed at the navy seals' base, Ram came to greet him. Mofaz shook his hand warmly. Ram introduced him to Shlomi Dahan, the commander of the fast-roping forces, but Mofaz knew him well. The combat fighters had already started drilling by fast roping down from two helicopters onto the landing pad. Mofaz was anxious to get up close and see the fast roping in action. He was the one who needed to give the green light. But first he spoke with the navy seals who would be clandestinely climbing aboard the ship from the commando boats. They were making final preparations for their helicopter flights to Eilat. All of their equipment, including their commando boats, were already being transported to Eilat on humongous trucks.

"If you bring the ship to Eilat, it will be like we dropped a five-hundred-pound hammer on Arafat's head," said Mofaz in explaining to the navy seals the strategic importance of the operation. He and Ram then returned to the staging area for the fast roping. A host of officers was there.

The fighters were fast roping was onto the landing pad. Mofaz got to see the fast roping for the first time and saw that it was not terribly difficult. He spoke to the commandos and gave them a goal—to slide down in the shortest possible time. The faster they slid, the less exposed they and their helicopters would be to potential hostile fire. He also spoke with the helicopter pilots and understood how important their skills were. When he asked to try fast roping himself, the air force commander wouldn't let him, but he did tell Mofaz that the Atara would be taking off at 1:15 p.m.

"Hopefully, it will find the ship," said Mofaz. The IDF chief could feel the fire of enthusiasm and determination to succeed that permeated those involved in the operation, and it made him optimistic. "I approve the fast-rope capability for action," Mofaz declared on the spot. The fast-roping training would continue, and in the meantime, Mofaz, the navy commander, and the air force commander flew to Jerusalem to meet with Prime Minister Sharon at his house.

Meshita got to the prime minister's house by the skin of his teeth, just in time. He was given coffee and cakes as he waited for Mofaz and his crowd of commanders to arrive—noticeably late. Arranging seating at the prime minister's conference table, Mofaz placed Meshita next to him: "Hezi, you sit next to me. I'll open, and then you'll present the intelligence and the operation."

When Sharon entered and asked where they were coming from,

Mofaz told him about the fast-roping training exercises. Mofaz said he had wanted to give it a try.

Sharon, who often was self-deprecating about his weight, seemed to mischievously imply that he was glad Mofaz and the young commandos were dealing with fast-roping issues as it would be too much for him. The prime minister was also often the first one to take sandwiches at meetings such as this one (he particularly enjoyed hot dogs in a bun with pickles), and he might even be known to take two sandwiches at a time.

Mofaz opened the meeting by presenting the strategic big picture, which he knew was Sharon's focus. Sharon wanted to know from him if there was any end in sight to the suicide bombings and other attacks that Arafat as well as terrorist groups such as Hamas were promoting against Israel. Mofaz was doing his best, but he did not have good news in that arena. But today Mofaz wanted to shift Sharon's attention from the daily battle against dangerous but small-time terrorist attacks to understanding the significance of the *Karine A*.

Sharon's decades-long opponent, Arafat, had figured out a way to potentially alter the balance of power and threaten large Israeli cities such as Ashdod and Ashkelon with massive rocket fire. Such an attack would cause great devastation and make the suicide bus bombings seem a minor footnote. Mofaz looked hard at Sharon and suggested he listen very carefully to Meshita's presentation about the *Karine A* threat, which could bring long-range powerful rockets from Iran and Hezbollah to Arafat.

Meshita presented all the details. Then he summarized, "We are 100 percent sure about the ship, and regarding the weapons we have very strong signs but have not achieved certainty. But just like a suicide bomber, even if you are not sure that he has an explosive vest, you shoot him. The same goes with this dirty ship."

Sharon interjected with questions about the *Karine A*: Were they sure the ship was connected to Arafat and the PA, and how could they be so sure? Sharon knew that even if Israel managed to catch the *Karine A*, Arafat would use all of his guile to cover up his involvement and avoid blame. What would be the plan if they were wrong, the ship was a legitimate commercial venture, and Israel faced global criticism for jumping the gun and grabbing the wrong ship?

Being a former general, Sharon also asked serious operational questions: How would the navy deal with capturing the *Karine A* if confronted with stormy weather? He also asked how the morale was among the navy seals, and he asked about Ram, whom he knew personally. Although the prime minister did not know every officer with the rank of captain in the navy, Ram commanded the navy seals. Sharon used the seals frequently in all sorts of extremely dangerous and sensitive missions, so he had made an effort to meet with Ram and got to know the commander who regularly risked his life and led one of Israel's elite units into battle.

Here and there, Mofaz interjected to back Meshita and to reassure Sharon. Mofaz also kept repeating to Sharon the mantra that the *Karine A* saga would have strategic and diplomatic importance of the highest order.

The prime minister approved the plan, praised its daring spirit, and moved on to a discussion with Mofaz about budgetary issues. When everyone else left the room but Mofaz, Sharon placed his hand on Mofaz's upper back, gave him a bear hug, and reassured him that he would have all of the backing he needed. The prime minister also specifically flagged that Mofaz had been smart to insist on putting a senior flag officer such as Chiny in the field, one who could make the rough judgment calls as the situation dynamically developed on the spot.

The last thing Sharon asked Mofaz before he left was whether he had found the ship yet.

Mofaz frowned. He did not like giving the prime minister bad news and an unclear path, but he had to confess that he had not found the *Karine A* yet. The Atara still had not found the ship.

The approval to draft the Atara and its staff into the IDF's reserves was signed by the defense minister and arrived around 1:00 p.m. "You can take off," said Zvi from the ELTA company to the aircraft's crew.

The pilots were from Israel Aerospace Industries, and the radar and picture-taking apparatuses were operated by Zvi's ELTA staff. The mission commander was from the navy's surveillance patrols, and he brought along with him six patrol staff. Lieutenant Junior Grade Tal from naval intelligence was aboard along with an air force navigator and a few navy operations command officials who were observing the aircraft's performance.

At 1:15 p.m., the Atara took off from its regular base. It could survey and get an in-depth look at targets from a very long-range. It was looking for any ships that were bearing north and were similar to the *Karine A*. The crew looked for a ship of around a hundred meters long, with three derricks—located next to the bridge, in the center, and at the bow—and traveling at less than fifteen knots, or about seventeen miles per hour. The accompanying aircraft would move in for a closer look and make a formal positive identification of any ship with these characteristics.

Around 5:00 p.m., the Atara was getting ready to leave the search area, having surveyed ninety targets. At about 518 miles southwest of the Straits of Tiran, it then found a suspicious target near the Sudanese coast and south of the Saudi Arabian city of Jeddah. It called on the accompanying aircraft to attempt an identification and turned to fly back to Israel. The accompanying aircraft could not confirm that the target was the *Karine A*, but it did photograph it.

The Crazy Day Ends

DECEMBER 20, 2001

Though he started to have doubts about whether the *Karine A* was really nearby, Chiny flew to Eilat anyway.

The base in Eilat was small. The base commander, Lt. Cdr. Yehuda Sisso, a missile boatman, was new in the role. His main forces were made up of two fast patrol boats, each containing ten fighters (including both those manning machine guns and those sailing the boat), and one Dabur, a smaller and slower but highly maneuverable patrol boat. At the start of December, the small patrol boat was in the shipyard for repairs. The night of the twelfth, Yehuda had received a telephone call from the navy commander's bureau chief. In a series of veiled references, he had brought him up to date on the *Karine A* situation and about the slim possibility that the ship would be captured in the Gulf of Eilat.

"This is top, top secret," he was told, "with the highest level of information security protocols." Only his deputy, his intelligence officer, and he himself knew the highly classified secret.

At the time, Yehuda put the base on a fast-paced operational footing. People didn't understand what was happening. "It's a drill," went the rumor in the city of Eilat, where there were always whispers of rumors and wild tales. But no one really knew.

Then the morning of the "crazy day," December 20, Yehuda was instructed to "find a civilian ship that will transport the navy seals from Eilat to the northern part of the Red Sea. Their commando boats will set sail from Eilat with only a pilot and a commander aboard. They'll sail to the northern part of the Red Sea—forty-six miles from the Straits of Tiran—where they'll meet up with the navy seals aboard the civilian ship."

He left the base and went to the marina at the port of Eilat. He knew the marina's administrator well. "How can I find a civilian ship and rent it for a few days?" he asked the administrator.

The administrator gave him a bewildered look and said, "Try on the northern end of the port. Maybe you'll find someone there who'll rent to you."

Yehuda searched but had no luck. As he started to despair, he finally saw a ship named *Miami*. He went closer and met a huge man with a long beard and large earrings who was dressed similar to a Robinson Crusoe–type character. Yehuda inquired about renting the boat.

"How many days do you want to rent my boat for?" asked the Crusoe-looking man.

"For about a week," Yehuda answered.

"What do you need it for?"

"We want to show some of our navy commanders a good time for a few days," said Yehuda.

Crusoe looked at him skeptically but eventually told him he

would need to rent it for a full week. Then he told Yehuda the price and added everything would need to be paid upfront and in cash.

Yehuda was shocked. The price was exorbitant. He tried to haggle but got nowhere. What was he supposed to do now? "I'll come back to you in a little while," said Yehuda, and he walked away.

"Upfront and in cash!" Crusoe yelled after him.

Yehuda had to pull some big strings. A defense ministry official flew in the cash, and the *Miami* was brought to the navy's Eilat base, where it was prepared for sailing.

At 6:30 p.m. in Haifa, Mofaz, Yedidya, and others watched the navy seals in a sliding drill from two Black Hawk helicopters onto a ship. Everything went successfully. While at the Haifa base, Yedidya updated Mofaz about the suspicious target near Sudan. They ate and held a status meeting. Mofaz was concerned. Everyone had talked so much about the Atara and its radar, but it hadn't found anything! And the suspicious target just made the dilemma starker: Was it the ship or not? Should they prepare for a capture operation as if it were the *Karine A*? Clearly he thought they needed to try to photograph it again immediately, but how? The air force commander suggested using an F-15I aircraft, and Mofaz approved.

The aircraft took off and photographed the ship, but it would take time for the photographs to be deciphered. By then, they might not be needed as new intelligence would likely come in. Everyone was on edge.

In Eilat, before he trailed off to sleep, Chiny kept asking himself, "Where the hell is the ship?"

Ram also was concerned about the ship and about his navy seals getting tired as well as their readiness eroding from waiting. He wondered, "What about the Americans?"

Meanwhile, Meshita thought, "We haven't heard anything from Stephanie. The defense attaché, Clark, just met with the IDF's planning commander and didn't give him any new information." So Meshita called Stephanie's office. An aide in her office told him that she was already on her way to see him.

When Stephanie arrived around 11:00 p.m., Meshita lost it with her: "You promised us intelligence, and there's nothing! Go check!"

Kobi and Gil calmed him down. Tensions ran high. Meshita was the one responsible for intelligence, and with his background in operations, he knew the lack of the ship's location was eating away at troop morale.

Stephanie, a veteran professional, also knew something about navy issues and understood Meshita's inner turmoil. She told him, "I'll check and get back to you."

Later, a bleary-eyed Stephanie returned and said, "I checked, and the result was, 'The commercial ship, the *Karine A*, was located on December 20 in the afternoon anchored at a port in Yemen.'"

Meshita thought he was going to faint. While Kobi ran off to check the exact spot, Meshita became furious and again went off on Stephanie: "Why didn't you say something? Do you know how important this is to us? What is the ship doing there? Are you sure it's there? Totally sure?"

Stephanie threw up her hands helplessly. She had no idea why the U.S. intelligence community had left Israel blindsided at this point, after promising regular updates, and she would never uncover a clear answer. She knew getting these updates in real time was crucial for the Israelis, but as it became clear a few weeks later in meetings in Washington DC, large swaths of the U.S. defense establishment had no idea about the *Karine A* or about its significance. As a small piece of a massive intelligence body, Stephanie could only do so much. But whoever's fault it was, the damage was done, and she didn't know if there would be a chance to repair it. Sometimes world history, success or failure, can turn on an unfortunate weak link in some random part of the intelligence chain.

In addition, she said that she didn't know why the ship was in Yemen, but she was completely certain that it was there. She promised that when the ship left, whether day or night, she would report it immediately.

Kobi returned and said, "It's right near the port of Hodeida. There is a small port there for Yemen's navy."

"I'm going up to Yedidya," Meshita said, and he brusquely left Stephanie, who was still brushing tears from her eyes.

Their interaction would have been tense under the circumstances, but the people involved made it even more intense. On the one hand, Meshita was a man and a high-ranking rear admiral, but he was from the United States' "little brother," Israel. On the other hand, while Stephanie was a mere lieutenant commander and a woman surrounded by aggressive, confident men, she represented the world's preeminent superpower. And here he had been yelling at her. Again, it was a low moment that would require some repairing later. Meshita, however, felt he had no alternative. He had needed to make clear to the United States—and Stephanie represented the United States, for all intents and purposes—how grave the situation was and how much Israel was depending on it to track the ship.

Meshita then updated Yedidya, who in turn briefed Mofaz. The chief set a consultation meeting for the next day. Then everyone was sent to get some rest.

Meanwhile, Yoni called the head of the helicopters desk at his hotel in Eilat. Waking him up, Yoni said, "Tomorrow, when you get up, make your way back to Tel Aviv. Now, go back to sleep."

After midnight, Kobi called and woke Chiny's intelligence officer, Shimon, in Eilat to update him. Shimon washed his face and thought, "We need to verify the Americans' information with the Blue and White! And from the moment that it's confirmed, I need to find out when the ship will leave the Hodeida area. I also need to request immediate satellite coverage of that area and to explain exactly where they can find the ship to ensure they don't miss it in their photographs."

Shimon spoke directly with the satellite surveillance unit. Surveillance using the EROS satellite could begin only as of December 25. For technical reasons, there was no other option. He then alerted Kobi and Meshita.

Thus, Friday, December 21, started with many questions: Could they rely on the Americans? What was the ship doing in the port north of Hodeida? When would it leave?

1. The *Karine A* docked in the port of Eilat after its capture. Courtesy of the IDF Spokesman's Unit, Navy photo lab.

2. The sign on the bridge of the *Karine A* showing its former name, RIM K, which was never removed. Courtesy of the IDF Spokesman's Unit, Navy photo lab.

3. *Left to right*: Israel Defense Forces chief of staff Shaul Mofaz, Defense Minister Binyamin Ben-Eliezer, and Prime Minister Ariel Sharon. Courtesy of the IDF Spokesman's Unit, Navy photo lab.

4. Israel Defense Forces deputy chief of staff Moshe Ya'alon (later IDF chief and defense minister). Courtesy of the IDF Spokesman's Unit, Navy photo lab.

5. *Left to right*: Naval intelligence chief Rear Adm. Hezi Meshita, head of naval intelligence operations Captain Kobi, and head of naval intelligence analysis Captain Gil. Courtesy of the IDF Spokesman's Unit, Navy photo lab.

6. Hezbollah military chief Imad Mughniyeh. Fars News Agency.

7. Naval intelligence chief Rear Adm. Hezi Meshita. Courtesy of the IDF Spokesman's Unit, Navy photo lab.

8. Israeli Navy Seals intelligence commander Lieutenant Colonel Itamar. Courtesy of the IDF Spokesman's Unit, Navy photo lab.

9. Incoming Israeli Defense Intelligence director Maj. Gen. Aharon Zeevi Farkash. Courtesy of the IDF Spokesman's Unit, Navy photo lab.

10. Outgoing Israeli Defense Intelligence chief Maj. Gen. Amos Malka. Courtesy of the IDF Spokesman's Unit, Navy photo lab.

11. Iran's Ayatollah Ali Khamenei. Khamenei.ir.

12. Palestinian Authority president Yasir Arafat. Government Press Office.

13. Islamic Revolutionary Guard Corps' Quds Force chief Qasem Soleimani. Khamenei.ir.

14. This photo shows a similar plane to the Atara aircraft, which provided long-range surveillance of the *Karine A* and later served as the forward command center for the IDF chief. Courtesy of the IDF Spokesman's Unit, Navy photo lab.

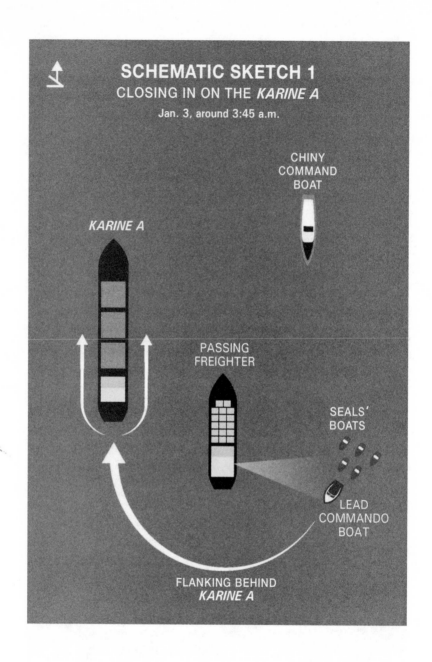

15. Diagram of the capture of the *Karine A*, sketch 1. Created by Zeev Eldar.

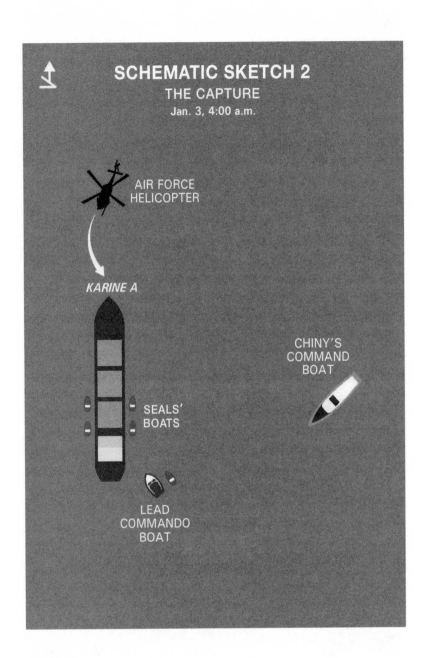

16. Diagram of the capture of the *Karine A*, sketch 2. Created by Zeev Eldar.

KARINE-A
איתור שם האניה

17. Footage identifying the *Karine A* from a surveillance aircraft. White lines indicate the area where surveillance aircraft saw the ship's name. Courtesy of the IDF Spokesman's Unit, Navy photo lab.

18. Footage of commandos taking over the *Karine A*. Courtesy of the IDF Spokesman's Unit, Navy photo lab.

4:06 / 5:53

19. The commandos raise the Israeli flag over the *Karine A*. Courtesy of the IDF Spokesman's Unit, Navy photo lab.

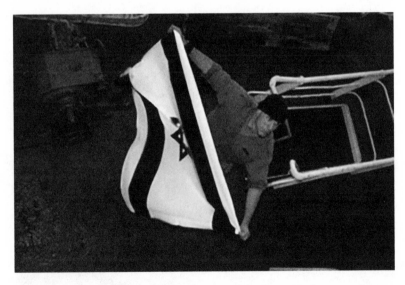

20. A commando holds the Israeli flag aboard the *Karine A*. Courtesy of the IDF Spokesman's Unit, Navy photo lab.

21. How the *Karine A*'s storage area 3 looked with the weapons in the crates. Courtesy of the IDF Spokesman's Unit, Navy photo lab.

22. A desk with navigation maps on the command bridge. Courtesy of the IDF Spokesman's Unit, Navy photo lab.

23. Displaying the captured weapons in Eilat. Courtesy of the IDF Spokesman's Unit, Navy photo lab.

24. More captured weapons displayed in Eilat. Courtesy of the IDF Spokesman's Unit, Navy photo lab.

25. Eilat monument commemorating Operation Noah's Ark. Courtesy of the
IDF Spokesman's Unit, Navy photo lab.

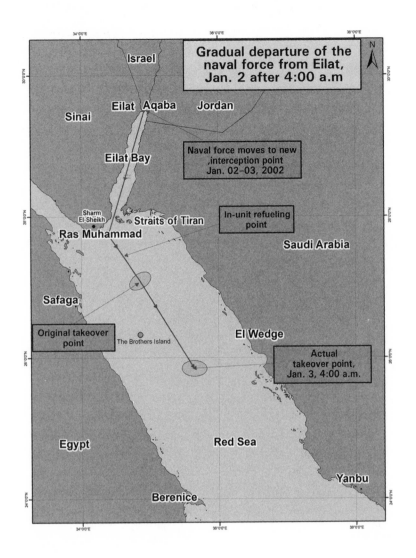

26. The naval force moves to the new interception point.
Created by Almog Hajaj.

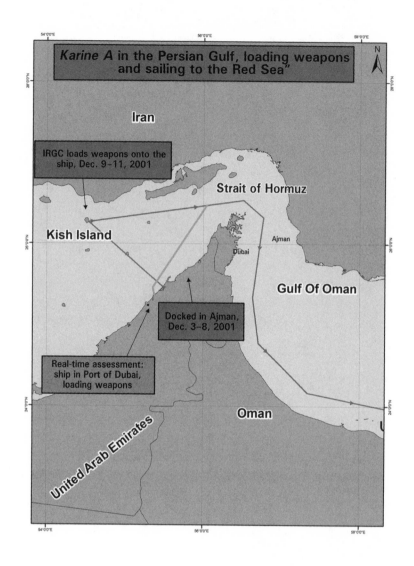

27. *Karine A* in the Persian Gulf, loading weapons and sailing to the Red Sea.
Created by Almog Hajaj.

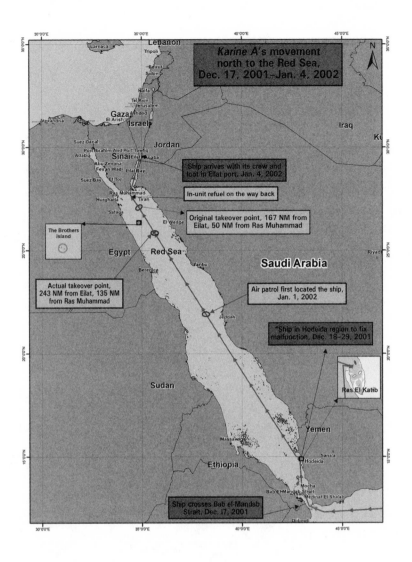

28. *Karine A*'s movement north to the Red Sea.
Created by Almog Hajaj.

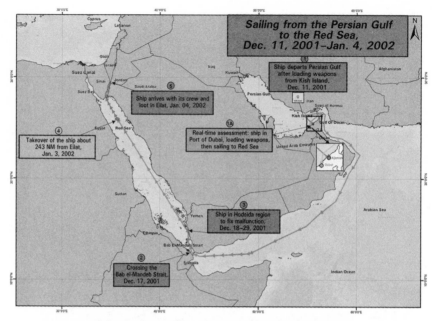

29. The ship's route from the Persian Gulf to the Red Sea.
Created by Almog Hajaj.

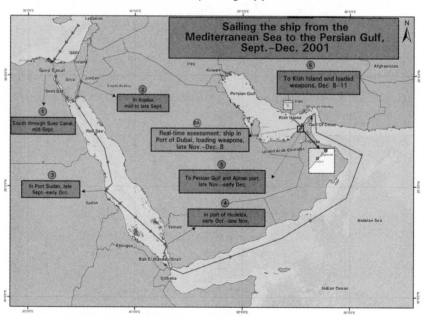

30. Sailing the ship from the Mediterranean Sea to the Persian Gulf.
Created by Almog Hajaj.

31. Navy chief Yedidya Yaari. Courtesy of the
IDF Spokesman's Unit, Navy photo lab.

32. Israeli Navy Seals chief Capt. Ram Rothberg (*right*; later chief of the navy). Courtesy of the IDF Spokesman's Unit, Navy photo lab.

33. Junior naval intelligence analyst Anat. Courtesy of the IDF Spokesman's Unit, Navy photo lab.

8

A Waiting Game

Mofaz looked over the intelligence dispatch alert of naval intelligence with its new information from the United States. According to the time, speed, and distance calculations based on the U.S. information, the ship would take about three to four days to travel from the Yemeni port to the Straits of Tiran. But what if the new U.S. intelligence was wrong about the location of the ship?

Mofaz then looked at Halutz, the air force commander, as if to say, "It's very important to me, very important, to confirm that the ship is in a port in Yemen. Everything about planning the operation depends on it."

Once again, Mofaz remembered the lessons learned from mistakes in the Syrian operation decades earlier due to incomplete intelligence. He was ready not only to expend extraordinary resources for training and gathering intelligence but also to take major risks earlier in the game to ensure that his special forces were not sent into an ambush or a situation from which they could not escape. If something was not impossible, he wanted his people to move mountains to do it so that his troops would face no surprises regarding the *Karine A*. Mofaz's navy seals would not be ambushed or caught by surprise as he had been in Syria.

The air force commander assured Mofaz, "We'll send surveillance aircraft there to take photographs. They'll refuel in midair

143

to travel the long distance [a round trip of approximately 2,500 miles]. We can get there. There is no place that we cannot reach."

Midair refueling and flying such long distances were off the charts from what the air force normally did. But these requirements were not impossible, and to catch the *Karine A*, the IDF's top echelons were getting used to finding a way to do even the impossible.

Mofaz felt better. "This will be a highly risky operation," he said to himself. "And it might get unwanted attention, but we need to do it." When they got up to leave, he leaned over toward the air force commander and asked, "Can we do the flight today?"

"No, it'll require lots of preparation and personnel. The surveillance aircraft will need to fly a thousand miles from Eilat—farther than Tehran!"

"On Saturday?"

"Yes."

Mofaz was left deep in thought. "Why did the ship stop in Yemen? Maybe the risk of an operation in the Red Sea was too great? Maybe the operational forces' capabilities were insufficient given the potential pitfalls, as IDF deputy chief Moshe Ya'alon had noted? What would the fast patrol boats and the commando boats be able to do if they ended up face to face with a larger Egyptian missile boat? Nothing!!"

Early in the morning, Yedidya contacted Chiny, and they agreed that Chiny should return immediately to Tel Aviv. They also agreed that Ram and his navy seals should return to their base to continue training for whenever the postponed operation might occur.

Chiny got back to Tel Aviv quickly and at around 10:00 a.m. went into Meshita's office. He saw a large vase of flowers on his desk. "What's that?" he said perplexed.

"I'm going to go over to see Stephanie soon at the U.S. Embassy and apologize for losing it with her yesterday," Meshita responded.

"Good for you," said Chiny. "Will we know when the ship leaves?" That was what he cared about.

"We'll know. Maybe with a lag time of a few hours, but we'll know," said Meshita.

When Meshita visited the U.S. Embassy in Tel Aviv, he offered the flowers to Stephanie and apologized. A senior officer such as Meshita giving a more junior foreign officer flowers was highly unusual. But from Stephanie's appreciative tears, Meshita could tell that she understood he meant well and that he recognized how close the U.S.-Israeli intelligence relationship was at all levels. If Stephanie had been a man, Meshita probably would have done something else. He believed it was important to repair the connection with someone he had worked with so closely, even as he also felt that the temporary anger he conveyed to her as the U.S. representative had been necessary on Israel's behalf at a crucial moment.

Then with an embarrassed smile, Meshita said to the still emotional Stephanie, "But I have a request."

"What is it?" Stephanie asked curiously.

"Give me the coordinates of the ship. We need them to take surveillance photographs."

Stephanie took the bouquet and gave Meshita the coordinates. She also added, "While you were on your way over here, I called Gil and told him that as of this morning, the ship is still anchored in the same place."

Before they parted ways, Stephanie said, "At the start of next week, it will be Christmastime, so you may not get any reports for a day or two. Don't worry. Later today, you'll get a call from U.S. Naval Intelligence director Rear Adm. Richard Porterfield."

Back at his office, Meshita updated Chiny and told the surprised Shimon the ship's coordinates. Shimon left and headed to the photographing desk at the air force's operations branch. Specifically, he went to the section for maritime maps at a scale of 1:500,000. He was very embarrassed and somewhat relieved to find that the air force's maps were not any better than the maritime maps. Shimon put in a request for a surveillance operation and ran through the area that needed to be photographed, the point where the ship was, and various technical issues. From the first moment, he felt resistance from the air force's desk for photographing. Personnel pointed out it was a very complex operation, and the air force had never performed a surveillance operation that far from Israel. Also, they asked, why did it have to be done on Saturday specifically?

Eventually, Shimon worked out a plan with the air force and returned to Meshita's office to update him. Following that, Meshita left for his house. When he was about two-thirds of the way home, he got a call on his cell. He pulled over. It was U.S. Naval Intelligence chief Porterfield.

"We trust and rely on you," Meshita repeatedly assured Porterfield.

Admiral Porterfield did not need to promise much. Simply his taking the time to reach out directly to Meshita spoke for itself. "You can count on us. As a superpower, we'll use all of our intelligence collection powers on your behalf."

Meanwhile, Kobi also returned to his house. On his way, he called Itamar, who was working at Ram's side in Eilat. "Are you coming tomorrow to the soccer game at Bloomfield Stadium against Ashdod?"

"From Eilat? Who's going to pick me up from the airport?"

"Me!"

"Fine. Do you have any new intelligence information for me?"

"Nope." Kobi also didn't imagine that there would be any new information to tell Itamar at Bloomfield.

It was Amit's turn to run the integrated intelligence operations room. Around midnight, the head of the international commercial ships desk got a notice from the gate to the base that an unexpected woman had arrived who wanted to see him. When he went to the gate, Stephanie handed him a large package, said a few words, and left. Still surprised and curious, he returned to the operations room. Once there, he opened it and was stunned: it contained the Spanish diagrams of the ship, now called *Karine A*, from the 1978 Vigo shipyards! He couldn't believe it. Thrilled, he immediately notified Gil, Kobi, and Meshita.

On Saturday, December 22, the surveillance aircraft took off during the afternoon and headed south toward Yemen. The operation was called Pundak Hajachnun in a reference to a Sabbath food that is part of Yemenite Jewish culture.

Around evening, Shimon brought the film rolls from the air force and put the film in the processing chemicals. Next, skipping through the surveillance photos, he moved straight to the target point, set the eyepiece on zoom, and started to examine them. Immediately he saw the ship sitting north of one of Yemen's ports and in the area where ships wait to enter one of Yemen's other larger ports. There was not even a shadow of a doubt. It was the *Karine A* in all of its glory. A fantastic shot! And he was the first Israeli to lay eyes on the ship.

That night, Yedidya had trouble sleeping. In the end, he decided to appeal to his counterparts in the United States and see if they would loan him some fast ropes. The readiness of the air force at that stage was minimal, and it was doubtful whether the Israeli fast-rope systems met international standards. "By the time we could buy systems like that on our own, we would already be working on the *Karine B*," he fretted.

Time-out with the Ship in the Shop

DECEMBER 23–26, 2001

Itamar, who was fluent in Spanish, was restless and practically shaking with anticipation to see the original Spanish-language diagrams of the *Karine A* from the Spanish shipyards. This information was the exact intelligence that his navy seals needed. Israeli intelligence analysts had already prepared photos and blown-up diagrams for him. He made some additional copies and grabbed the original copy for himself. He traveled to the navy seals' base, closed himself off in his office, and started to familiarize himself with the schematics: every door, every opening, every window, every staircase, and every derrick—all with an eye to how these details would impact the two-pronged sea- and air-based operation.

He called Hanania at his house. "Hanania, I have the original diagrams of the ship!"

"Are they similar to what I wrote up?"

"Yes, you were eerily close. Hanania, you are incredible!"

"I'll be coming to see you tonight."

"Perfect. Tell me, when the ship sails, are its derricks straight, or do they tilt at an angle?" Itamar also wanted to know whether the sliding doors on the surface of the deck were closed or slightly open. These details were very important as they could make the difference between life and death when carrying out the fast roping. It would be a problem if they slid down thinking they would land on solid, closed doors, only to find the doors open and fall through them.

All of the navy seals were back at their base that Sunday, December 23. Their focus was on preparing for the full drill of the operation the next day, December 24. They would carry out the drill at night with a full stand-in crew complement, just as the operation would run in real life. The rental ship looked similar to the *Karine A*. Chiny would be in a fast patrol boat with his forward command group; Ram would be in the lead commando boat. The initial infiltration force would be on the four commando boats, and support staff would also be at the ready.

Meanwhile, Itamar called in two architects for reserve duty to make a model of the ship using a standing carton. They would work all night so that a perfect model of the ship at a scale of 1:100 would be ready by Monday. Another set of staffers prepared a full-size model of the ship out of iron and jute—a vegetable fiber that can be woven into more solid material—that the navy seals would use for their drill. Hanania was with those staff members most of the time, giving them tips for building the model, and he gave advice to the navy seals. Around the middle of the week, each of the navy seals would receive prepared intelligence about the ship with photos, schematics, diagrams, and three-dimensional photo views of the ship and its individual parts, as well as explanations and information regarding its crew.

Itamar mainly wanted to find the best way for the seals to absorb all the information. During one of the meetings Ram held that day with the commanders, Itamar was adamant in explaining, "We've had some luck. It's good that we didn't find the ship a few days ago. Now we've gotten the most important prize—time to prepare properly and to gather more intelligence."

In Tel Aviv, as the sun rose on Sunday, Kobi and Shimon went to meet with Yedidya. Chiny was already there. Shimon presented his blown-up photographs of the ship and a map that showed its exact location. He explained what they were looking at and compared it to the picture of the sister ship. No containers were on the ship; the deck was clear. They also found the ship's radar. Yedidya and Chiny reviewed the blown-up photographs. Ultimately, they were relieved to be able to eyeball the ship that naval intelligence had been telling them about since December 5. It really did exist!

Kobi updated them about the plan for more satellite surveillance: Efforts were underway to maximize the potential of the satellite coverage on December 25, 26, and 28 of the area where the ship was docked so that Israel would not be solely reliant on the ongoing goodwill of the United States. There were also efforts being taken by Unit 8200 and other initiatives.

"Do the Americans give us a report about the ship once or twice a day?" Chiny asked curiously.

"They committed to at least once per day, but I think they're taking pictures of the target area at least twice a day," said Kobi. "So far, they have been solid."

"The diagrams of the ship—that was huge," Yedidya interjected.

"Did the Mossad contribute anything?" Chiny asked.

"We'll be turning to them also," Kobi answered. The Mossad, along with IDF Unit 8200, would continue to contribute a variety of human intelligence, photographs, surveillance, and other helpful details.

"So why is the ship anchored there?" Yedidya asked interrogation style.

"We have no information," said Kobi. "The possibilities are that either it is waiting to load another round of weapons or maybe it's had a malfunction."

"Okay, our job is to get constant coverage and to exploit every intelligence resource," said Yedidya.

Very little time had passed before the intelligence agencies provided the answer: The ship was in Yemen because of an electrical malfunction. One estimate was that fixing the issue would drag out until December 27. Next, the ship would head to Egypt and on to Libya. Finally, top Palestinian smuggling sponsor Adel Mughrabi was in Egypt—and that was for sure.

Stephanie maintained constant contact with Gil. Every day she updated him and provided reports about the ship's location. Some days there were two reports, with one in the morning and the second in the afternoon. All the reports said the ship remained docked, with no change. According to satellite surveillance, the ship was docked four kilometers north of the same Yemeni port. The highest resolution photos from the Israeli satellite revealed that there were no containers on the ship's deck. The intelligence officials were zoned in on the ship and had its pulse.

"We need to be on alert, to be on alert," Meshita kept repeating to Gil and Kobi. That was the watchword for every naval intelligence update. There was nothing like a waiting period to kill readiness.

All that day, Chiny was busy organizing the full model ship for the takeover drill. In a series of meetings, he finally and for the first time started to coordinate the timing of the sea- and air-based commandos with the air force commanders. The plan was for the sea-based commandos to first take over the ship's bridge and deck in a lightning-fast raid of seconds to minutes. Next would follow the fast-roping commandos from the helicopters. Once aboard, the seals would spread out to take positions at various strategic locations on the ship. The exact timing would be set during the drill itself.

On Monday morning, December 24, the day of the drill, Chiny was due to give a speech at the naval intelligence course. The topic was the capturing of the *Santorini*. It was a full and unusual day, so his natural inclination was to instruct his bureau chief to tell the officers he was busy and that they should postpone it. This was a very common occurrence in the IDF, but he stuck to his commitment. With the *Karine A* model standing before him, the *Santorini* operation was hot on his mind, and he knew the *Karine A* would be the mother of all weapons-smuggling operations thus far. Who was aboard and what was the significance of the fishing boat *Santorini*, which had been caught in the Mediterranean Sea, when compared to the cargo ship *Karine A*—at a hundred meters long and with the ability to transport four thousand tons—that would be captured in the distant Red Sea?

"And maybe I am just fantasizing?" he said to himself as he delivered his speech to the engrossed officers. At the end, he couldn't contain himself and said to the future intelligence officers, "You have no idea at what point you grabbed me. In the future, you'll hear about it."

They did not understand and would never have dreamed about what he was referring to.

"We just need to make sure that the ship doesn't get away from us," he muttered to himself on his way to see the IDF chief.

When he arrived at Mofaz's office, Chiny was formally granted the position of the head of the Naval Operations Command. Now it was official. Mofaz shook his hand warmly and laughed: "So, how are the drill preparations going?"

"Everything is super!"

"Too bad that I can't come," said Mofaz apologetically. "I have meetings all day about budget cuts."

As Chiny left the room, he glanced at Mofaz. When their eyes met, they exchanged a look that conveyed an unspoken bond about the lives at stake and the history they were making together.

From the high command's headquarters, Chiny traveled to the navy seals' base to meet with Ram. Itamar saw Chiny's car maneuvering through the base's small parking area.

When they met, Itamar told Chiny, "We now have unparalleled intelligence for our navy seals about the ship, and I have no doubt that each of them will have memorized every nook and cranny of it until they know it better than their own homes. But there are still many things that we don't know yet."

"What are you missing?" asked Chiny.

"We have no information about the ship's security efforts, what the crew is armed with, where the weapons are stored, or even if they armed at all. But in our planning, we are going with the assumption that there will be armed resistance, and we are prepared to address that issue."

"I don't think that they are all-star fighters. I don't think the crew on the ship is there to fight," Ram commented. "But for planning purposes, we'll be ready for that scenario."

Itamar continued, "We don't know what the full crew complement is. For example, we don't know who the captain is for certain. We don't know where the larger weapons being smuggled are concealed or how they are being concealed—"

"I understand you don't even have certainty about whether there are weapons being smuggled," Chiny cut in.

"That's right. But I understand from Kobi that all signs suggest there are high-quality weapons," Itamar answered.

Chiny felt solid about the intelligence efforts when he later boarded the *Miami*, which had been brought from the port of Haifa to the navy seals' port. After a sumptuous dinner on the ship, Chiny left for his fast patrol command boat. All members of his forward command group were there. Ram went down to his lead commando boat, and the drill began.

The forces involved in the drill included the navy seals' emerging from the commando boats and the navy seals' sliding down from helicopters. The rented ship was labeled *Karine A*, as planned. For the first time ever, the IDF carried out a drill of taking over a ship simultaneously from the sea and from the air sliding down from fast ropes. With the accidents that had happened to U.S. forces, tensions were high. People have died in such drills.

But the drill came off without any casualties. Chiny and Ram were able to breathe with some relief. They said, "We can do this."

Yoni and the navy's head of the Operations Division worked on the drill and put together the model materials. They also were tracking specific distance and timing issues. They determined how close the helicopters could get to the ship without being heard in calm weather as well as about how long it would take the helicopter to reach the ship from that point. The drill and its evaluation afterward also showed them how long it took for the navy seals to climb onto the ship from any pair of commando boats (with one on each side of the ship). They decided that the moment the first navy seal started to climb onto the ship from the second pair of commando boats would be the same moment that the Black Hawks with the fast-roping commandos should break their holding patterns and start flying toward the ship. That way, at the moment when all of the sea-based seals were on board and had completed its takeover, the first Black Hawk would be directly above the drop point, and its commandos could start sliding down onto the ship.

Synchronizing these disparate sea- and air-based commandos was critical for the operation and for Ram and Chiny as the commanders in the field. The air force also had learned a lot of the potential pitfalls and risks to the Black Hawks through participating in the drilling process. The drills also included scenarios of having to rescue injured navy seals and whisk them off for medical attention, as well as having to react to various situations where the Black Hawks might come under fire.

That coming Wednesday, December 26, was set as the day for critiquing the drill and adopting the lessons learned in the actual operational plan. Unlike the drills on the "Crazy Day," December 20, now the forces involved had some additional precious time to improve the operation's execution. But what about the *Karine A*? When would its technical malfunctions be fixed? Why was it taking so long to repair a simple electrical issue? They all wondered sarcastically: What, were there no good electricians in Yemen? Ironically, they would learn later that the additional delay, which had the whole Israeli military on edge, was in fact because of a lousy electrician.

On Tuesday, December 25, Mofaz held a status update meeting with only the short list of the high command's principals dealing with the operation. He felt it was important to show that the issue of the smuggling ship was a high command issue and one in which he was personally involved. Yedidya updated everyone regarding the full-scale drill and shared the new surveillance pictures. He also explained the possibility of bringing a missile boat through the Suez down to the Red Sea had been explored, but that was not going to happen. Primarily, there were concerns that such a move would raise suspicions in Egypt and could reveal Israel's intentions. Mofaz approved the continued drills and recommendations by Yedidya.

After the meeting's attendees left, Mofaz sat with his chief of staff. In one more week, on January 2, 2002, Mofaz was due to fly to the United States. This important visit had been planned for some time, and he already had a set schedule of meetings. What should he do?

"I'm going to leave the decision until the last minute," he told his chief of staff, "so keep preparing for the trip as if nothing unusual is happening."

"Yes, sir!"

"But in the event I have to postpone the trip, let's already figure out a cover story," he added.

When his chief of staff left, Mofaz surveyed reports about an agreement between Foreign Minister Shimon Peres and top Palestinian official Abu Ala. One of the clauses in the agreement included the PA's collecting unauthorized weapons from the Palestinian population. Mofaz laughed to himself bitterly. These documents with the idea that the PA would crack down on terrorists at that point seemed more from a fantasy novel than from a serious diplomatic deal.

Karine A Stays in Yemeni Port

DECEMBER 27–28, 2001

"So what do you think about the new information that came in?" Gal asked Anat. Gal had uncovered the *Karine A*'s original name, RIM K, while Anat was the young star who had found key aspects of the *Karine A*'s weapons-smuggling background and plans. Both discoveries had helped naval intelligence figure out which ship they were looking for.

Junior intelligence officials such as Anat were the ones who first reviewed the intelligence information that came in from the Mossad, Unit 8200, and the other intelligence agency counterparts. They were the ones who built the initial analytical framework for approaching the intelligence. Also, they were the ones who did both the grunge work and the creative work in taking a first crack at piecing together the puzzle that would be the foundation for operations. Most important, they were the ones who first flagged the *Karine A* for the higher echelon as the big fish within the disorienting sea of fish.

"The sources are very trustworthy, and in the past, they gave us information about the PA's establishing a smuggling network in Yemen," Anat said decisively about some of Israel's gems in the intelligence world.

"That's also my opinion," said Gal. "Now, the question is: Are they looking to load up the *Karine A* with weapons from Yemen in addition to the weapons they loaded onto it in Dubai?"

"That's definitely a possibility. Look, we received a good piece of information that the ship came to the port in Yemen because of an electrical malfunction, but it wasn't a major malfunction. So why is it taking them so long to fix it? A full week to fix something small?" Anat said in disbelief.

"I'm asking myself the same question," said Gal.

"It stinks!"

"I agree! Maybe they are loading weapons?"

Gal thought for a moment and then said, "Anat, pop over to Shimon. Ask him if the satellite or aerial surveillance photos show any ships next to the *Karine A* that might be used for loading weapons."

Later, Anat came back and said, "We got lucky! Yesterday, the IKONOS satellite got a good shot, and there were no ships next to it."

"And you asked him to continue checking the photos going forward to see if any ships next to the *Karine A* might be used for loading?"

"Of course. But he said that it's impossible to load anything onto it in the place where the ship is located. In order to load anything, the ship would need to sail to one of Yemen's larger ports."

Outside was a torrential downpour along with lightning and thunder. Anat was drafting an update when a new piece of information came in. Gal glanced at it and called out, "Anat, come and read this over with me."

They read it over and were in shock. The conclusion was unambiguous: The ship was as dangerous as a hive of wasps. The ship was smuggling weapons, its captain was Omar Akawi, and it was still being repaired.

"Start preparing the update, and we'll integrate the part about the possible Yemenite weapons into it. I'm going up to see Gil, but I'll be back soon," said Gal.

Gil was in great spirits after hearing the new information. He patted Gal on his upper back and called to Yoki: "Get me a picture of the crew as soon as possible, with a focus on the Palestinian Naval Police and those connected to Adel. Get all the data you need from the Mossad, the IDI, and the Shin Bet, and send it to Itamar and the navy seals," he instructed. "Obviously, include any data you've collected in the materials you are preparing for our prisoner interrogators," said Yoki. "I've always said that Akawi was leading the smuggling and that we needed to keep tabs on him."

"There are questions about whether Akawi is even on the ship," Gal said. Then he explained the issues, prompting a debate.

"What are you talking about?" asked Yoki. "Akawi is the one who would take the lead for a smuggling operation like this emanating from the network. This is a major smuggling operation, the first of its kind. It makes sense that the most experienced ship captain would take the lead."

"But what about the information we've gotten that Akawi is in Egypt, at least according to intelligence collection officers?" Gal retorted.

"Forget about them," Yoki said. "Do you know how often they've made mistakes? They are good people, but they're young, and

I never rely solely on them—that is, unless it's regarding issues directly related to their intelligence collection."

Despite Yoki's views, Gal still harbored doubts.

Naval intelligence put out an intelligence dispatch alert. The key part said:

> The ship's crew has thirteen members. The captain appears to be Omar Akawi. Some of the crew members have been identified as also being members of the Palestinian Naval Police who are involved in weapons smuggling.

Later that night, Shimon updated Chiny on the issue.

"It doesn't really matter to me," Chiny responded. "If they are loading more weapons and if Akawi is there, then when we catch the fish, it will just be an even fatter catch for us. What's really important is, do we know when the ship is leaving the port in Yemen?"

"No. We received information indicating that the repairs might be done today, but we don't know if they were finished, and, if they were, we don't know when it will set sail. Just as it has been every day, today the United States again sent us three reports that the ship is still docked with no status change."

"Do we have satellite coverage set for tomorrow?"

"Yes."

On Friday, December 28, Stephanie sent two updates—one in the morning and one in the evening—that said the ship was still docked with no changes. The satellite photos from the morning showed the same result.

Later that day, at a celebratory ceremony, the new IDI director took over the reins. Speaking at the event, Mofaz said that the PA was covered from head to toe in terrorism.

On Saturday, December 29, the PA notified the Americans that as far as it was concerned, it had secured the seven days of quiet that Sharon had been demanding. Zinni would return to the region during the coming week. Meanwhile, the country experienced heavy rains, which kept most Israelis preoccupied. But some were preoccupied with the *Karine A*. And they continued to ask, When would it set sail again and in which direction?

9

The *Karine A* Disappears

The *Karine A* Is Not in the Port in Yemen

DECEMBER 29–30, 2001

On Saturday night, December 29, Kobi called Gil: "We didn't get any reports from the Americans today. I asked the integrated intelligence command center a bunch of times, and they said nothing came in from Stephanie."

"That's weird," said Gil. "Because in recent days, they've been reporting to us two to three times a day."

Kobi said, "Maybe you should call Stephanie?"

"Let's give them a little bit longer, then I'll call," Gil decided.

"100 percent," said Kobi.

A short time passed until Gil's home telephone rang. Stephanie was on the line. "It's not there," Stephanie said anxiously.

"What do you mean, 'not there'? Since when is the ship not there?" Gil said in shock.

"The last time we saw the ship was midday."

Gil, a bit angry, asked aggressively, "What time? Twelve noon?"

"Correct."

"Okay, when was the first time that the ship wasn't there?" Gil asked, though this time a little bit more gently.

"At 6:00 p.m., December 29, the ship was gone."

The picture started to become clearer to Gil. Then he spoke to Stephanie very slowly, carefully enunciating for emphasis. "Now,

I'm going back over what you said, word for word, and you confirm to me if I have it right."

"Fine."

Gil repeated what Stephanie had said, and she confirmed it. He thanked her and immediately called Kobi and Meshita. Meshita updated Yedidya, while Kobi updated Itamar and Shimon.

"Shimon," Kobi said, "you need to immediately put together a satellite coverage plan for the port in Yemen as well as other ports on the way toward the Red Sea—most importantly Port Sudan. And make sure it is the higher resolution of the two satellites we have been using."

"Wait one second, commander. What's going on?"

Kobi explained the situation. Then he added, "Since they saw the ship at 12:00 p.m. but at 6:00 p.m. they didn't see it, our working premise is that the ship left one minute after noon. So all of the calculations regarding the time and the ship's pace as it advances on a north trajectory in the Red Sea will be based on noon as the starting point."

"Does Chiny know?" Shimon asked curiously.

Chiny had received a call at home that the ship had sailed. He ordered a status update for Sunday, December 30, in the morning. The question was: Where did the ship disappear to? Did the ship enter a port in Yemen to load more weapons? Or was it going north toward the Suez Canal? The clock was ticking.

On Sunday morning, December 30, the entire high command of the IDF above the rank of brigadier general went to a hotel on the coast in the Tel Aviv corridor. There they would attend three straight days of seminars for "The Year 2020—Possible Directions."

Chiny was given dispensation to step out of the conference to conduct a status meeting for those involved with the *Karine A* operation, including Ram. Everything was tailored around the expected timing of the ship. Their working premise was that the ship left the port in Yemen the day before at 12:01 p.m. Thus, if the ship moved at its fastest speed of twelve knots, it still wouldn't reach the capture point before Tuesday, January 1, in the afternoon.

Ram hit on the key first conclusion: "This isn't imminent." So he, his navy seals, and all their equipment did not need to dash down to Eilat. Rather, they would head south the next day, December 31. Chiny agreed.

The second takeaway came from Yoni, who said there was no reason to use the aerial surveillance to start looking for the ship at this point, as the ship was still too far away. Instead, they would wait until the ship traveled farther north. But the next day, they would need to start sending out the Atara aircraft again and use its longer-range surveillance capabilities. Tomorrow afternoon, the ship should be north of Jeddah, Saudi Arabia, if it was traveling at its top speed. Chiny accordingly ordered the air force to issue directives for sending out the Atara. As they were getting ready to finish and walk out of the meeting, Shimon's hand hesitatingly went up.

"Shimonel," said Chiny, using his nickname for him, "what do you want to add?"

"Tomorrow around 10:00 a.m., our higher-resolution satellite will take photos of all of the area around the port in Yemen, and if it does not find the ship there, then that means for sure that the ship is on a northern trajectory."

"And if it finds the ship in one of Yemen's other larger ports?" someone asked.

"Then we go back into a waiting cycle, and we have the Atara and the navy seals stand down," said Chiny.

The Atara and its staff, including Zvi of ELTA, essentially had remained in a state of readiness for ten days after having been drafted into the IDF's reserves. Every day, Zvi would receive a message from the navy along the lines of "Be ready to fly out tomorrow afternoon." He got the same message that day, but this time with the added phrase, "Now it's serious." The Atara and the aircraft accompanying it were ready to fly for the next day. The new radar and scope for taking photographs both during the day and at night were also ready to go.

At naval intelligence, the morning update conducted by Gil was different than usual. Everyone could feel the anticipation in the air that something big was waiting for them right around the corner. The naval intelligence analysts were on the verge of reaping the fruits of all of the sweat and labor that they had invested. Sometimes they had felt as if they could almost taste the water of the Red Sea. An operation was in the winds, making everyone excited. It seemed even more certain from the information presented that the *Karine A* had had a malfunction and was heading toward the Suez Canal. But they still were not certain.

An urgent intelligence dispatch went out that day with these clarifications:

The *Karine A* was not seen at the port in Yemen on the evening of December 29, and it had already set sail. It is likely that it is sailing north on a trajectory through the Red Sea. The PA is making preparations for the ship to pass through the Suez Canal.

All of the intelligence collection deployments, the preparations, and the coordination efforts among the agencies were starting to reach a critical point. They would now be on call, tied in to the operational plan. Information security also quickly became an issue. Naval intelligence started operating twenty-four hours a day.

Later that evening, Yoki and another staff member sat exhausted in Kobi's office. Kobi comforted both of them and himself: "Another two days and we're done."

The secretary brought in coffee for them. The branch chief of Kobi's naval intelligence operations would be the head intelligence officer for the operation. He would be positioned in one of the commando boats with all of the intelligence materials, including maps, photographs, and other items.

"Are you and Chiny's intelligence officer, Shimon, on the same page?" Kobi asked Yoki.

"Yes, and we're meeting tomorrow in the early morning."

"Fine. Who from our staff is going to be on the Atara surveillance flight tomorrow?"

Yoki named a surveillance photography decipherer. "And the

satellite desk will switch over to two shifts tomorrow, with each shift covering twelve hours."

"Remember that Shimon will be with Chiny at all times, so that all of the organizing, ensuring intelligence collection officials are carrying out their roles, ensuring their information is passed on— it all falls on *you!*" Kobi emphasized.

"What will happen if we don't find the ship tomorrow?" Yoki tossed out.

"Guys, we'll find the ship—if not tomorrow, then in two days," said Meshita with a light laugh as he entered the office and injected himself into the conversation.

Did We Lose It?

DECEMBER 31, 2001, 7:00 A.M.

Chiny held his last status update in Tel Aviv and then headed down to Eilat. By the afternoon, all of the forces other than the fast-roping commandos, who remained in the center of the country, would be in Eilat. Its weather in December is moderate, and the city wasn't crowded. By a stroke of luck, the large volume of people streaming into the naval base in Eilat as well as those filling up some of the hotels didn't get much attention. The base commander's office was converted into Chiny's forward command group post. The cooks worked nonstop. It wasn't every day that a rear admiral, the head of the navy's Operations Command, spent time there. It wasn't every day that they got to see and interact with the navy's most elite team, the seals, as well. The atmosphere was a mix of relaxed banter and underlying tension. When would they find the ship?

Around noon, Shimon had a call from his chief decipherer. Everyone in the room who saw him pick up the red phone anticipated that he might be receiving an important update.

"Tell me what the results are," he said loudly. Shimon knew that his decipherer was at the satellite photos station and was due to be deciphering photos from Israel's high-resolution satellite.

"We didn't find the ship. It isn't where it was at the port in Yemen before, not at the larger of Yemen's ports, not in the surrounding areas—nothing."

"How was the quality of the surveillance?"

"It was excellent—top-notch resolution and no clouds."

"Did you get a second opinion to look over the surveillance?"

"Yes."

"Good. Tomorrow, the other Israeli satellite will be over Port Sudan?"

"Yes, don't worry."

Once Shimon updated Chiny, the chief said, "Okay, so now we'll see if the Atara finds the ship." Chiny and Ram were talking constantly. They were debating when was the right time for the group to leave Eilat and travel to the capture point, around forty-six miles south of the Straits of Tiran. It was not a simple dilemma. On the one hand, if they went too early and before the Atara had located the *Karine A*, the sitting and waiting at the Red Sea capture point would wear down the navy seals' readiness. On the other hand, if they didn't go early enough, and during the course of the day the Atara didn't find the ship, they might arrive at the capture point too late and squander the opportunity to seize it. It was a case of damned if you do and damned if you don't. Everything was in the hands of the Atara. It needed to bring in the crucial golden intelligence.

Meanwhile, the Atara took off. Its goal was to find the *Karine A* about 345 miles south of the Straits of Tiran, taking into account its highest speed of twelve knots.

The head of the navy's aerial patrols commanded the mission. The Atara carried out surveys in circle-style runs over dozens of ships. The tense but focused navy patrol staff meticulously checked every ship that matched the *Karine A*'s characteristics: a hundred meters long, three derricks, and a speed of under fifteen knots. There was no sign of the *Karine A*. It was as if the water had swallowed it. The staff didn't even find a ship that had similar characteristics. Zvi, who was reaching despair, tried to distract himself by reading the newspaper.

In the evening, the Atara returned empty-handed to land in the center of Israel. You could read the disappointment on all the faces of the patrol staff. What was going on?

At the same time, Stephanie met with Gil and the naval intelligence analysts and collection staff. She was making strong efforts to lobby her American counterparts for a direct, secure connection in case of an emergency, but she couldn't solve the problem. The Americans didn't know where the ship was. All they knew was that as of that moment in the afternoon, the ship was not in either of the ports in Yemen.

At the conference hotel in the Tel Aviv corridor, Mofaz held a situation update with his high command officials, including Yedidya and air force commander Dan Halutz. Metaphorically, they were all hopping between the theoretical year 2020, the focus of the conference, and the very real immediate realities of what was transpiring in the Red Sea. Where had the *Karine A* gone?

Mofaz was in a lousy mood. "We can't miss catching the ship," he said to himself as he opened the meeting. He addressed the others: "Okay, let's start with the intelligence briefing."

Meshita gave an update. Essentially, most of it was speculation about where the ship was and why they hadn't located it.

Mofaz was pouring over a map in front of him, especially the area where the Atara had patrolled. As time passed, he grew even more irritable. "First of all, we've got to find the ship and be basically attached to it, so we can see what it's doing. It could still have another malfunction or just dock at the Saudi Arabian port of Jeddah. As soon as we identify it moving along its trajectory, we need to have it under constant surveillance. We have no choice!"

The head of air force operations tried to calm him. "Tomorrow, at 10:00 a.m., the Atara will find the ship! The Atara will carry out surveillance of an area where we estimate the ship should be coming through, assuming it is moving at one of its lower speeds. It's very possible that the ship is just moving slower than we anticipated—maybe only at a speed of eight knots. Also, maybe it didn't leave the port in Yemen in the afternoon on Saturday, as we assumed, but closer to Saturday evening."

The air force operations commander projected confidence, but Mofaz continued to worry that maybe everything was slipping through their hands. "Maybe the ship had passed the point where Atara was patrolling?" he asked and pointed to the relevant areas on the map.

That's not possible, they explained to him. That day, the Atara had patrolled the entire area where the ship would have been if it had been moving at its maximum speed.

Mofaz continued to be skeptical. Suddenly, someone interjected that Egyptian president Hosni Mubarak and British prime minister Tony Blair were meeting at that time in Sharm El-Sheikh, close to the Straits of Tiran. Mofaz exploded: "I don't care about that! First, I want to get onto the ship. After that, anything is possible. Regarding Mubarak, the foreign affairs people will deal with that. We need to capture this ship . . . I'm just worried about missing this chance. Everything else is irrelevant."

Mofaz was practically in pain from the weight on his shoulders. He wanted to prevent the firing of rockets on the southeastern Israeli city of Ashkelon, which would be in range from the Gaza Strip if the *Karine A*'s rockets reached the Palestinians. He was envisioning this scenario and knew that it could transpire if they missed the chance to capture the *Karine A*. He looked around him. Did they all understand the gravity of the situation and the strategic consequences at stake?

He said, "Listen, this is a five-hundred-ton bomb. This is ten F-16 aircraft strikes on Arafat's head!"

In a low-key professional tone, Yedidya explained, "We need patience. At sea, you need patience. There are no miracles at sea, and ships don't skip from place to place. Ships *sail*. We'll send out more Sea Scan patrols tonight and tomorrow at dawn to check out the northern area of the Red Sea and to make sure the Atara didn't miss anything. We'll hold another status update tomorrow afternoon and take it from there."

The *Karine A* Disappears

Meshita tried to calm Mofaz also but from a different angle. He explained that Mughrabi, who was in the Suez area, had received funds that matched with the possibility of paying for the ship to cross through the canal. This meant that the ship's plan was "to enter the Mediterranean Sea, that is for sure—there is no question. The takeaway is that we'll also be able to carry out our Mediterranean Sea option."

But this did not soothe Mofaz. He thought to himself, "Sure, the ship could pass through the canal, but maybe this will be after it has unloaded its weapons around the western Sinai coast!" He looked at those present and said, "If it gets to the Suez, we're done for!"

All of their questions regarding intelligence at the end of the day had consequences for operational decisions: When do we tell Chiny to set sail into the Red Sea with Ram and his navy seals? What if we order him to go too early or too late? When do we send the Black Hawk helicopters and the attack helicopters south with their fast-roping commandos aboard? Now?

The meeting's attendees clearly saw that tomorrow, Tuesday, January 1, 2002, was a fateful day, especially for the surveillance apparatus. "Would they meet the challenge?" Mofaz asked himself. "Would the massive resources invested for developing these surveillance capabilities prove worth it?" Everything he had heard from those present encouraged him, but shreds of doubt still haunted him.

Right before finishing the meeting, as Mofaz delved into details about how the seals would know where to find the concealed weapons, Meshita remembered a piece of information had come in about the commercial goods loaded onto the ship when it was at Port Sudan. "Chief, there is an abnormal level of camouflage and concealment surrounding the weapons. There are rice, toys, and other things they can use to cover up the weapons."

At that point, Mofaz also remembered the importance of having prisoner interrogators involved. Mofaz said as he concluded the meeting, "Our working premise is that the *Karine A* headed north around the afternoon of December 29, and in light of that, we need to be ready."

All night he envisioned pictures of the ship and a terrifying giant bomb falling on Arafat's head. How would things look for him on the first day of 2002? The weather forecast was no good.

Karine A Found, but Storm on the Way

JANUARY 1, 2002

Forecasts regarding weather conditions at sea only go as far as three days out. Beni Ben-Porat, in charge of meteorology for the navy, went over the forecast for Tuesday, Wednesday, and Thursday (January 1–3). The forecasts showed that barometric pressure, a southern wind, and very dynamic temperatures were coming toward the Israeli coast and would arrive at the coastline on Wednesday evening. It would be a harsh winter day with winds of twenty-five knots at sea whipping stormy and wavy waters. He looked over the Red Sea—1,150 miles of water whose brutal waves sometimes reached three to four meters—and the unreliable forecasts. He had served on fast patrol boats in Sharm El-Sheikh on the Egyptian Sinai Peninsula in 1970 and knew the waves from up close. They were terrible and threatening.

He was deep in thought. The northern winds, which blew about 90–95 percent of the time, created the waves, but the low pressure in the Mediterranean Sea would offset the northern winds from the Red Sea. The rain and storms from the Mediterranean Sea's southwest would cause the Red Sea arena to be calmer and the waters to be flat. When would this be? He figured on Wednesday and in the middle of the night between Wednesday and Thursday (January 2–3). Then, as morning came on Thursday, the pressure from the Mediterranean Sea would collide with the coast. Next, the wind would circle in a northerly direction, grow stronger in the Gulf of Suez, and arrive at the Red Sea as a storm around the area of the Straits of Tiran. According to his calculations, all of this would occur around 9:00 a.m. on Thursday. After Thursday morning, the water would go completely out of control.

He sent out the forecast bulletin to everyone on the navy's long distribution list and went to see Kobi. The captain was with Meshita, who had updated the IDF chief of staff at an earlier status review meeting. The large Weather Man popped into the room as Meshita was still talking. With a friendly wave, Meshita said, "Weather Man, come on in and take a seat."

The Weather Man sat down slowly and started to explain the weather forecast. Meshita listened very carefully. The operational implications for him were clear.

Gil entered the room, having finished his own morning update. He said, "I homed in on the activity at sea between Sharm El-Sheikh and a central Egyptian military port off the Red Sea. This activity could impact both the operation and even the travels of dignitaries coming through the area. Today or tomorrow there will be satellite coverage of the relevant nearby ports."

"Mofaz is not that interested in hearing about Egyptian president Hosni Mubarak and other dignitaries," laughed Meshita. "He is only interested in one thing: where is the ship?"

The specialized Sea Scans, which were tailored for patrolling maritime areas, had revealed nothing. Again, it was as if the Red Sea had swallowed the *Karine A*.

At around 8:00 a.m., the Atara took off from Lod in central Israel. Its flight to the area where the Atara was due to perform surveillance would take ninety minutes. In the center of the rectangular zone was a part of the Red Sea near the Saudi Arabian city of Jeddah, the second-busiest port city in the Arab world.

Zvi, the ELTA man, was pessimistic after the previous disappointing day of searches. Today the flight also included Deputy Commander of the Navy David Ben-Besht and the mission commander, who was also the head of aerial surveillance for the navy and who brought six airborne lookouts with him. The sea was full, with many ships traveling north. The surveillance team looked for a specific set of criteria and immediately disqualified ships traveling at a speed greater than fifteen knots, that were more than a hundred meters long, and that did not have three derricks. The team focused on slower ships, shorter ships, and ships with three derricks.

Immediately after the reconnaissance started, a suspicious target appeared on the far northern end of the group of ships. An accompanying aircraft for taking pictures was dispatched to identify the ship. The results were again disappointing: it was not the *Karine A*.

Time passed. The team had checked dozens of ships from the air, and none of them were the *Karine A*. Mofaz, the navy commander, the air force commander, and everyone else who knew of the secret mission all felt the same tension. They could have cut it with a knife.

Zvi's pessimistic mood worsened. Soon their dropping gas levels would force them to end the mission and return home empty-handed. He stretched out on his side and lost himself in reading the newspaper. Some time passed. At 11:40 a.m., the group was following ship number 86 from a distance of dozens of miles, and it fit the criteria. The surveillance scope was set on a mode to zoom in for a high-quality picture of the target. A few seconds passed and a few more, and suddenly the mission commander screamed out, "That's it!"

Everyone ran over to get a look. They crowded together and started to call out in unison, "That's it!" It was the *Karine A* itself.

The surveillance commander ordered the pilot to fly close enough to see the ship with the naked eye. It was the *Karine A* in all its splendor. The team used the aerial photographic systems to take pictures. At a distance of around 345 miles north of the Atara, the accompanying aircraft took reports from the Atara regarding the coordinates of the ship, its speed, and its bearing. Then the Atara circled the ship to make sure the identification was accurate. The people in the accompanying aircraft reported immediately to the land-based command center regarding the identification made by the Atara:

11:40 a.m. The location of the *Karine A* ship—40 miles northwest of Jeddah. Course .026 with a speed of 6 knots.

Dudu Ben-Besht, deputy commander of the navy, was deliriously happy. On a scratchy satellite telephone call, he was able to reach Yedidya, and the first words that came out of his mouth were, "We found it!"

The *Karine A* Disappears

"There are no miracles at sea, and ships don't skip from place to place," Yedidya remembered saying the previous evening to Mofaz. The moment of truth grew near. In his mind, Yedidya was calculating the time and the distance. It was just shy of 460 miles from the spot where they located the ship to the area where they were setting up the ambush. At a speed of six knots, the ship would only get there on Thursday night, January 3, 2002. At a speed of ten knots, it would arrive around Thursday afternoon.

The aerial photography decipherer for naval intelligence was in the accompanying aircraft. Its aerial photography and surveillance platform was positioned next to the window, while he was in the crowded cockpit with reinforced binoculars. Around 2:00 p.m., the accompanying aircraft escort flew closer to the target. He looked at it through the binoculars.

"They are right. It is the *Karine A*," he said. He got up and moved next to the window in one of the airborne lookouts' spots, took another look, and again identified it. This ship was the *Karine A*. Bull's-eye! He envisioned all the pictures of the ship. Everything matched.

He felt the thrill of solving a mystery. Their efforts had been worth it. After everything that had led up to this moment—all of the imagery desk's satellite photos, the sorties, and the pictures of the sister ship—the real thing was right in front of him and almost close enough to touch.

He needed to make sure that Shimon in Eilat knew as soon as possible.

10

A Stormy New Plan

The Weather Factor

JANUARY 1, 2002

Hagai, the IDF bureau chief, bent toward Mofaz, who was sitting in the first row, to give him a note: "The *Karine A* has been spotted by the Atara at a distance of around 460 miles south of the ambush point."

Mofaz stopped breathing for a moment. He folded up the note, placed it in his shirt pocket, and continued to listen to the speaker at the podium. Those participating in the seminar could not have known what was going on inside him. He waited patiently for a break in the seminar and then initiated a hastily thrown together meeting with those who were in on the secret. He shared Hagai's information. A debate started around the central question of timing: would the navy seals approach the ship during the day or at night? According to the current speed of the ship, the confrontation would occur during the daylight hours of Thursday, January 3, unless the ambush point was moved deeper and farther south into the Red Sea. The discussion was very short.

Mofaz also raised his personal issue: The next night, Wednesday, he was scheduled to fly to the United States. Obviously, he was leaning toward postponing the trip. He would finalize the issue with Prime Minister Sharon later that day.

With the Atara on its way back to Lod in central Israel, Dudu's thoughts went into overdrive. In the past, he had set up command groups for the IDF chief of staff on missile boats. Why couldn't he set up the command group on the Atara? It was a large and wide aircraft. And looking down from the sky, the chief would be able to watch the operation with his own eyes and hear it with his own ears.

Immediately, Dudu started to outline his model of the preferred setup on the aircraft and the needed support staff. He called Yedidya again, reported the idea to him, and got his approval. Both of them remembered well that only a week ago, in one of his summaries, Mofaz had directed, "Be ready to run the command group from the air above the operation."

Dudu summoned Cdr. Ben Tzuk, the deputy head of the navy's Equipment and Weapons Division, to the airport. He handed him a diagram of the proposed setup and said, "Start to prepare the aircraft. Get assistance from the air force."

When Dudu got to his office at headquarters in Tel Aviv, the head of the navy's Equipment and Weapons Division, Ben Tzuk's boss, was waiting for him. He was against setting up the command group on the Atara.

"I don't think you can change a civilian aircraft into something military," he said definitively.

"So we'll go to Yedidya, and he'll decide," said Dudu.

Since the discovery of the *Karine A*, Yedidya had been restless. He was regularly speaking with Chiny and Ram. What were they doing about the weather forecast? How would they carry out a takeover of the *Karine A* in the Red Sea forty-six miles south of the Straits of Tiran? At what time would the takeover take place? Would it be late Thursday night as planned based on the ship's slow pace? When would the seals leave Eilat? And maybe they should still drop the commando boats from the capture operation as they might not be able to pull alongside the ship in stormy waters. This scenario was exactly the kind he had warned them of! Instead, maybe they should just carry out the operation with commando forces sliding down from a fast rope?

A Stormy New Plan

"I'll hold a status review meeting with everyone shortly, and we'll see," said Chiny in the end.

Meanwhile, on Tuesday, the fast-rope commandos, under the command of Shlomi Dahan and his deputy, were aboard helicopters and heading to the airport. The Black Hawks would move into position tomorrow.

What Yedidya wanted most of all was not to lose the *Karine A*, and he wanted to know and see where it was at every moment. Mofaz, who was also deeply concerned about not losing track of the ship in the stream of ships coming north from the Red Sea, called air force commander Halutz. Shortly after, Yoni Man arrived to meet with Yedidya.

"I want continuous surveillance of the *Karine A*," Yedidya explained to him, though he kept getting cut off by urgent telephone calls throughout their conversation. Despite the ship's importance, the commander of the navy had to continue handling a range of issues—not only the *Karine A*.

"So you're saying you want aircraft continuously monitoring it in real time," said Yoni.

"How can it be done?" asked Yedidya expectantly.

"Listen, sir," began Yoni, who went on to explain how all of the aircraft pilots would become worn down under those conditions.

"The pilots will become worn out, but I still need to know where the *Karine A* is at all times," the commander of the navy answered.

"Not only that," Yoni said, adding, "the continuous presence of aircraft could tip off the ship and lead the *Karine A*'s crew to identify them as suspicious."

But as always, necessity led to solutions. The air force promised to conduct continuous surveillance to provide intelligence to the navy so it would have the coordinates and speed of the *Karine A* at all times.

Dudu and the navy's head of the Equipment and Weapons Division met with Yedidya. The division head expressed his opposition to using the Atara as a spot for the command group. Yedidya called and asked if the IDF chief of staff was available to talk for five minutes.

"If you run over fast, he'll have time," Mofaz's staff answered. Yedidya and Dudu went and presented the issue to Mofaz. They included the opposition from the navy's expert on equipment and weapons.

As Mofaz listened, his face lit up. "This is what I've wanted from the beginning. This was my idea," he said enthusiastically. "I wanted to watch the capture from overhead. In every operation, I was always at a forward point in the field; it's in my blood. The commander's place is in the field. There are risks, but the positives outweigh them. This time I will be in command from overhead."

Mofaz went quiet for a moment and then suggested, "We'll fly tonight in an aircraft, and we'll model it and work out the kinks. Is that possible?"

"Yes," Dudu responded.

In the end, the flight exercise did not happen because Mofaz had to meet with Prime Minister Sharon in Jerusalem. But the preparations for the command center aboard the Atara continued.

Mofaz's move to be in "the field," overhead in a flying command center, was anything but routine and posed a huge logistical headache for his subordinates. But his commitment to his troops, his audacity, and his readiness to take risks where others might have balked were part of what set him apart from a mediocre, play-it-safe, military paper-pusher kind of chief. Mofaz was not worried about personal blame if one of the medium risks went sideways; his eye was on the bigger game—stopping the Karine A at all costs.

Chiny held a status review meeting on Tuesday with Ram and the other officers running the operation. Before the meeting, Chiny had spoken with Beni Ben-Porat to get the forecast and to understand the issues underlying the forecast predictions. He had known the Weather Man for years and had been his commander when Chiny was the head of operations for the Naval Intelligence Command.

"That man is a gold mine," he thought. "Only a lifelong navy man can understand the importance of nailing the weather forecast precisely."

They checked the movements of the ship. Clearly the ship was moving slowly, which was why they did not find it yesterday. All of their calculations had been based on assuming a speed of ten to twelve knots. Thus, when the Atara searched for the ship north of Jeddah, it was still trudging along south of that area. Now everyone saw that by Thursday morning the ship would still be 160 to 170 miles south of the Straits of Tiran in the Red Sea. That was as far as it would move by then; even if it sped up, it could only go slightly farther. So all of their problems were being caused by the ship's moving at turtle speed.

"If we combine this with the weather, which will be rotten on Thursday," Chiny thought, "and we wait for the ship to get to the planned ambush point forty-six miles south of the Straits of Tiran in the Red Sea, we'll only be able to engage it Thursday afternoon in stormy waters. That means we won't be able to use the sea-based commandos."

This was the heart of the terrible dilemma: If they waited for the ship to reach the planned ambush point, it would not get there until Thursday afternoon or evening, and the waters would be too stormy, blocking the involvement of the forces from the commando boats. But what could they do? Should they just decide already to drop the commando boats' part of the operation?

"No," he said to himself. Then Chiny said out loud, "We're not going to wait for the ship to get to the planned ambush point. We're going to take over the ship using the commando boat forces at a point 150 to 160 miles south of the Straits of Tiran in the Red Sea. We're not giving up on using the sea-based commandos. The takeover will happen at night, and it will happen in calm waters. The middle of the night between Wednesday and Thursday—just before dawn!"

He looked at Ram and the other officers. Did they agree with him?

Ram sank into deep thought. The room was silent. He was the commander who would need to put his commandos in harm's way. He was an operations man who thought in operational terms. While he had many issues to weigh, Chiny's concern—which led him to propose moving the takeover operation farther south so they could still use the commando boats—seemed to make sense. Ram said, "That sounds right, but let's play out the implications."

The first and most prominent implication was that this proposed ambush point was beyond the operational area of the Black Hawks. The officer serving as Chiny's air force command group representative, who was also a helicopter pilot, pointed to a line on the map and said clearly, "The Black Hawks can operate up until this line without needing to refuel. Beyond this line—and your plan, Chiny, is to capture the ship significantly south of this line—we'll need to refuel the Black Hawks."

"Which means?" Chiny and Ram asked together, somewhat already anticipating the disappointing answer.

"That means," said the air force officer, "we would need to drop the fast rope part of the operation. The Black Hawks cannot do a mid-air refueling. They can only refuel on land, and there is no land that far out."

All eyes rested on the air force officer.

"Maybe we can overcome this," he said. "The air force will try to come up with some kind of idea, even if it's risky."

The air force officer called Yoni, his boss, and updated him about the idea of bringing the capture operation farther south to around 150 to 160 miles from the Straits of Tiran in the Red Sea. "Yoni, start to think about refueling options for the Black Hawks. Without one, we lose the fast-rope option."

Yoni was a bit confused, as this was the first time that he had even heard of this possibility. But he started to look into options anyway. A lot was resting on the idea of deploying the commando forces from Eilat.

Meanwhile, other problems arose. The hardest to deal with was refueling the navy boats, including the fast patrol boats and the commando boats. This issue troubled Chiny and Ram. It had been obvious that the boats would need to refuel twice. That meant they would need to load more tanks of gas on the fast patrol boats and find all kinds of tricks for storing the gas. An assistance ship loaded with tanks of gas could travel to the original ambush point, but because of its slow speed, it could not keep pace with the fast patrol boats and commando boats to the *Karine A*.

And, of course, there was the issue of time. If they wanted to go south and get to the ship around Thursday morning while the water was still calm, they needed to move up their schedule and leave Eilat Wednesday morning, January 2, instead of Wednesday late at night.

Chiny held another status review meeting at 7:00 p.m. after receiving intelligence regarding the location and speed of the *Karine A*. And who knew? Maybe the Weather Man would change his meteorological forecast. Afterward, Chiny dozed a little bit, disconcerted by the idea of galloping south without the additional commando forces who were supposed to fly in on Black Hawks and land on the *Karine A* by fast rope.

After receiving some updates regarding the ship's varying speeds, Chiny updated Yedidya. "So we're talking about a capture point 280 to 300 miles south of Eilat. That would mean going without the fast-roping commando unit."

Yedidya was in a slight state of shock. He asked several clarifying questions and noted the serious risks.

Chiny responded, "If the weather forecast is wrong and the water is good on Thursday, and the target is moving slowly, then we can take it over at the originally planned spot—forty-six miles south of the Straits of Tiran in the Red Sea—and with commandos both from the sea and from the helicopters. But if the weather gets worse, as the Weather Man predicts, then we are running with this new plan that I just presented. That's the only option! That is our window of opportunity—the middle of the night between Wednesday and Thursday."

"Everyone agrees with you?" Yedidya asked.

"Yes," Chiny immediately answered.

"Get everything ready. I will come in the evening, and we'll see," Yedidya said.

The Weather Man Can

Naval Intelligence Command still didn't know about Chiny's new plan. The default plan was to carry out the operation on Thursday in broad daylight. Intelligence reports from the aircraft following the ship were showing that the ship was adjusting its speed. Around 4:00 p.m., the ship slowed to seven knots and later it slowed to five knots. Subsequently, it sped up to nine knots and then bounced between six and seven knots. At that speed, it became clear that the ship would get to the original ambush point—forty-six miles south of the Straits of Tiran in the Red Sea—around Thursday afternoon or evening just as the impending storm reached its height.

Meshita and Kobi were driving Beni Ben-Porat crazy with frequent check-ins. "Is there anything new with the forecast?" The same was true of the bureaus of the commander of the navy and with the navy's Operations Command. The Weather Man gave the same answer to everyone: "There are no changes. We'll see what happens with the pressure on the Mediterranean Sea around us tomorrow."

The weather had become the Archimedean point of the entire operation. The forecast, which would significantly impact the timing and success of the operation, was all in the hands of one person— the sharp forecaster, Ben-Porat.

In the meantime, Gil met with Stephanie. In their frequent meetings, Stephanie's warmheartedness and genuine desire to help made things flow fluidly. Gil updated her: Israeli forces had found the *Karine A* already north of Jeddah, and they were continuing to follow the ship. The whole time he was bothered by the lack of information about how highly armed the ship's crew was. The intelligence officers in Eilat, Shimon and Itamar, wanted to know more about this point. Though she wanted to be helpful, Stephanie had nothing to add.

Meshita, meanwhile, held a long meeting with many attendees about the importance of maintaining a media blackout. The meeting's purpose was to coordinate communication responses depending on differing outcomes, including the possibility of Israel's forces in the Red Sea being exposed. He said, "The foundational point is that the danger to our forces becomes bigger following any media coverage. So we need a complete media blackout until we have a new status meeting about the issue."

Kobi and Yoki were constantly running around, coordinating and tying up loose ends. They also planned what to do with the ship when it arrived in Eilat.

Toward the evening, Chiny wrote a status review. As the lights in the ports around him began blinking, he envisioned the *Karine A* and started to write. This was the moment when the senior commander in the field needed to write out the final plan—personally and alone. He needed to do this without the staff. He wrote:

INFORMATION

As of 0119 on January 1, the target, which is being followed, is at a distance of around 400 miles south of the Straits of Tiran in the Red Sea.

The weather is expected to get worse throughout Thursday.

The target, *Karine A* and code-named Noah's Ark, is expected to get to a point around 160 miles south of the Straits of Tiran in the Red Sea around Thursday morning.

GOAL

Capturing the target in good weather.

PLAN

In order to capture the ship in good weather, we need the flexibility to launch a takeover of the target on Thursday at the point around 160 miles south.

We can get to a state of readiness for taking over the ship around that area on Thursday, January 3, around 0500 based on the following schedule:

0204—the assistance ship for refueling leaves and afterward the civilian ship carrying the navy seals.

0209—the fast patrol boats leave.

0210—the navy seals' commando boats and their command boat leave.

0218—the ships pass the Straits of Tiran in the Red Sea.

0221—completing the refueling of the ships south of the Straits of Tiran in the Red Sea.

0305—this is when there is a time window for capturing the *Karine A* 160 miles south of the Straits of Tiran in the Red Sea.

SCENARIOS AND RESPONSES

When we get to the area south of the Straits of Tiran, if the ship is moving slowly and the waters are expected to remain calm for longer than currently expected, we'll carry out the takeover 46 miles south of the Straits of Tiran in the Red Sea with both the sea-based and helicopter-based commando teams.

If the weather is okay only at that moment, but is still expected to get worse, the priority remains capturing the ship at the point around 160 miles south.

If the waters are rough, then we'll carry out the capture around 23 miles south of the Egyptian port of Sharm El-Sheikh with a combination of high-speed patrol boats and helicopter-based commandos but without navy seals' commando boats.

At another status review after 7:00 p.m., Chiny presented the time line, the different options, and the preferred option. Two key factors dictated the plan—the weather and the speed of the ship's progress. Chiny would receive ongoing reports regarding its location every hour or two. But the weather was in the hands of god and his messenger on earth—Weather Man Beni Ben-Porat. In one of the hardest areas to forecast the weather in the Middle East, he had declared the window of opportunity in calm waters as running from Wednesday until early Thursday morning. By later Thursday morning, the waters would change to stormy. But what if his weather forecast was wrong?

"When we leave from the Gulf of Eilat, we'll pass the Straits

A Stormy New Plan

of Tiran and travel south for refueling. We'll get a chance to feel out the waters and see if the waters really are calm as forecasted," said Chiny.

Preparations for leaving according to the time line, including a complex second refueling, started to roll forward.

Around 10:00 p.m., Yedidya arrived in Eilat. He was dressed in his civilian clothes, just as field security had directed for all of those traveling south to Eilat. In the office of the commander of the Red Sea arena, the meeting opened with a late dinner, and there was a lot of chatter. A large stack of carrots was brought to the commander of the navy. He loved carrots.

Chiny presented the plan and the key factors. Ram, who sat with Chiny, supported him regarding each point. Yedidya reread Chiny's personal status review memorandum. He envisioned the serious risks: the proposed ambush point, 160 miles south of the Straits of Tiran in the Red Sea and 288 miles south of Eilat, was beyond the standard operating umbrella of the fast patrol boats and commando boats. It was deep in the treacherous Red Sea. Every complication could turn the operation into a catastrophe. What would happen if one of the navy boats capsized and sank along the Saudi Arabian or Egyptian coasts? What would happen if an Egyptian missile boat intercepted the Israeli Navy's boats? Even the air force might get involved, leading to a mega disaster.

After multiple rounds of debating different scenarios, around midnight, Chiny said, "Let me go out to sea according to my time-table. Approve my plan. If you want, you can always stop me as I'm on my way."

Yedidya thought about it. The problems and risks of sailing south were so clear and unambiguous, but on the flip side was a small rare window of opportunity if the forecast predicted by the Weather Man turned out to be correct. The weight of responsibility felt heavy. His uncertainty tormented him. Hesitation was not an easy feeling to cope with. Then Yedidya recalled the daring operation he had been involved in when he was injured in 1969. The injury helped crystallize that moment in time for him. He remembered that no operation was without risk and that he himself had paid a serious personal price for the risks involved in that operation. But the operation had sent a message to the Egyptians and had been important for his country. Sometimes personal sacrifice, whether his in the past or with his commandos now, was necessary to keep the nation safe. He emerged from memory lane more resolute.

"Approved," said Yedidya, with renewed confidence and a sense of history in the making. He added that they still needed final approval from the IDF chief of staff.

They tried to reach Mofaz but did not get through. He was with Prime Minister Sharon. Mofaz did not take calls during those meetings.

Chiny was tired and wanted to go to sleep. "Let me go out," Chiny said again to Yedidya. "If you don't call me during the night to let me know that you've changed the plan, I'll start moving the plan forward in phases starting at 4:00 a.m. on Wednesday, January 2."

Yedidya looked at him and thought about the tag team of Chiny and Ram. He felt an awesome weight of responsibility about reaching a decision, but it was time to trust his commanders. Finally, he quietly muttered, "Yes, okay."

On his way to his hotel, Yedidya decided that he would need to speak with Mofaz and get his approval. But he still felt some sense of security since he still had a card to play; this was not really the point of no return. That point would be Wednesday night when Chiny and his forces were at the forty-six miles south location. From there, they would be able to feel out the traitorous Red Sea before deciding.

Mofaz was holding a working meeting with the prime minister about the *Karine A* and about Mofaz's planned trip to the United States. Mofaz updated Sharon regarding the ship, including conveying that the air force was continuously following it, as well as the potential weather problems.

For Sharon, this was a major moment. There would be no middle ground. In this round, either he or Arafat would win. He realized that any hesitancy came from the enormity of the moment and said that he was satisfied with the presentation and would not require changes. He relied on Mofaz's judgment and ability to accomplish the complex job. The issue of Mofaz's planned trip to the United States for the evening of January 2 was more complex. "It's important to me that you fly there and explain the situation to the high echelons of the U.S. government and to lay the groundwork for my unofficial planned visit there."

"As IDF chief of staff, I'm obligated to stay and to be present here with my troops during the operation. You need to understand that," Mofaz said to Sharon firmly. Sharon seemed to become combative, and Mofaz nervously thought the prime minister would reject his request.

Then Sharon started to laugh and said, "Okay, you can cancel your trip to the United States. But how will we explain this to the media? It will immediately create a wave of rumors about the reasons for the cancellation. The left-leaning *Haaretz* newspaper, which is often critical of our government, will exaggerate it. And who knows? Maybe there will even be speculation that we are staging an operation behind the scenes. We need a cover story for pushing off the visit."

"We'll publicize that we put off the visit because of General Zinni's arrival in Israel on January 3 to discuss his proposal of a seven-day quieting down of the Second Intifada."

"Smooth. I like it," Sharon said, backing him up.

"Also, people know that I have close relations with the general since Zinni was a commander in the U.S. Marines in 1982. In an Israeli-U.S. exchange program, I was in a U.S. military course as a colonel, and he was helping conduct the course for the special forces. We became close during the course."

After discussing the question of who would eventually succeed Mofaz as IDF chief, Mofaz went home.

At around 1:00 a.m., the telephone woke him up. The commander of the navy was on the telephone. Yedidya updated him and briefly explained the issues related to the timing of meeting up with the *Karine A*. He added that he wanted to start sending naval forces out to sea in phases on Wednesday at 4:00 a.m., meaning in three hours.

"We should move up our sailing from Eilat to maintain all of our options. Chiny and Ram are making the same recommendation." Yedidya did not go into all the details about how deep into the Red Sea Chiny's forces might go depending on the weather and other factors.

Mofaz already felt as if he held a golden egg in his hands and gave the green light.

11

D-Day Minus One

Chiny's telephone did not ring that night. So just as he and Yedidya had agreed, at 4:00 a.m. the refueling ship, practically covered in fuel canisters, set sail in the dark. More ships would follow.

At 7:00 a.m., with the navy seals aboard, the civilian ship *Miami* left the port. At 9:00 a.m., two fast patrol boats—patrol boat 860, Chiny's command boat, and boat 862—slipped out of the port. At 12:14 p.m., patrol boat 861 left the port, and on board were the prisoner interrogators; a chief engineer; an electrician; a bomb squad officer; the navy seals' intelligence officer, Itamar; and other officials with special roles. At the same time, five commando boats set sail. Each one was manned only by a helmsman and a subcommander; the seals themselves would only move to these attack boats at a much later stage of the trip. The lead commando boat also left along with its staff, while Ram, commander of all the commandos, rode on the lead patrol boat with Chiny, the overall commander of the forces in the field.

Chiny scanned the stately red mountains. He didn't know what the future would bring, but one thing was clear to him: he would not come back to Eilat without the *Karine A* in tow. The full-scale drill and the prior drills gave him confidence in the navy seals and in the operational concept of capturing the ship from the commando boats while coordinating commandos slid down fast ropes onto the deck from helicopters. He received continuous reports about the location and status of the *Karine A*, which maintained a speed of seven to eight knots. At that speed, it would be around two hundred miles south of the Straits of Tiran around Thursday morning.

It would take the command boat six hours to traverse the 115 miles from Eilat to the Straits of Tiran. Some of the staff were dozing, some were playing backgammon, some were gorging themselves with food, and others were lost in thought.

The air force officer advising Chiny asked him, "It's weird. Why can we still see Eilat?"

"This isn't an airplane," Chiny answered him. "At sea, you need a lot of patience."

"You know," the officer said, "when I get on a plane, no one says goodbye to me. But with how emotional you all get when a ship sets sail, it reminds me of *The Love Boat*."

"Stop bothering me about movies," Chiny growled at him. "Will the air force be ready to refuel the Black Hawks so that I'll have my fast-roping option available? Why else are you here?"

The officer did not have a chance to answer before Chiny comically answered his own question: "You're here to advise me regarding all aerial issues as the head of the helicopters desk. That's why you're here. Otherwise, as far as I'm concerned, you are no more than a mouth to feed and a butt that craps."

The officer was a bit shocked. Chiny, with his sailor's visor and in his informal sailing outfit, then added: "You're here in your pilot overalls because during the full drill, I noticed, luckily for you, that you didn't puke."

After this exchange, the air force officer immediately reached out to Yoni, his boss. Yoni said, "We're reviewing options. We've carried out different photographing runs. There are a lot of issues to work through. But don't worry. Just tell Chiny that we'll figure it out."

Although he sensed some hesitation in Yoni's voice, the officer reported to Chiny that the air force would find solutions and that he wouldn't be stuck capturing the *Karine A* without his fast-roping capability. He transformed into Chiny's chief optimist about the air force's ability to solve the issue.

In the command group, Chiny's deputy adopted the officer and coached him about understanding a sailor's mentality. "Woe to us if someone goes on to the deck and whistles. Chiny might get angry enough to throw him into the sea," he said to him.

"Why?" asked the air force officer.

"Because the legend among sailors is that it could upset the waters," Chiny's deputy answered with a gleam of pleasure in his eye.

Around 3:00 p.m., Chiny's command patrol boat and boat 862 passed through the Straits of Tiran. The Egyptians had received advance notice that the Israeli Navy was carrying out a drill in the Red Sea. Chiny surveyed his forces' situation and debriefed his staff about plans for the refueling point being set at 40 miles south of the Straits of Tiran. Then he reported to navy headquarters: "The capture will take place at 6:00 a.m. on Thursday around 160 miles south of the Straits of Tiran."

Until that moment, all the officials at navy headquarters understood that Chiny had left Eilat a bit early, but they didn't view that as anything unusual. Now, little by little, they were starting to grasp that something else might displace the standing default plan. The capture might not take place at 46 miles south of the straits on Thursday afternoon or evening; rather, it might go forward around 160 miles south of the straits and as early as Wednesday night or Thursday morning.

Meanwhile, at around 10:30 a.m., or five hours before Chiny sent his message to Yedidya, Mofaz read the papers. He repeated the headline of the *Haaretz* newspaper's lead story with unconcealed glee: "IDF Chief Mofaz left yesterday for Washington to meet with the Secretary of State. Sharon briefed Mofaz yesterday in view of his planned trip."

"I hope that tomorrow they print that I didn't fly to the United States due to Zinni's arrival in Israel," he said to his bureau chief and asked him to bring in the officials who were to meet with him regarding the *Karine A*.

Two new participants were in the meeting—the new IDI director Aharon Zeevi-Farkash and navy deputy chief Dudu Ben-Besht. Meshita opened with a review of the intelligence picture. He focused on the ship's slow speed for calculating times and the indications that the ship would not reach the designated capture point forty-six miles south of the straits until Thursday night or later. At the same time, they were facing a three-day weather forecast in which Wednesday and Friday would have calm weather, but Thursday would be stormy. Meshita added that Egyptian president Mubarak was leaving Sharm El-Sheikh that day but was leaving behind his special naval guards.

Mofaz's intelligence bureau chief glanced over at Meshita, Yedidya, and Ben-Besht. All of them were in pure white uniforms and were giving off the vibe that they were about to accomplish something of great importance, complexity, and risk. It wasn't every day that the navy ran the show for an orchestra that included the air force and the full range of the Mossad, Unit 8200, and the other intelligence collection agencies. All of this effort was to support a mere three patrol boats and five commando boats.

Meshita himself sounded very focused on the professional minutiae while exuding a confidence and commitment to the operation that filled the room. He had already come before Mofaz in the past to present the *Santorini* saga, but this operation was on an entirely different level of magnitude. He was the lead intelligence agent and in the center of the spotlight.

Mofaz asked, "How certain are you that this ship is the *Karine A*?"

"Ninety-nine percent!" Meshita said.

"I want 100 percent certainty," Mofaz responded. He studied Meshita as if to ask, "Can you do this for me?" It was disturbing Mofaz. He wanted certainty so he could approve the fast-roping aspect of the operation without a heavy heart. "I'm missing something," he thought. "What happens if the navy seals slide down onto the ship, and they find out that they've landed on a legitimate commercial ship? What a royal mess that would be! How will it look, and how will we be able to explain it?"

"I want to see the name *Karine A* on the ship," Mofaz stressed with a dead-serious face. Something else was bothering him and led him to ask another question: "How much certainty do you have that there are weapons being smuggled on the ship?"

"Eighty-five percent," Meshita answered. "Regarding the ship, I am certain. Regarding the weapons, I have a high level of probability. Don't hang me if we don't find weapons, but we do need to seize this ship."

Mofaz turned to the head of the IDI's Research Department Brig. Gen. Yossi Kuperwasser. "Our estimate is the same as naval intelligence's estimate, but personally, I put the probability of there being high-quality smuggled weapons on the ship at 100 percent," Kuper said decisively. Still, as an intelligence agent who knew nothing is certain, on the inside he wondered, "Did I just exaggerate? What if I'm wrong?"

They moved on to other issues. Mofaz's thoughts skipped from the tactical arena to the strategic arena. They discussed the profound impact that capturing the *Karine A* could have on the diplomatic situation as well as the significance that the weapons would have for the region if they got into the PA's hands. Almost trembling, he reemphasized that this was a unique operation. And on top of his concerns of keeping round-the-clock surveillance and what would happen if they failed were others about the stormy weather forecast for Thursday and the fact that so many disparate pieces had to come together perfectly. They had arrived at a singular moment where all of the planning was coming together. He felt pride, yet his heart raced with anticipation.

Ben-Besht updated them that the Atara would be used as the aerial forward command center. Personnel were outfitting it and installing all the required systems. That afternoon they would carry out a drill using it as the forward command center. Mofaz was ecstatic.

"I'm going to be on it," he told those present. "I need to be in the forward area. With all of my paratroopers' operations, I was in the lead. When one of our soldiers died in the field defending the tomb of the biblical Joseph and was facing a multitude of Palestinians, I came to his side. If there is a failure, it's my responsibility, and I need to be there on the spot and in the field."

"If there's a communication issue while you are on the plane, you won't be able to be in control or have command," someone warned.

"I'm ready to take that risk," said Mofaz.

Then they debated about tactical issues, and finally Mofaz summarized a range of operational, intelligence, and information security issues. His mantra was that the goal of Noah's Ark was to bring the ship clandestinely to Eilat. The estimated timing of the capture would be between Thursday, January 3, and the morning of Friday, January 4. Photographing the ship's name was critical to ensure that the ship they were capturing was in fact the *Karine A*. Overall command would be on the Atara, where the IDF chief, Yedidya, Halutz, and other officers would be aboard. No one at this point was raising Chiny's daring idea of cutting in early before Thursday's stormy weather. Mofaz himself was not aware of it; he had only approved Chiny's forces leaving Eilat early.

Mofaz hurried to finish his meeting summary. Then he headed to the opening of a new center for studying intelligence at the armor training school.

The meeting's attendees went their separate ways. They likely did not even consider that on that very night they would take off in the aerial forward command center to keep up with Chiny, following his sudden decision to move the capture time of the operation forward and deeper south into the Red Sea. All of these changes would be necessary to avoid the stormy weather forecasted for Thursday and to take advantage of the window of time when the water was still calm.

When Meshita got back to his office, Kobi and Gil were already waiting for him impatiently. "So?"

"Come with me, guys," said Meshita as he entered his office. His bureau chief followed him with a pile of notices. Meshita quickly reviewed them. "The chief approved all of the different operational scenarios," Meshita opened. "But he wants to see the name *Karine A* on the ship with his own eyes!"

"The King Air [patrol aircraft] could pull that off," Kobi responded. "We have one ready to go."

"So send it to get Mofaz his 100 percent certainty."

"I'll head right over to the air force to handle it. By the way, I'm holding two large meetings today. The first is a status update with all of the intelligence agencies. It's the first time that we're holding such a meeting. The second is to wrap up the information security issue and what our responses will be to the media and foreign actors, including the various military attachés. We're dealing with different scenarios, including what must be completely blacked out, what issues will be dealt with by official press releases, and so on. I'll bring it for your approval."

When Kobi left, Meshita turned to Gil. They started to talk, when suddenly the secretary came in and announced: "Kuper wants Gil at his office for a meeting immediately."

With his hand, Meshita signaled him to go. After Gil left, Meshita called Stephanie and asked, "Can you come to meet with me now?"

"I'll be there in fifteen minutes."

Shortly after, Stephanie entered his office out of breath. After they greeted each other, Meshita showed her a color photo of the *Karine A* that the Atara had taken on Tuesday. "I want to ask you— tell me, is this the ship?"

Stephanie took the picture with her and left, promising an answer.

Meanwhile, Gil and other intelligence officers had rushed over to Kuper's office. Once everyone was gathered, Kuper said, "I'm just returning from a meeting with the IDF chief. This operation has huge, and I mean mega, consequences. If we make a mistake in identifying the ship, the state of Israel will be in for a disastrous diplomatic mess. Let me be clear: Recheck every intelligence item and every source, and make sure this thing is airtight with not a single error."

Gil then held an intelligence update meeting. All of his officers who had dealt with the *Karine A* issue were there.

"Are we 100 percent sure that this is the ship?" Gil asked, but he already knew the answer.

One after the next, they all answered, "Yes, 100 percent."

The head of the international commercial desk added, "Today, I met with the navy's engineering and equipment branch head. The engineer's conclusion was that this was the *Karine A* almost to a practical certainty."

"Based on what?" Gal asked.

"They did a comparison between the pictures from the earlier surveillance of the ship when it was docked in Yemen to the original schematics of the *Karine A* as well as to its sister ships. They were identical."

"What about the cargo?" Gil immediately asked.

"It's likely that it has a cargo aboard of at least a hundred tons."

The King Air B-200 patrol aircraft's advanced electro-optical scope was the most advanced aerial photo system available. The crew had two pilots, two patrol staff, and a mission commander. They took off around 11:00 a.m. with a two-part mission: to locate cables and other obstacles on the deck of the *Karine A* that could obstruct the helicopters and their commandos, and to give information to the helicopter pilots for choosing where to drop the commandos. The two leading options were between the cabin and the middle derrick or between the middle derrick and the bow of the ship. One of the Black Hawk helicopter pilots had joined the crew of the King Air for the flyover to make that call.

But the mission included another objective: on the ship's stern they looked for the name. There was no mistake. Two patrol staff persons saw *Karine A* clearly, and the aerial photographic system snapped it. They reported:

> We clearly saw that the name of the ship is KARINE A. We didn't see the flag of the ship and could not gauge what kind of radar it uses. We didn't see weapons, containers or chests on the deck of the ship. We saw one man on the deck who was walking from the bow to the stern. The patrol staff do not believe he was doing any kind of guard duty or security rounds.

The report went on to discuss the cables and other potential objects of obstruction.

The King Air landed around evening time. One copy of the photographic film was sent to the surveillance desk of the navy, and another copy was sent to the air force decipherer. The decipherer's findings would be vital both for the navy seals on the commando boats and for those sliding down the fast ropes. They would also assist the Black Hawk pilots who were very concerned about the derricks. The largest question remaining was: Could they prove for sure that the ship was smuggling weapons?

In the afternoon, Kobi and Yoki met with Meshita. Yoki updated him that he'd coordinated all of the intelligence assistance aboard the Atara and was just returning from a related drill.

"How was it?" Meshita asked curiously.

"Yedidya was there. He checked the visual surveillance scopes. But everyone was interested to see where their bosses would sit. Everyone was trying to get the best seat for their boss."

"Where am I sitting?" Meshita asked, now even more curious.

"Right behind the IDF chief. Your name is tagged to the chair. Don't ask about how many fights there were," he said, grimacing slightly.

Kobi cut in: "Did you hear what they're saying?"

"That Chiny wants to capture the ship deeper into the Red Sea as early as Thursday morning?"

"Yup. Exactly."

Meshita got up to look at the map. Beni the Weather Man happened to enter the room with his heavy steps. He looked agitated.

"Speak!" Meshita said to him.

"I've told the entire world now that my certainty about the forecast has increased. Tomorrow, the Red Sea will be hell with threatening winds coming down from the north to the south." Then he began giving scholarly explanations about weather in general and the weather pattern in the Red Sea specifically.

"The ships can't wait until tomorrow at the original point of capture of around forty-six miles south of the Straits of Tiran. There's no time to waste. Listen to Beni, we need to go south right now— and I mean *right now*—to capture the ship while there is still decent weather. The faster they can go the better," Meshita said with an air of determination. Then he turned to Kobi and said, "Let's go up to Yedidya's office."

Also that afternoon, Yoni was called to the navy's Operations Division. For the first time, the navy officially told him that the capture operation might take place as early as later that night and at a much farther distance of 150 to 160 miles south of the Straits of Tiran.

Though the navy had not officially told him about this possibility before, Yoni thought to himself, "Luckily, I have an officer embedded with Chiny who gave me an informal heads-up about this possibility some time ago." Responding, Yoni said, "Of course, you know that the Black Hawk helicopters don't have that kind of a range."

"Yes, but we need to do the fast roping," the navy operations official pressed him. "Find a way."

Yoni updated his direct operations commander and then went up to see air force commander Dan Halutz.

"What are the options for refueling the Black Hawks?" asked Halutz. Yoni presented an option to him. Halutz listened, glanced over at Yoni, and said, "There's no way that will happen."

Disappointed and depressed, Yoni returned to his office. He updated navy operations, which then reported to Chiny: "At this stage, there's no fast-roping capability."

Every Second Counts

JANUARY 2, 6:00 P.M.

After dark, Chiny's remaining forces passed one by one through the Straits of Tiran and traveled toward the refueling point forty miles south of the straits. There they could feel the water change. While they were sailing in the Gulf of Eilat, they had been shielded by Sharm El-Sheikh, and it had been impossible to know what the true state of the Red Sea was. It would have been easy to underestimate the situation and to conclude from the Eilat area's waters how calm the Red Sea would be. But the Red Sea was also actually calm now, exactly as Beni the Weather Man had forecasted. Still, Beni's last weather report indicated that later that night, the northerly winds would start to move in to the Suez Canal. By morning, they would wallop the Red Sea like a bullet coming out of a gun barrel.

"Now, every second is priceless," Chiny thought.

At 6:10 p.m., he called Yedidya. The operations room in the small command patrol boat was crowded and dark, but he could see the lights of the different machines were blinking. The *Karine A* was around 201 miles from their forces and around 247 miles from the straits, trekking along at the slow speed of eight knots. At that speed, the ship would only get to Chiny's current position on Thursday afternoon—during the height of the storm. Chiny described the state of the water to Yedidya: "Our Weather Man came through. Right now, we have a window of calm weather until Thursday morning."

They needed to take advantage of the calm weather to seize the ship clandestinely and in the dark of night. He wanted to do the takeover at 5:00 a.m. Chiny knew that going another 115 miles farther south with such a small force and beyond the operating range of some of the helicopters was a gamble. His accompanying air force officer was constantly assuring him that the air force could handle the refueling of the Black Hawks, but Ram felt an ache in his chest, worrying he might not have his fighters from the Black Hawks on hand. But he trusted the commandos in the boats to take over the *Karine A* without too many issues. Each of them knew exactly what their individual roles were. Each of them knew every meter of the ship. Like Chiny, he understood the rare window of opportunity that they had. At the end of the day, pulling off the fast-rope operation would be more of a bonus prize.

"We'll be living on the edge regarding the timing of the operation," thought Chiny as he waited for Yedidya's decision. "But whoever balks at the risk of living dangerously will get nowhere, and I trust my men."

The responsibility was on Yedidya as commander of the navy. For what seemed the millionth time, he weighed the various factors and risks. He considered that in the worst-case scenario, they could stop the *Karine A* in broad daylight using the fast patrol boats and have the fast-roping, helicopter-based commandos as a fallback force. That option would be open and not clandestine. It went against what Mofaz had hoped for, but it would still lead to capturing the ship and its weapons. He and Chiny agreed on some updated basic principles:

> The takeover would take place at night at a distance far beyond the Black Hawk helicopters' operating envelope.

> If this could not be accomplished, then the takeover would take place closer to the original capture point, employing the fast patrol boats and various aerial means.

But they also needed Mofaz's approval.

Chiny's air force officer was in a bad mood. "What! There won't be any helicopters?" he asked Chiny after the chief had agreed on the updated plan with Yedidya.

"No! The air force won't approve it," Chiny said to him, though he still hoped and believed that Halutz and the air force would come through.

"I can't believe it. I can't believe it," Chiny's air force officer practically shouted. "There are definitely options. The air force can find a way."

Around 6:30 p.m., Yoni called Halutz's bureau to check if he'd changed his mind. About a minute passed, and Halutz's bureau chief told Yoni, "He hasn't changed his mind. No way."

Within a few minutes, Chiny, whose boat was refueling, received a report from the navy: "You don't have a fast-rope capability."

Shlomi Dahan, the commander of the navy seals' fast-roping forces, got a call at the airfield where they were stationed that the fast-roping piece of the operation had been cancelled. He couldn't believe it. He and his deputy sat with the Black Hawks' commander and tried to clarify different options. They found it hard to accept that the air force would fail to show up for the operation and that it had declined to offer some kind of a solution to the refueling problem.

At 6:30 p.m., Yedidya and Halutz met with Mofaz. Yedidya presented the weather situation and Chiny's updated plan, including all of the costs and benefits. Then he recommended approving the plan. He said, "Chiny, who is currently around forty miles south of the Straits of Tiran in the Red Sea, has said that the Weather Man's forecast of calm weather for today is right on even as we are facing rainy weather in Israel."

Mofaz said, "So what you're saying is, tomorrow the weather will be the stormiest."

Yedidya nodded his head and emphasized, "We can carry out another refueling for our boats. The problem is the fast-roping issue. The updated plan would require Chiny traveling another 115 miles south from where his forces are currently stationed. The Black Hawks don't have the range to make it there and would need to refuel. My understanding is that the air force can overcome the issue and figure out a way to refuel."

Mofaz looked at the map. He remembered his talk with Chiny on Thursday, December 20, when he had looked directly into his eyes and told him he would back his calls in the field. Now the moment of truth had come. From the questions he asked, evidently Mofaz supported the plan to sail 115 miles farther south toward the *Karine A* to take over the ship while the weather was still calm, but he was also the biggest fan of the fast-rope tactic. Why should they give up on that? He turned his glare on Halutz.

Halutz explained the different risks entailed and the problems the air force would encounter if it tried executing a refueling option so that the Black Hawks could operate beyond their standard envelope. Halutz had solid and convincing objections, including diplomatic issues. But Mofaz was still dead-set on the fast-rope option.

"Do it," he said to Halutz. "I'll take responsibility. Do serious checks to try to overcome some of the risks." He then asked Halutz what other aerial forces would be in play besides the Black Hawks with the navy seals.

Halutz told him that two Apache helicopters would accompany and provide a security envelope for the Black Hawks. One of them also would provide airborne medical assistance if needed. Two Hercules aircraft would serve to refuel the Sea Stallion helicopters, and the King Air aircraft would take pictures of the *Karine A* to assist the navy seals in taking over the ship from the sea. The navy's Sea Scan aircraft would also be under his control as well as the Boeing Atara aircraft for communications and electronic relays. Finally two fighter planes at an airport in the south would be on call to assist on a moment's notice.

Satisfied, Mofaz paused and muttered, "It's crucial for me that we do the fast roping."

"Sir, you'll have it!" said Halutz. "We built the fast-roping capability in record time, and we've carried out the farthest surveillance run in our history. We'll do everything we can to make this happen."

Mofaz was in high spirits. "We'll do a broader situation update at 8:00 p.m. and see where things stand," he said.

At 7:00 p.m., Yoni was sitting in his office and feeling down. Then the air force's head of the Operations Division called: "Yoni, Halutz came back now from meeting with the IDF chief. He's approved the option we recommended to him. It's going to happen tonight. The air force's fast-roping option is a go. Get everything ready."

Yoni was dumbfounded at the 180-degree turn. He needed to change all the orders for the relevant pilots not only to reflect the time change from tomorrow to this evening and the new, longer distances that his forces would need to fly but also to account for the necessary additional refueling. The Atara aircraft also needed to be prepped for flying out that night to serve as the forward command center. This wasn't just a matter of paperwork. At the lower levels of military officials who had to carry out the orders, including for the pilots, it was a major change of plans and a daunting task. Would they be able to accomplish the new plan in the brief time they were being given?

Meanwhile, on the water, they started to refuel the navy's boats at 7:00 p.m. Chiny called the head of the navy's Operations Division and said emphatically that the operation would be a go at 5:00 a.m. and that they would carry out another refueling before the takeover.

The refueling continued. Around 8:00 p.m., the navy seals boarded and got ready in their commando boats. At that point, Ram was still by Chiny's side in the command patrol boat. The rest of Ram's command staff, including Itamar, transferred to the lead commando boat. All forces started moving south in an organized formation. The *Karine A* was about 184 miles south of their position.

Mofaz heard the radio report that the reason he had not ultimately flown to the United States as scheduled was because of the expected arrival of General Zinni in Israel on Thursday. Satisfied, he chuckled to himself. Yedidya was giving him constant updates. Around 8:00 p.m., he held a meeting of select members of the high command. Halutz brought the three-minute video taken by the King Air. Mofaz saw the name *Karine A* written on the ship with his own eyes. That was it! He took in the video of the ship, asked his standard round of questions, took notes in his yellow notebook, and said to himself for the millionth time, "This is a five-hundred-ton bomb on Arafat's head."

Meshita gave an update: Mubarak and his accompanying ships had left Sharm El-Sheikh as expected. He added that the *Karine A* had sped up a bit to nine knots, though its average speed was still around eight knots. The weather was starting to get worse.

The head of the navy's Operations Division presented Chiny's plan: He would come into contact with the *Karine A* sometime between midnight and 6:00 a.m. on Thursday. The exact time would vary depending on speed, refueling cycles, and other similar factors. The expected new capture point would be around 120 miles south of the Straits of Tiran at around 5:00 a.m.

"We'll get it done," said Halutz regarding the refueling dilemmas.

Mofaz looked around at those present and his gaze rested on Yedidya. This operation was Yedidya's biggest ever, and he would command it from the Atara aircraft.

All that was left was to set the actual exact strike time. The die had been cast. The next status update meeting was set for 11:30 p.m. in the navy's control room. Mofaz wanted to speak to Chiny directly from there. Mofaz's bureau chief updated the military secretaries of Prime Minister Sharon and Defense Minister Binyamin Ben-Eliezer. Later, Mofaz spoke personally with Prime Minister Sharon and got the green light.

Anticipation had seized everyone in naval intelligence. The rumor spread like wildfire: the mission was happening that night!

Anat had no idea what to do with herself. Meshita held a final status update where he reiterated the importance of avoiding leaks and established what each person would be doing as they followed the operation: Yoki would be with him on the Atara, another officer would be in the King Air, and Gil and Kobi would run the intelligence station at the navy headquarters' command and control center.

During the meeting, Meshita took a call from Stephanie. Regarding the photo he had given to her earlier, she confirmed, "This is the ship!" He thanked her warmly.

Meshita was still briefly distracted by a variety of other last-minute doubts, but then he recovered. He looked around at those present and, after a short hesitation, said, "Friends, I want to thank all of you for the fantastic intelligence research you've done. You, and no one else, led us to the *Karine A*. A 100 percent bull's-eye. I couldn't be prouder."

Sitting at his desk in the meantime, Kobi looked at the decipherer's report from the King Air. Usually, decipherer's reports didn't need his personal approval, but the stakes were different this time. There would be no time to fix things. He requested to see the video and a hard copy. Under the glass tower set on his desk, he reviewed the pictures and compared them to the diagrams of the ship. He used the pictures to write a special report addressed to the sea-based forces that were in the Red Sea and the helicopter forces getting ready to depart. His report outlined the obstacles on board the *Karine A*, most notably the various cables strewn around on the ship's deck. When Itamar received the report on the lead commando boat, he updated Ram and Dror, who would be commanding the navy seals during the takeover.

Meanwhile, Kuper met with Foreign Minister Shimon Peres in Jerusalem about issues related to Syria. After other meetings, he headed back to Tel Aviv around 10:00 p.m. On his way, Kuper's bureau chief called: "Kuper, there've been changes. Come quick. Everyone is walking on eggshells."

"What are you talking about?"

"Come quick!"

D-Day Minus One

Continuing on a dangerously wet highway, he eventually arrived at IDF headquarters in Tel Aviv. He practically sprinted to his office.

"This evening you'll be flying with Mofaz in the airborne forward command center," his bureau chief said excitedly, adding that Kuper should head downstairs for a meeting with Mofaz. It was about to begin.

Kuper went one level down to Mofaz's bureau, where he was told, "The meeting is in the navy's underground command and control center with the navy at 11:30 p.m."

At 9:40 p.m., Chiny's forces continued south. The *Karine A* was about 140 miles south of their position. The ship was moving at eight knots.

At 10:00 p.m., Chiny gave a status update in which he told his forces that the patrol boats would refuel the commando boats at 1:00 a.m. and that the operation would go forward at 3:00 a.m. If the weather deteriorated faster than expected, then they would initiate the takeover even earlier and perform the refueling after the takeover.

Yedidya told Mofaz that Chiny wanted to move the takeover up from 5:00 a.m. to 3:00 a.m. as he was concerned about the deteriorating weather situation. He could feel the change in the water; the larger waves signaled that the deterioration could happen at any moment. Mofaz was physically in his bureau, preparing for his meeting the next day with Zinni, but his thoughts were in the Red Sea.

Mofaz approved.

"The operation is a go for 3:00 a.m.! Approved!" Yedidya told Chiny. "And the fast rope is also approved. The air force will make it happen."

Chiny was thrilled. It was 10:30 p.m. Chiny sent for his air force official, who had been depressed, given up, and gone to sleep when he thought the fast roping was cancelled. The air force official came up on deck and saw Chiny waiting for him with a smile. He said, "You've got what you wanted. We're running with it. It's been approved. Tel Aviv didn't disappoint."

Chiny's forces continued their southward trajectory, while the

Karine A sailed north toward them at a speed of between seven to nine knots. The gap between them and fate was closing.

Everyone sat waiting for Mofaz at the navy's command and control center. The hall leading to it was full. All the navy personnel wanted to get a glimpse of the IDF chief. He sat at the head of the table in silence. His eyes homed in on Meshita. He remembered Meshita had told him that very morning there was a 99 percent likelihood—not yet 100 percent—of having correctly identified the ship. "So," Mofaz said to him, "now we've identified the ship with 100 percent certainty."

Meshita held in his hand the official confirmation from Stephanie that the United States had officially and completely confirmed that the ship was the *Karine A*. He responded with a little bit of tongue in cheek: "Halutz and the air force gave me an extra half percent to add to my 99 percent from the morning." He continued, "The other half percent, I got from our U.S. partners."

Yedidya then explained the takeover was currently scheduled for 3:00 a.m.

Mofaz considered the issue. From what he was hearing, the patrol boats would refuel the commando boats. How long would the refueling take? Did they have experience with this kind of a refueling plan with these boats and at sea? "I want to speak with Chiny," said Mofaz. Quickly they got Chiny on the line. The discussion was short. Mofaz was curious about the refueling and about when Chiny thought they could execute the takeover.

"My guess would be around 3:30 a.m. or 3:45 a.m.," Chiny answered. He sounded confident and was constantly keeping tabs on the *Karine A*. The weather conditions were still ideal, though the continuing feeling was that they were at most hours away from getting worse. Their window of time was small.

Mofaz was satisfied. The circle had closed. Yedidya informed Chiny that the operation was now a go for 3:30 a.m. on January 3, 2002. From their airfield near Eilat, the helicopters would have to fly about two hours to arrive in the area around that time.

Mofaz called Sharon once again to give him the updated operation start time. Sharon approved and wished them luck. He trusted

Mofaz. Sharon understood they were about to roll out a complex military operation much farther from home than usual, but at that point, for Sharon, it was still just an operation. In his mind, the strategic significance and diplomatic consequences were still off in the distance.

When Meshita left the meeting with Mofaz at the navy's command and control center, he saw Kobi. In a spontaneous moment, he said, "Kobi you go on the Atara with Yedidya in my place. I'll take your place at the command and control center." Kobi was shocked, but before he could say anything, Meshita had already turned to get Yedidya's approval.

The secretarial staff gave Kobi a hug and a copy of the book of Psalms to take with him. A rumor had gone around that the Atara aircraft had problems and was unsafe to be aboard. Maybe the Psalms would bring him good luck.

Although Mofaz had said the mission should be a go at 3:30 a.m., the air force wasn't ready. It had to alter its plans when the operation moved from Thursday morning to the middle of the night between Wednesday and Thursday. Yoni worked like a demon in his final sprint. On top of everything, the heavy winds meant it would take the air force longer to reach the capture point. Around midnight, the air force notified everyone it needed more time, and the operation was pushed off until 4:00 a.m., January 3, 2002.

At the same time, the intelligence officer for the Eilat base started making preparations for taking the *Karine A* into custody after its capture. The staff set up the quarters for questioning the prisoners, the communications for intelligence collection officers, the equipment, and the storage areas.

At 1:30 a.m., Mofaz climbed the Atara's ramp in the midst of a raging storm. "This was when I was supposed to take off for the United States," he thought to himself. "Instead, I'm flying out to drain the terror swamp—to drain it!" he recited to himself as his mantra.

He entered the aircraft and took his seat next to Yedidya. The media was still reporting that he had delayed his flight to assist with Zinni's visit. "There's some truth to that," Mofaz chuckled to himself. "In the end, all of these details connect to one strategic framework."

At 2:00 a.m., the refueling was finished. Ram moved from Chiny's lead patrol boat to his lead commando boat, which also had a ship's helmsman and a subcommander to attend to the ship. Ram was directing the commandos on all five ships, Itamar, the staff to operate the electro-optical scope, and two crew members to man two small machine guns.

Chiny's forces started moving south again.

12

The Capture of the *Karine A*

Showtime

JANUARY 3, 2002, TOWARD DAWN

At 3:00 a.m. on Thursday, Chiny was packed in with his command staff in the command center on a fast patrol boat. The situation with the *Karine A* had him on edge. He could not stop pondering the current time and distance for intercepting the target. The helicopters with the fast-roping commandos would arrive around 3:30 a.m., and they could only stay in the field until 4:15 a.m. Calculating the timing was critical. Where was the *Karine A*? According to all the calculations based on the ship's movements and speed, at this point it was supposed to be only twenty-three miles south of his position and moving at a speed of six to ten knots. They were supposed to meet up in forty to fifty minutes.

"In the radar we see a group of ships at a distance of twenty-three miles," one of the radar monitors said. But which one of them was the *Karine A*? The radar was not giving a clear answer. A patrol by the navy's Sea Scan aircraft, using its electro-optical capabilities, did not succeed in identifying the target.

"Shimon," he said to his intelligence officer, "when do you think we'll see the *Karine A* using the electro-optical imaging?"

"The weather is making it harder to see. I assume that from a distance of eight thousand yards, we'll be able to see it," Shimon responded. His face was glued to the electro-optical scope, and he was completely focused. "I need to give this my all, 100 percent of my knowledge and experience. Stay focused, stay focused," he repeated to himself. But it was hard for him not to think of his wife, Adi, and young son, Liad.

Around 3:30 a.m., Ram's navy seals started to move forward. The command boat led the way with five commando boats right behind it. The surveillance scope on the command boat followed the *Karine A* but could not identify it with complete certainty. The estimated distance to the *Karine A* was now eight miles. Itamar's biggest concern was that when they finally pulled alongside the ship, either the ship's sides would be higher than estimated, making them harder to scale, or they'd face some other unforeseen challenge. He was at peace with the level of tactical information they had given the commandos about the ship.

On the *Karine A*, Omar Akawi woke up in a fright from a bad dream. The small captain's quarters, which were located under the bridge, were pitch-black. For over two months, he had served as the captain of the *Karine A*. Under orders from Adel Muhgrabi, in September and October he had recruited his crew. In October Fathi Ghazem, the deputy chief of the Palestinian Naval Police who had authority over weapons smuggling, had sent him to Yemen; there he took command of the ship, which had arrived from Sudan. "Omar," Ghazem's voice rang in his ears, "this is the most important national mission you have ever been given. Forget all of the smuggling you have done until now."

Akawi had found the ship in terrible shape, but he had complete confidence in his long experience at sea. The ship traveled successfully to the Persian Gulf, and now it was crossing through the Red Sea. He raised his arm to check the time on his watch. His bad dream of Egyptian police throwing him into a stinky cell continued to trouble him. He was a wanted man by the Egyptian regime because of his past smuggling, and he knew he was taking a risk now by trying to pass through the Suez Canal. During their conversations in Ajman north of Dubai, Mughrabi had repeatedly promised him that he had nothing to worry about. Mughrabi explained that he would handle all of the paperwork with the Egyptians and that he would not allow them onto the ship to inspect it.

"All of them are friends of mine," he had said to try to calm Akawi.

But Akawi did not trust the slippery Mughrabi. Anger flooded over him. He had served the Palestinian revolution in the maritime arena for over twenty years. But when the Second Intifada broke out, he was back in the business of tedious journeys and smuggling. Would they finally pay him back? And whom in his crew could he trust? Definitely not the Egyptians, all from the same village, whom he had recruited. They had tried to rebel and abandon the ship when they accidentally learned that the ship was smuggling weapons. The incident came up when the weapons were being loaded onto the ship near the Iranian coast. The most trustworthy were the three Palestinians who were veteran smugglers.

Little by little his eyes adjusted and made out the time on his watch—3:30 a.m. "No big deal," he muttered to himself. "Anyway I was going to need to get out of bed in another half hour."

It was his regular habit to go to the bridge around dawn to see that everything was okay, and then he went back to sleep for a few more hours. He got out of bed, rubbed his eyes, and picked up the navigation map that he had dropped on the floor next to his bed. He lit a light and carefully looked over the map. Since they had left Yemen, he had traveled 805 miles. Another 135 miles and he would arrive at the entrance to the Gulf of Suez, which was along the way to the Suez Canal. They would reach it later today, Thursday, around evening time.

"And then," he repeated to himself, "we sail toward Alexandria, Egypt; meet up with three fishing boats at the agreed-upon coordinates; and give them the containers. Then I'll have finished my job." He put the map down, got up from his bed, and headed to the bridge, where two observers were already watching the seas.

The fateful moment of 3:40 a.m. was approaching. Where the hell was that ship? The intelligence officer Shimon, dressed in a water-resistant suit and wearing a warm knitted black hat, was using the electro-optical scope to search for it. Then at a distance of eight thousand yards, he saw the amorphous shape of a ship. Its chimney was distinctive, along with the billowing black smoke and sparks of fire coming out of it. He peered over at it excitedly but kept quiet. Eventually he could see the image that had become so familiar to him—the *Karine A* with its three derricks, including a large derrick in the middle of the ship. He took a deep breath and yelled, "We found it!"

Chiny looked at the monitor. The picture was a bit obscured, but he completely trusted Shimon's identification. His adrenaline shot up. Chiny also received a report that the helicopters had arrived in the area.

Ram on his command boat and the navy seals on their commando boats were edging in even closer to the *Karine A* from the east. The distance between them became even shorter, and Itamar was now able to examine the ship with binoculars. He felt as if he were on cloud nine. This was the ship! This was the ship! He tried to figure out how much activity was on the ship—an issue that had been eating away at him up until now. He thought he could spot the outline of only one person on the bridge.

Chiny's fast patrol command boat stopped a thousand yards southeast of the ship. The navy seals closed in on the ship from the east and curved around it from behind. From that point, from only a few hundred meters from the ship's stern, they cut in toward it to begin the raid. But as the commando boats started their maneuver to circle around the ship from behind, an unrelated commercial ship started to sail into the same area. The commercial ship lit up the pitch-black area with its strobe light as it passed.

Luckily the unwanted attention from the light was only a temporary distraction, and the navy seals in their commando boats zeroed in on a point only a hundred meters from the ship's stern. Months of intelligence work and weeks of constant operational preparation were about to confront reality as the commandos would try to take over the ship and seize its weapons. Ram on his command boat got close enough that he saw the ship's name on the side with his own eyes. There was just enough light for him to make out the letters K-A-R-I-N-E-A.

At 3:55 a.m., Ram confirmed the sighting of the *Karine A* to Chiny. When he gave Ram the green light, the commando boats jumped into action and went alongside the ship. There was already complete radio silence. Ziv, one of the navy seals' subcommanders, sat in his commando boat along with eight of his troops. They would be the first to jump into battle, scaling the *Karine A* from its right side. Sweat dripped down Ziv's neck from the humidity.

He peered over at the third-quarter moon and saw its pale light glistening on the small waves, which were growing in size by the minute. It was a complicated moment. He felt the usual human anxiety and adrenaline that accompanies every operation. Paradoxically, Ziv's navy seal unit, which was specially trained for combat at sea, had been used mostly for land-based commando raids. Palestinian terrorists and suicide bombers in the West Bank near Nablus had kept them busy. They had carried out ambushes and operations where they had burst into enclosed areas. Their operations included messy, close contact gunfights and hand-to-hand combat. A number of Ziv's fellow seals had been injured.

Then they had been called back from the West Bank and returned to their base near Haifa on Israel's northwest coast. Cdr. Dror Friedman, one of Ziv's commanders, told them, "Your new mission will be to capture a mega Palestinian weapons ship in the Red Sea." Relief was mixed with anxiety. They would finally get to put their sea-based combat training to the test.

The commando boats sped up. They inched closer and closer to the aft portion of the *Karine A*'s sides. For a moment, Ziv's sight of the *Karine A* was blocked by a series of foamy waves. He mentally was rattling off his checklist for the operation. His thoughts were not about making history, but about synthesizing all their intelligence about the *Karine A* for the impending surprise attack. Suddenly, the moon disappeared from sight. It was obscured by the *Karine A*. In only a few moments, they would launch their surprise attack.

Two lookouts were on the bridge of the *Karine A*. The first lookout, a Jordanian named Taysar al-Asalaki, was an expert sailor who was serving as the first officer with a salary of $1,500 per month. He and the ship's captain, Omar Akawi, were constantly at each other's throats about one thing or another. From the beginning, the ship's commercial cargo had made no sense to Taysar. In Sudan, they had loaded hundreds of tons of sesame and rice. In the Persian Gulf off Dubai, they had sold the food items and purchased toys, furniture, kitchen items, clothes, cosmetics, and pens. What was this ship, an old-fashioned general store? It seemed bizarre.

The second lookout was a Palestinian named Salem al-Sankari. He was also a diver and affiliated with the operations unit of the Palestinian Authority's Fatah movement. He was on Captain Akawi's short list of crew members who could be trusted.

Beams from a speeding commercial ship's strobe light passed the *Karine A* on the right and caught the lookouts off guard. A few minutes passed. Then Taysar thought he saw boats coming alongside the ship.

"Let's wake up the captain," said Taysar to Salem.

"We don't need to. Let's wait," Salem responded.

Taysar didn't argue with him, but he looked toward the starboard side of the boat. Suddenly, the captain himself appeared and started to question Taysar.

Four key navy seal commanders participated in the assault: Ram, Dror, Dan, and Ziv. Ram was in charge of both the sea-based and helicopter-based commandos. Under him was navy seal squadron commander Dror Friedman, who was commanding both the boats and the commandos as they approached the *Karine A*. Under Dror, Lieutenant Commander Dan would lead the thirty-two commandos during the clandestine assault. He was built like a brick wall and physically intimidating. Reporting to Dan was Ziv, the subcommander of the two commando boats on the starboard side of the ship; they would be the ones to make contact with the *Karine A* and its crew. Dan was with the two commando boats on the port side.

Israeli naval support and command vessels and their surveillance cameras moved closer. Suddenly, Shimon, the intelligence

The Capture of the *Karine A*

officer on Chiny's command bridge, wiped his eyes in disbelief. On the *Karine A*'s bridge, he could see a slightly overweight man with a mustache wearing what looked like pajamas.

"Isn't that Captain Akawi?" he asked himself. He didn't have time to check the pictures in his intelligence file. He told Chiny.

The Israeli Air Force's lookout King Air B-200 was flying overhead. It would transmit images in real time to the naval forces at sea. A few minutes later, all surveillance footage was sent directly to navy seal commander Ram.

The raid was about to start.

This was the moment of truth for the Israeli Navy Seals. In the first operation of its kind, they would clandestinely take over a moving ship with one team of commandos climbing onto it from commando boats and another team fast roping down to the ship from Black Hawk helicopters. From March 2000 to August 2001, no fewer than four elite U.S. Navy SEALS had died in similar, but less complex, training missions and operations. Three more U.S. Navy SEALS would die in 2002 on similar missions, including a forty-one-year old commander who died while fast roping down from a Black Hawk helicopter in El Salvador. Other U.S. Navy SEALS died from boats capsizing during mobility training exercises that took place in much calmer waves than the Israeli Navy Seals were having to contend with on this raid.

If the Israeli Navy Seals succeeded in climbing up the ship unscathed, their next moves for taking over the ship were clear: First, they must capture the bridge, where most of the ship's command functions were centered; it represented the high ground in any ongoing battle. Then they would go for control of the ship's other critical areas—the engineering room and the communications room. If they did not capture the captain in any of those rooms, their next priority would be to track him down and subdue him. Meanwhile, others would be subduing the rest of the crew, securing the storage areas and other parts of the ship, and getting ready for the helicopter-based commandos to come in and reinforce them.

At 4:00 a.m., the commandos in the two boats on opposite sides of *Karine A*'s stern used a classified device to project a grappling hook with a rope ladder twenty-three feet above and onto the ship. As they scampered up the sides of the boat—one after another—the ladder shook with the wind, threatening to toss them into the merciless waves.

Ziv would be the first one to reach the top and set foot on the *Karine A*'s deck. After carefully planting his feet, he started to climb. He felt the wind rushing through his hair and brushing the small portion of his skin that was not covered in combat gear. He had trained for this dozens of times, but now it was the real thing. The moon seemed to be smiling at him now, but as he climbed up one hand after another, questions streamed through his mind: "Will they fire on me? On my unit?" With all of the impressive intelligence they had assembled, naval operations intelligence never figured out whether the *Karine A*'s crew was armed. If the men were armed, then with what? Because of that gap, the Israelis had trained for the worst, assuming that the crew was armed.

Finally, Ziv reached the top. In a vaulting motion, he hopped onto the deck, landing with a carefully planned roll and rising in one fluid move before rapidly dashing toward the bridge. Showtime! He could already start to see the crew close-up—no longer from a distance through binoculars or electro-optical scopes. One after another, the men of his navy seal unit hopped over the ship's edge onto the deck, rolled, and followed his lead toward the bridge.

They had memorized every nook and cranny of the boat and had practiced the best way to move around and open each door they came across. Two to three seals would position themselves on both sides of the doorway. One would turn the handle slowly to ensure it did not creak. Another would squat, ready to fire at knee level if necessary. A third would aim his weapon at eye level for the moment the door opened.

They used silent hand signals, a secret code between elite fighters, about when to move and maneuver forward. So far, they had achieved surprise. They met no resistance or shooting as they got to the deck. That did not mean their luck would continue when they tried to take the bridge. The quiet was welcome. But they also feared that it might conceal a dangerous threat lurking in the dark.

As Ziv's first unit made its way toward the bridge, more commandos continued to scramble up the side of the ship and onto the deck.

The remaining two commando boats waited for their turn. After only three minutes, all of the commandos from the first two boats were already on the deck. Then the commandos from the second two boats joined them. Ram used the electro-optical scope and watched the commandos throughout the operation from the starboard side. The King Air surveillance aircraft's live feed allowed him to follow the commandos' progress on the port side of the ship.

Ram's job was to synchronize the different sea-based commandos' infiltration of the *Karine A* from opposite sides and to ensure various sections of the ship were taken simultaneously. This was crucial for maintaining surprise and preventing a distress call. Then he would orchestrate the fast-roping commandos' arrival by helicopter.

Meanwhile, Taysar told Akawi about the commercial ship that had suddenly lit up the area with its strobe light.

"Why did they flash their lights?" Akawi asked.

"Maybe they were concerned about colliding with another ship," Taysar responded. "It seemed to me that I also saw boats coming in from behind us."

"Get down immediately to the deck and check!" Akawi ordered.

Taysar hurried out to check. Akawi remained at the railing of the bridge, his mind racing anxiously, but he was not remotely dreaming about an Israeli attack this far out at sea. Instead, he was worried about what would happen if Egyptian naval forces came up to inspect the ship and identified him. "The water is too rough for the Egyptians to bother with trying an inspection," he said to reassure himself.

For a moment Akawi relaxed and even felt some pride. Two weeks earlier, he had heard PA president Arafat's speech announcing a cease-fire from all Palestinian terrorism and violence directed against Israel. "Is this for real?" he had asked Mughrabi, who had recruited him for the mission. Mughrabi just laughed and said that of all times, now was when "the Rais," a title reserved for Arab rulers such as Arafat, especially needed the Iranian weapons that Akawi would bring to the PA on the *Karine A*.

Akawi knew he was taking a risk now in trying to pass through the Suez Canal. Again he cursed Mughrabi for convincing him that the Egyptian patrols would not be a problem. Also, he was angry that the PA had not given him greater recognition for his years of service and that he was stuck on this ship with a crew he mostly did not trust. He squinted at his watch. It was around 4:00 a.m.

Taysar started down the stairs to the deck to check if anything was happening. Since he was not talking and his shadow was not visible in the pitch-black dark, the Israeli commandos had no real warning that he was coming. But the commandos were trained to pick up on any hint of an incoming enemy. Any military force could win a loud gunfight with a numerically inferior force. But that was not their job.

The elite Israeli Navy Seals' job was to win the fight clandestinely, quickly, and without drawing unwanted attention. Even as Ziv and his men hustled forward, they heard a series of thumps and creaking noises as Taysar descended the stairs toward them. Ziv held up his hand to signal his commandos to stop moving. They concealed themselves from the incoming crew member's gaze.

Just as Taysar started around a corner, Ziv grabbed him in a headlock, gagged him, and handcuffed him. It only took seconds. Taysar barely had time to breathe, much less sound the alarm. Now time was even more important. Akawi would be suspicious if he did not report back soon. Ziv raced up the stairs toward the bridge.

Captain Akawi had only been on the bridge a few minutes. He gave a soft encouraging pat to one of the other crew members and glanced at the radar. Peering through a glass window as he approached, Ziv spotted Akawi. He saw an opening to take him by surprise from behind. Creeping up slowly from behind, Ziv seized him and put him in a headlock. Then he dragged Akawi down backward, blindfolded him, and handcuffed him.

Akawi was as shocked as if he had been struck by lightning. At first, he had assumed that his nightmare of being caught by the Egyptians had come true. Then he realized it was worse. His captors were Israelis! He heard them barking orders at each other in Hebrew, a language he knew well from an earlier era when he had worked with Israeli sailors. As he started to orient himself despite the blindfold, he was thrown off again by the piercing sounds of the Black Hawks streaming in with the fast-roping commandos.

Four seals were assigned for taking down the other crew members, most of whom were sleeping. They crept up on them until they had surrounded them in their beds. Then all at once the seals pounced. Quickly, they handcuffed the crew members' arms and legs. The Egyptians offered no resistance at all, while the remaining Palestinians resisted a bit more.

Since they were near Egyptian waters, the crew members first assumed they were being attacked by Egyptian inspectors. Once they realized they were being nabbed by Israelis, they were overwhelmed with confusion and gave up even faster. What were Israelis doing this far out from Israel, and how in Allah's name did the Israelis know they were here?

Soon after seizing the bridge, the commandos took over the engineering section and the rest of the ship. Meanwhile, the second round of commando boat–based navy seals started climbing the sides of the *Karine A*. Shortly afterward, Ram told Chiny that it was time for him to call out the code word, "Harry Potter!" Like the magical wizard Harry Potter on his flying quidditch broom, the helicopter-based commandos began to move in.

Chiny ordered the Black Hawks to descend on the *Karine A*. They were hovering nearby but at a sufficient distance so that the crew would not hear them. Ram's decision to have the commandos in the helicopters wait to board the ship until the sea-based commandos had taken down the crew was a tough call. The *Karine A*'s crew had failed to resist the takeover, and there had been no gunfire. But all it took was one armed crew member waiting in ambush, and the commandos sliding down from the helicopters would be easy targets. So Ram had decided they would only join the takeover forces once the whole crew was subdued.

Around 4:05 a.m., the two Black Hawks arrived and hovered above the ship at a height of thirty meters. "Dudu" (his real full name is classified), a commando on one of the Black Hawks, felt his hands were hot. He was wearing special custom-made gloves that allowed for fast roping from a helicopter. Without the special gloves, even the strongest fighter's hands would be torn apart by the friction on the ropes.

At this point, a lot could go wrong. A rope could shake too much, leading a commando to fall to his death. The whole apparatus holding the commando and the rope could fall off, which had happened with U.S. Navy SEALS in March 2000 and led to their 167-foot fall. But the biggest risk the Israelis faced was that they were dropping down onto a moving ship in the pitch dark. They could not see where they were landing. Intelligence indicated they would land in an area without cables or sharp objects. But if anything was slightly off, they could land on something dangerous. All the training in the world would still leave them defenseless.

Dudu had almost missed out on this mission. Navy seals are sent to do additional military-related academic studies from time to time, and Dudu was in the middle of a study period when the mission was announced. His commanders initially brushed him off when he tried to join the sea-based commandos, but they eventually relented.

Dudu was used to bursting into a chaotic scene of gunfire, but that was on dry land in the West Bank. He had a completely different feeling landing on the *Karine A*'s deck. He sprinted toward the ship's first storage area to secure it with the rest of his team. They faced no resistance. Dudu and his unit then secured the remaining storage areas. Finally, his adrenaline started to subside.

At 4:06 a.m., Dror Friedman reported to Ram: "We have control and have secured the crew." Ram informed Chiny, and eventually both of them boarded the *Karine A* along with two experts in prisoner interrogation and other staff.

Throughout the operation, top Israeli armed forces' commanders were watching it unfold on three large monitors on the Atara aircraft as opposed to from their quiet offices at the Tel Aviv headquarters. One monitor showed the picture from that aircraft's aerial scope. A second monitor showed the King Air aircraft's overhead view of the operation. A third streamed a picture from headquarters of a map showing the positioning of both the Israeli Navy and other hostile naval forces. Top intelligence officials who had been involved in discovering and tracking the *Karine A* and the chiefs of the navy and the air force were along for the ride.

High fives followed Chiny's report to the navy chief: "We have control of the bridge. We are steering the ship toward the Straits of Tiran and the final destination, Eilat. In a few minutes, we'll start inspecting the ship."

Mofaz let out a sigh of relief. He later jotted down in his yellow notebook: "Eight minutes and the whole thing was over."

Next, the navy seals' small commando boats, with only a few naval personnel on each one, were all given orders to start traveling north at the fastest possible speed. Forty-six miles from the Straits of Tiran, a refueling and assistance ship was waiting for them, but the waves were getting higher and wilder. The waves would get worse as the storm they had anticipated moved into the area.

The entire thirteen-man *Karine A* crew, eight of whom were Egyptians, were held in the officers' dining room. Their hands were tied behind their backs, and they were blindfolded. Three commandos guarded them, making sure they did not make a peep. In the room next door, Shin Bet intelligence interrogators were quickly setting up an ad hoc interrogation center.

"Send in Akawi," they told one of the commandos as they looked over a classified detailed analysis of Akawi that naval intelligence had prepared. Akawi was sitting on the floor, slightly separated from the crew, still in shock.

It finally had sunk in that this was a moment of deep failure. After months of planning and getting so close, his mission of bringing the Iranian weapons to Arafat to bolster the PA's ability to hit the Israeli home front had ended in a matter of minutes. But how had it happened? With all of the precautions they had taken—falsifying their destination papers, changing the ship's name and flag, and arranging their byzantine maze of travels—he never thought Israel had a chance of tracking them. In his worst-case scenario, he thought they might be caught in the Mediterranean

Sea. And that was what was so brilliant about their idea of dropping the weapons in their special Iranian-made floating tubes off the Egyptian coast before continuing toward the Mediterranean: The weapons would already have been delivered. There would have been no trace of them, and Israel would have had to let them go. No one imagined a scenario where Israel would somehow track them and seize the ship deep in the Red Sea.

His only consolation was that the Israelis wouldn't torture or kill him. He was sure if the Egyptians had captured the ship, his fate would have been extremely dire. His thoughts turned to an old close Israeli friend, Hanania Peretz, who had dined with him in fish restaurants in the Haifa area and had conducted some joint commercial business before the Second Intifada broke out in late 2000.

Maybe Hanania could get him some lenient treatment. It never occurred to him that Hanania himself was a key part of the naval intelligence team that caught him. Hanania had figured out that the *Karine A*'s stated travel plan and the commercial goods it planned to transport made no economic sense. He had surmised that the ship had a more nefarious purpose.

As Akawi sat on the floor, his only hope was that the weapons were so ingeniously concealed that the Israelis wouldn't discover them. If he pretended no weapons were aboard and the Israelis could not figure out their hiding place, then he had an outside shot that they would still need to let him go.

At the same time, at the naval command center in Tel Aviv, another set of top officials sat around a large conference table. Meshita had followed the operation since the start, watching the monitor to follow developments on the ship, but his mind was elsewhere. The navy seals were on the ship, but he still harbored lingering doubts. He had told Mofaz that the probability of finding weapons was 85 percent. But were they really there? If so, was the Palestinian Authority really behind it all?

He looked at Anat. She had started all of this. She was the first officer to sense something big. He asked someone to bring her

The Capture of the *Karine A*

over. Anat was surprised, nervous, and excited to be escorted over to the table of the "big shots."

Just as Meshita had reassured Mofaz, now he needed reassurance. "Tell me," he asked Anat, "how sure are you that the ship has weapons—that it isn't just an innocent commercial ship?"

Anat was short and young, but she displayed that rare indomitable quality of an intelligence analyst who would go far. She did not care about rank or red tape. She and some of the other naval intelligence analysts had just dived into the *Karine A* more deeply than their fellow IDF intelligence analysts. Others appeared to have just scratched the surface. She had instincts that you could not teach and an encyclopedic memory. A whole room of senior officers might be wobbly about the risks of sounding certain when the evidence was mixed, but she would still give an unambiguous answer.

At times, higher-ranking officers had told her they had strong intelligence that there was no ship, that this was the wrong ship, or that the ship was not where she said it was. Anat did not give an inch. She steamrolled her doubters until she proved them wrong time and time again. She did so not because she was arrogant, but after a string of late nights and intense focus, she and the other naval intelligence analysts just had penetrated the intelligence picture more deeply. Anat reminded Meshita of those moments when she and the staff painstakingly rewound and rechecked every piece of data going back months. There had been some dark moments of doubt. But in the end, she was 100 percent sure the weapons were on board.

Within a short time, however, the commandos had searched the areas where they had expected the weapons to be concealed. They found nothing. Doubt once again spread like wildfire up the chain of command. In the aerial command center circling above the captured ship, Mofaz went from relief to practically being unable to breathe. If they did not find the weapons, even the heroic takeover could be overshadowed by disaster.

After All This, Are There Weapons?

Itamar split off from Ram and started to debrief the navy seals. "So, tell me?"

"Nothing."

"What do you mean, nothing?"

"We've found nothing."

He went toward the bridge and met up with Ziv, the navy seal who took down and captured Akawi. "Come over here, Itamar," said Ziv. "There's nothing here!"

Itamar's heart sank. "What? No weapons? There's nothing?" he said, trailing off in disbelief.

On the Atara and at the navy's command and control center, everyone was tense with anticipation. Everyone was waiting for the report of redemption—that they had found weapons on the *Karine A*.

The ship had three storage areas. Where were the weapons? Ram, Itamar, Dror, another navy seal officer, and a group of navy seals went down into the first storage area. The pitch-black environment reminded them of the biblical plague of darkness that had enshrouded Egypt. They used flashlights to check the area but found it empty. They looked at each other in shock. Chiny joined them.

Dan, one of the commanders, went up to the bridge to talk with Akawi, while Chiny, Ram, and the others went to the second storage area. They opened the door. It was also empty! They looked and looked, but there was nothing in the storage area other than grains of rice. They went back up to the deck. Collectively, their hearts sank.

"Maybe we're on the wrong ship," was the horrifying rumor that started to go around. Then came the thought that maybe they needed to cut their losses and abandon the ship, returning it to its crew, but Itamar saw a lifeboat on the deck with the writing RIM K on it. That was the old name of the *Karine A*. This find reinvigorated him, and with a second wind he said, "We're fine. This is the *Karine A*. We're on the right ship."

Everyone breathed a sigh of relief. But still, they all wondered, where were the weapons?

On the Atara, Mofaz was waiting for news of redemption. But it had not come. Chiny reported that until that point, they had only found some rice. Kuper was trembling. He had said only yesterday that he was 100 percent sure there would be weapons on the ship, including high-quality weapons. Mofaz rotated and glanced over at Kuper. "So, you said 100 percent?"

Kuper weakly said yes and that Chiny and Ram's commandos should keep looking. Mofaz told them to keep looking.

But already Kuper wanted to disappear. What a failure this might be! Another five minutes passed, but it seemed like hours. The Atara was starting to head back to Israel. Then it got another report from Chiny: the third storage area contained toys, no weapons. Mofaz, a stubborn commander with nerves of steel, looked over at Kuper again and said, "You see the window?" It was as if to hint that if no weapons were found, Kuper should jump out of the plane in a form of seppuku, or honor suicide for failure, as the Japanese samurai of old would perform for their samurai master.

Kuper was trying harder and harder to magically disappear. He thought, "Where were the weapons? What a screw up!" But at the same time that he was getting rattled, deep inside he hadn't yet lost faith. "It can't be," he continued to mutter. "There have got to be weapons. All of the information indicated that. Not in any explicit and unambiguous way, but all of the signs were in the direction of proving that there were weapons."

At the same time, Yedidya turned to Kobi with a worried face that was also asking, "So there aren't any weapons?"

Kobi was taken aback like everyone else, but he was still adamant: "Just wait. There are weapons. They'll find them."

At the navy command and control center in Tel Aviv, tension was also rising, especially in the intelligence apparatus. Ship's captain Hanania was also there. He was the first one to give the navy intelligence staff confidence that the ship was not a legitimate commercial ship but a weapons-smuggling ship. He was also the one who estimated, as an experienced sailor, that the weapons had been loaded onto the ship when it was close to the Iranian coast and not when it was in Dubai.

"Why is it taking them so long?" Anat wondered. Her thoughts were jumbled. "Of course there are weapons, but maybe they won't find them. Then what do we do? What happens if all we find are a few bags of rice? They'll accuse us of a colossal blunder." It was hard for her to cope with the tension and the nerve-racking worst-case scenarios running through her brain. Her husband was at her side. "You know, if they find weapons, we'll all be heroes. If they don't, we're done for."

She then envisioned all of the intelligence and information she had reviewed. "Where did we screw up?"

Chiny and Ram were losing it, when suddenly Ram's walkie-talkie lit up with a cry: "It's in the front! Dan just got it out of Omar Akawi!"

They went to the bridge. Dan, with the stare of someone you would never want to meet in a dark alley, was interrogating Akawi in a tiny room. The two Shin Bet interrogators were furious. According to the mission protocols, they were the only ones allowed to question the *Karine A*'s crew. Chiny said that they were right, but in any case, the focus should be on their interrogating the prisoners starting now. They set up a proper interrogation room, and a more organized initial interrogation began. Shimon took pictures of the thirteen crew members with a digital camera. The navy seals searched the ship and clarified there were no booby traps on the ship and returned to Akawi.

"You've got nothing to worry about," he told the interrogators.

As they went down into the third storage area with Akawi, the darkness surrounded them again. There were cartons, furniture, mattresses, toys, shoes, bags, and combs. They saw an incredible volume of junk. Everyone stared at Akawi.

"Where are they?" came the question from the angry and disheartened crowd.

"It's under here," said Akawi pointing to a giant pile.

All of the navy seals rolled up their sleeves and started moving the equipment that was in the way. Only their flashlights made it

The Capture of the *Karine A*

possible to get anything done in the pitch-black storage area. Little by little, they reached a large wooden crate. They immediately sent someone to the bridge to report to the forward command group on the Atara: "We've found a crate!"

"What's inside it?" asked Yedidya.

"We're checking now," was the answer.

Dan found a crowbar and started to yank open the crate. Akawi sat with an expression of despair. Surrounding him were the navy seals, the Shin Bet interrogators, and the bomb squad officer. The forward command group on the Atara kept nagging: "Come on, what did you find already?"

Finally, Dan succeeded at getting the crate open. Inside the three-meter-long crate was a green container.

"It's inside that," said Akawi.

They brought him back to the interrogation room and asked him about the container and about whether it was booby-trapped. Akawi took a diagram of the container out of his pocket and explained how the system worked. The containers held the weapons, and parts of the containers went a couple meters underwater while leaving an above-water footprint for whoever was supposed to pick it up (the Palestinians). "There are eighty-three containers like that," he said.

Itamar followed Akawi's explanation and became so excited, he almost forgot who he was with and was ready to start yelling in his native Spanish, which only he would've understood: "Now, I get it! Now, I get it! This is the same mystery equipment the Iranians were experimenting with a few months ago!"

They took Akawi back down to the storage area. He used special items to open the container that had been inside the crate and started to unscrew a bunch of bolts. It seemed as if time was standing still. Everyone was peeking and trying to get a glimpse of what was about to be uncovered. Chiny was tense. And then the container opened. What was inside?

Kalashnikov rifles! This reveal was a bit disappointing. They were hoping to intercept weapons of greater importance, such as a bomb, or at least a high-quality weapon that would have been a strategic game changer. And what was in there? Kalashnikovs! Nothing special.

"A bummer," said Itamar, disappointed.

Still, it was the first successful sign, and using the code word for weapons, Chiny reported it to the Atara: "There are 'candies'!" With his knowing smile, he said, "Just wait, we have another eighty-two crates to open. Who knows what's inside them?"

Mofaz heard the report "there are candies" and breathed a sigh of relief. Several euphoric officers around Mofaz jumped out of their seats. Kuper was about to join them—better to jump out of his seat in victory than to have to jump out of the plane in failure—but then he thought twice about it. This was a big step in the operation's being a success, maybe the largest. Yet at the same time, not until they returned to IDF headquarters in Tel Aviv would they receive a report on the full scope and enormity of the weapons the seals had captured. Also, the *Karine A* had not returned safely to Israel's port in Eilat yet. He would hold off his full euphoria until then. But he was far more relaxed and back to feeling confident that he had kept Mofaz and the IDF on track.

Now the Atara was sent back to Israel. The air-to-ship communications between the Atara and Chiny's forces were of low quality. On the way, Mofaz's thoughts trailed off and alternated between the diplomatic-strategic arena and the operational-tactical one. "There's no doubt," he thought, "this will be the tipping point in the confrontation with the Palestinians. The operational success will lead to a strategic win. The navy intelligence people along with the Mossad and Unit 8200 really nailed this one."

On the communications hookup, he heard the voices of Ram's navy seals working on finding more crates in storage area 3. He felt the exhaustion hit him. He ordered a situation update for 6:45 a.m. at the navy's command and control center and was lost in his thoughts before drifting off to sleep.

Yedidya was thrilled. He had carried out the operation way beyond the navy's comfort zone. The navy had broken records and punched above its weight, including with the airborne for-

The Capture of the *Karine A*

ward command center. The navy would still conduct a review of the fast roping to improve its execution, but this operation was a slam dunk win across the board for both the sea- and air-based commandos. When Kobi got up to tell him something, Yedidya gave him a big hug and told him, "Well done!"

Then some of his other concerns came back. How would the commando boats return through stormy waters? How would they refuel? How would they cross through the Straits of Tiran?

Ram, who went up to the *Karine A*'s deck for a minute to get some air, saw the waves starting to crash higher against the sides of the ship. He began worrying about the small commando boats and his navy seals.

Finally, Chiny's report also came into the navy command center. When the group heard the words "there are candies," there was a round of hugs and cries of joy. Everyone's spirits went through the roof.

"Incredible. Incredible," Anat kept muttering. Gal threw his hands up above his head in a sign of victory. Gil was overwhelmed. Hanania allowed himself a short-lived modest smile, as was his way.

Then Meshita came out of the central room and went to the intelligence center's bridge position. Everyone was smiling and on cloud nine. He thanked everyone. He emphasized the special contributions of Anat, Hanania, and Gal, and alluded to others who had a big part in the operation's success. Anat listened as if she were in a dream. It was not often that the chief of naval intelligence publicly mentioned a junior officer such as herself along with two far more senior officers. His speech was a warm one about success and had an electric feel. It made her think of the historic 1976 Entebbe rescue operation, taught in detail to all military personnel, in which Israeli commandos rescued a group of hijacked civilians from terrorists holding them hostage in Uganda.

"Am I in the middle of an operation of the same magnitude?" she asked herself. "I'm so lucky that I was hurled into these historic events!" Still, even as the success seeped in, she—as did so many others—wondered, "Where are the game-changing weapons?"

Aboard the *Karine A*, the seals cleared out more and more furniture and junk from storage area 3 and placed them in a giant pile. They also kept finding crates. Row after row. Column after column. It was almost suffocatingly hot and humid, so they opened the roof above the storage area. Air and light started to pour in. The seals opened up some more crates as well as the containers inside them, finding Sagger launchers and anti-tank missiles. After that they discovered other high-quality weapons hanging from the underbelly of the deck above them. And dozens of crates were still unopened. Who knew what kinds of "candies" they would find?

Chiny's air force officer joined the inspection group. He was hoping to find shoulder-held antiaircraft missiles. The seals would not finish opening all the crates until they got to Eilat. Only there, in another two days, would they reveal the full scope of the game-changing weapons. They would learn that the ship was carrying rockets with a range of twenty kilometers; if fired from the Gaza Strip, they could hit the large Israeli southwest coastal city of Ashkelon. The Palestinian Authority had nothing like that at the time, and Israel had not even started to seriously develop any kind of competent missile defense solution. The *Karine A* also held 120 mm mortar artillery rounds and over one and a half tons of high-grade plastic explosives and more (detailed in appendix B). These weapons would have given the PA a game-changing ability to cause more destruction and death in Israeli towns and cities.

On the deck of the *Karine A*, Itamar was deliriously happy. Suddenly, he recognized the significance of the operation. Until then all of his adrenaline had been invested in planning the takeover itself with his team of seals. It was dawn, and the sun was rising. The navy seals came over to him. "Itamar, give it up!" they said with high fives. "Your intelligence was right on! The placement of the stairs, the doors, the right direction to open the doors—it was all exactly as you said."

It was music to Itamar's ears. "It was my small part in this miracle," he said to himself as he moved to the bridge to join Ram and Chiny. On his way, he already could feel the change. Waves of confidence and of success were replacing the tension that had followed him and everyone else for days and even only minutes before.

Immediately after the seals had taken over the *Karine A*, the five commando boats and the lead commando boat headed for the Straits of Tiran and ultimately for Eilat. The *Karine A* could handle whatever the impending storm dished out, but the small commando boats would have far more trouble and needed to get out of there, pronto. Four people were aboard each commando boat: two helmsmen and two commanders, enough for a rotating watch. Ram knew they would be sailing into hellish northern winds. Everyone was already feeling the increased wind speed. The six commando boats were led by the navy seals officer who was generally in charge of the ships (as opposed to the fighters themselves). He would need to lead the boats around 115 miles through dangerous waves that could reach four meters high, and they would be mostly alone. Moreover, the waters they would traverse were hostile and not far from the unfriendly Saudi Arabian coast. (This was long before the Saudis began cooperating with Israel against Iran.) He had one communications line to the navy command and control center but nothing with Ram or Chiny. At the same time, he was one of Ram's top guys, and Ram trusted him.

The commando boats accelerated to their maximum speed. Every minute they got closer to escaping the Red Sea was critical. They left the *Karine A* far behind. They had about an hour until the storm kicked into full force, but there was still a fuel problem. After about an hour, right before the storm was about to explode, they met up with the fast patrol boats, as planned, to refuel. Then they continued north through the stormy waters of hell. Their next refueling would be from the navy's assistance ship, which was about seventy miles north of their position or around forty miles south of the Straits of Tiran. Would they be able to refuel in the midst of the storm? From the *Karine A*, Chiny received updates from the navy assistance ship that the captain wasn't positive he would be able to carry out a refueling during the storm.

The northern wind covered the commando boats in a deluge of water, and the noise was horrific. The boats were barely advancing, and the navy seals aboard were near exhaustion. What would they do? Like his commander, Ram, the ship's officer thought outside the box. He saw a large and long commercial Greek ship carrying cars. All of the commando boats came alongside that ship and used it as shelter from the harsh winds and waves. All of the seals were soaked and shaking from the frigid weather, but they could finally breathe easier. They had some refuge for a few hours from the raucous sounds of the wind that had been battering their eardrums.

Then, as if the devil was intervening against them, one of the commando boats ran out of fuel. The other boats needed to tow it, slowing them down further, and they couldn't keep up with their shield, the Greek ship. Again, they were at the mercy of the humongous and deadly waves and the shrieking winds, but they did finally reach the navy assistance ship for their final refueling. The process was difficult. The winds strained the commando boats' ability to stay close enough to continue the refueling, but they ultimately succeeded.

By that point, it was the middle of the night between Thursday and Friday morning. The seals had fought through nearly twenty-four hours of horrendous weather but still needed to push through a few more. The stormy weather threatened to sap their remaining strength. From the navy command and control center, Yedidya ordered them to find a place to rest, no matter what! Toward dawn on Friday, they found a sheltered spot behind an island that was in international waters and not far from the Straits of Tiran. There they rested until the vicious northern wind died down.

Heading Home to Eilat

JANUARY 3, 2002

Chiny was now looking at the same escalating waves that had plagued the commando boats. He and the *Karine A* still needed to make it another 110 miles to the Straits of Tiran. The storm had started going crazy in the area near the straits. He envisioned the image of the hulking Weather Man, Beni.

"He got a bull's-eye! He got us the window of calm weather for the operation. We were right on the line. If there had been a single delay, we would have lost our chance to take the *Karine A*," Chiny thought.

A little after 6:00 a.m., the Atara landed back in Israel. Mofaz disembarked and headed down the ramp. Now that he had pocketed the successful operation, it was time to begin the public relations and diplomatic campaign. In the spirit of all of the hard work that had led to this moment of great success, he remembered a poignant phrase from the Talmudic tractate Megillah, which tells the story of the Jewish holiday of Purim: "Rabbi Yitzhak said: 'If a person says to you: "I worked hard, but didn't succeed"—don't believe him. If the person says: "I didn't work hard, but succeeded"—you still shouldn't believe him. But if he says he worked hard and he succeeded—then you can believe him!'"

Yedidya gathered the entire staff from the aircraft, including the ELTA staff. Standing next to the ramp, he thanked all of them and explained that night, the IDF had leaped forward to a new level of operational capabilities. He spoke from the heart, and many of those present were genuinely touched. Zvi of ELTA would never forget it.

The rain battered the windshield of Mofaz's car on its way to central IDF headquarters in Tel Aviv. The rays of the morning sun started to cut through and erode the enveloping darkness of the night. His driver turned the radio on. The broadcast was filled with coverage of Zinni's imminent visit, the decisions to ease the West Bank and Gaza security closures, and the cancellation of Mofaz's own trip to the United States. Not a word on the operation.

"Beautiful!" he thought and made some notes in his yellow notebook. "We need to maintain the media blackout on the operation until the ships are home. Then there will be an abrupt transition." Would the public relations campaign be as successful as the military operation? Would they succeed or fail to convince the world, and especially the United States, to shift paradigms in how they viewed the PA and Arafat? Would the United States understand that Iran and Hezbollah were behind the weapons-smuggling plot involving Arafat? Mofaz continued to ponder these questions as he headed to the navy's command and control center.

What was the best way to steer and direct the captured *Karine A* home? Chiny's air force officer worked in the navigation room. The GPS system there was similar to the systems used by the Sea Stallion helicopter. After a little bit of playing around with it, the air force officer started to use the *Karine A*'s GPS system to navigate. But with the water getting rougher, it was difficult for the ship to advance. It rocked back and forth, and the bottom part of its hull was briefly drawn down into the water after every large wave. Crossing the Straits of Tiran would be dangerous; with a large reef in that area, it was a prime spot for a collision for a ship that was bobbing up and down. As the air force officer navigated through the straits, he briefly imagined the ship colliding with the reef and sinking.

Chiny was positioned on the bridge and reported developments to Yedidya. The chief of the Israeli Navy yelled at him: "You're telling me that you're letting an air force pilot navigate the ship? Have you gone mad?!"

After listening to Chiny and Ram clarify with Yedidya what was happening with the commando boats, who were then between a rock and a hard place, the air force officer left behind these psychological distractions and refocused on navigation.

On the morning of Friday, January 4, the lead patrol boat and the *Karine A* crossed the Straits of Tiran. The commando boats all made it as well, and after noon, all the Israeli naval vessels had made it.

The censor removed the blackout. Suddenly, all of Israel and the world started to learn about the operation and what had happened. A press conference set for 2:00 p.m. would include Mofaz, Yedidya, Halutz, and the IDF chief's spokesman.

At this point, out of nowhere, a Saudi Arabian ship appeared and started to trail the *Karine A*. The seals signaled the Saudi ship to stop following them, but it ignored the signals. Next, they aimed their weapons at the Saudi ship. It got the hint and retreated.

Two navy seals— one from the sea commandos and one from the sliding commandos—approached Ram. They produced two Israeli flags. "We want to hang the flag," they said. Ram was overcome with their patriotism and hugged both of them. Immediately, they organized a flag-raising ceremony by the central flagpole. The navy seals exchanged hugs, and Ram was close to tears.

The water and its inhabitants also seemed to salute the navy seals. Dozens of dolphins leaped out of the waves alongside the ship as if they were dancing in celebration.

At 8:00 p.m. on Friday, January 4, the *Karine A* entered the port of Eilat, was towed in, and dropped its anchor. Shimon, the first to see the *Karine A* in the Red Sea twenty minutes before they captured it, looked out at the welcome party waiting to greet them at the port. He called his wife.

"Where are you?" she asked.

"I'm on my way home. Everything worked out. Listen to the radio."

At the port were floodlights, cameras, and TV crews. Yedidya and Meshita boarded the *Karine A* to shake everyone's hands and to thank those aboard on a job well done. Ram and his navy seals disembarked. The crowd went wild. It was like a rock concert. There was an emotional reunion with the navy seals who had come in a bit earlier on the commando boats and were waiting for the seals from the *Karine A*. They exchanged hugs and kisses with the wives and girlfriends who had shown up. As thrilled as Ram was, he kept himself at an even keel but felt the unique gratification of a commander who had led his elite unit successfully through a high-stakes operation.

Chiny went down to the platform. He envisioned the entire operation—all of the dilemmas, misgivings, and preparations—all at once. A moment later, a thought flickered in his mind: "Now, the navy is really on the map!"

Later that night, Yedidya, Chiny, Meshita, the Eilat base commander, and the navy intelligence staff had a festive dinner. Ram handed out drinks, congratulated them, and then left. The navy seals had earned a rowdy night off in Eilat.

The next morning, the seals boarded buses to take them to their base near Haifa. They would not have the weekend off. Instead, they would immediately be training for a new impending operation in Gaza.

From Friday, January 4, until Sunday, January 6, large volumes of IDF soldiers unloaded the crates from the *Karine A*. They opened them, removed the weapons, and set them up to be displayed on one of the port's platforms. Prime Minister Sharon, the defense minister, and Mofaz would present the weapons at a major press conference on Sunday. The interrogations of the *Karine A* crew, especially of Akawi and the three Palestinians known as weapons smugglers, continued throughout. They produced a constant flow of intelligence for real-time use.

The operation was completed, and the public relations campaign and the push for a diplomatic shift were just starting. Stopping the weapons and their game-changing power was one thing, but the real goal now was to turn the tide of global opinion, most importantly in the United States, against the PA and Arafat. Israel hoped that the heroism and courage of its fighters had laid the groundwork for a major diplomatic watershed.

One story had ended. Another was just beginning.

13

The International Ramifications

During his visit on Friday, January 4, Bush envoy General Zinni visited Prime Minister Sharon at his farm for a sumptuous breakfast. Foreign Minister Shimon Peres and Defense Minister Ben-Eliezer were also in attendance. Upon Zinni's arrival in Israel the evening before, he had met with the Israeli intelligence high command. This morning's gathering would now be his first diplomatic meeting during his four-day trip to meet with the Israelis and the Palestinians. His next stop would be with Arafat.

"You can tell Arafat not to worry about his *Karine A* ship," said Sharon to Zinni mischievously. "We're bringing it to Eilat right now. By evening, it will have docked, with all of its weapons."

Most of the conversation that morning dealt with the *Karine A*, the PA, Arafat, and terrorism. General Zinni was not the first American to hear about the capture of the *Karine A*. A little before their meeting, Sharon had called Secretary of State Colin Powell to update him.

That afternoon, Meshita invited Stephanie to his office. After she arrived, he said, "Can you connect me with U.S. Navy Intelligence chief Adm. Richard Porterfield?"

"Sure, I can do that," she said.

It was 6:30 a.m. eastern standard time in the United States. Meshita assumed that the prime minister had updated Zinni that morning about the operation, but he knew it was important for him to call Porterfield directly. "So get him on the line for me," he said.

When Stephanie had Porterfield on the phone, Meshita told him about the operation. He also told him that in less than an hour, the operation would be publicly announced and thanked him.

On Saturday, January 5, the new IDI director Farkash updated Sharon that the intelligence clearly showed that Iranian supreme leader Ayatollah Ali Khamenei knew that Iranian weapons were being sent on the ship. Farkash emphasized that this information was hard, and not speculative, intelligence. Many prime ministers were somewhat intimidated by intelligence chiefs and would just accept these kinds of reports. Sharon was different. He asked why Farkash was so sure and what the basis of the intelligence conclusion about Khamenei was.

Hesitating a bit, Farkash said it was mostly based on Unit 8200's interceptions of electronic communications as well as on data from a highly placed Mossad double agent with whom Sharon was familiar (but whose identity remains classified to this day).

Sharon nodded his head and understood.

The signs of the Iranians' handiwork regarding the weapons and the intelligence basis were also strong evidence of two points: first, the personal involvement of Arafat and his top aides in the PA, including Fuad Shubaki; and, second, the strategic and operational connection between Iran and the PA, both directly and indirectly, via Hezbollah-Iran's top operative Imad Mughniyeh. The connection started in April 2000 with a series of Palestinian-Iranian meetings in Russia, Oman, and the UAE—all of which took place with Arafat's specific approval. Not only did the Iranians prepare the floating containers for the weapons but also the weapons themselves were loaded onto the *Karine A* at a small island near Iran and not in Dubai, which was naval intelligence's theory until the ship was captured.

Sharon also spoke with Mofaz that day. Both men understood the strategic importance and opportunity that the ship and its weapons presented for making inroads with President Bush regarding his view of Arafat and the PA.

The International Ramifications

And how had Arafat, Mughniyeh, and Khamenei dealt with the seizure of the *Karine A* when Israel revealed its intelligence coup to the world?

The *Karine A* Saga's Losers

There was no way around it. The *Karine A*'s capture was a humiliation and defeat for Arafat, Mughniyeh, and Khamenei.

Arafat was beside himself. While the Iranians clearly expressed their rage at the failure, they still did so in a restrained and channeled fashion, but the PA leader yelled all the time, even when something small did not go the way he liked. This operation had been his chance to turn the tables on his nemesis from Lebanon decades earlier, Ariel Sharon. With the ability to fire powerful long-range rockets at the large Israeli cities of Ashdod and Ashkelon, he could have brought Israel to its knees with new demands for land concessions on the diplomatic plane. Or he could have just fired rockets on Israel, sat tight, and saw how things transpired before deciding what to do. He probably could have even shot rockets, then later stopped shooting them, and blamed the uptick of violence on the Israelis when they retaliated and invariably killed Palestinian civilians whom his operatives would use for cover.

Maybe he could have won the Nobel Peace Prize again after that. Now he had no options. The small-time terrorist attacks and suicide bus bombings would hurt Israel, but knowing Sharon, eventually the bulldozer would start punching harder than the Palestinians could counterpunch, especially without the rockets. Also, unlike the Iranians, Arafat was more likely to punish his top lieutenants for their failure by cutting them off from the leadership and the levers of power for months or years at a time. At different points in his life, he would play Mahmoud Abbas and Ahmed Qurei and other top officials off against each other, sometimes favoring one and sometimes another.

Arafat was also paranoid about failure. Ayatollah Khamenei had multiple levels of secret police and ruffians who were so loyal to him that his authority was never in question. In contrast, Arafat was the titular leader of the Palestinian nation, but in some areas already, especially in Gaza but even in parts of the West Bank such as Hebron, Hamas was more popular than he was. He was always terrified of being assassinated or otherwise replaced. (In fact, only a couple of years after Arafat's death in November 2004, Hamas would take over Gaza from the PA.) With all of his bizarre, unstable, and idiosyncratic behaviors, however, he knew how to maintain Palestinian unity in a way that no one else did. He might need to penalize some top aides, whether they were involved in the *Karine A* or not, to keep all of his potential competitors off balance.

In a crisis such as this one, his lips often started to tremble, and his jaw would start to quiver. Already in 1997, medical observers had caught his exhibiting physical symptoms resembling Parkinson's disease, and the shaking was always exacerbated when he was under stress. Regarding his global supporters, whom he had hoodwinked into believing he was a statesman who had abandoned his warrior ways of Lebanon and the past, his instinct was to scream at his lieutenants to issue denials across the globe and to talk about the possibility that—if the Israelis were not faking the whole incident—maybe the weapons were destined for Hezbollah. Israeli intelligence said Arafat told his staff not to receive communications of any kind from Hezbollah for the near future. His only chance to escape Sharon's wrath now would be to return to his peacemaking image. Arafat would appeal to the world for a return to negotiations and accuse Sharon of trying to break apart any progress, just as in Lebanon twenty years earlier.

If Arafat started to feel a little better from these machinations, around this time his secretary told him that U.S. general Zinni had arrived after having met with Sharon. Arafat switched quickly into action mode, trying to pull off his best acting and obfuscating show ever. The stakes could not be higher. In that meeting, Arafat famously assured Zinni by oath that he did not know anything about the *Karine A*. Arafat hoped Zinni could sway Secretary of State Colin Powell to accept Arafat's denial.

Likewise, Mughniyeh probably did not feel like a hero. His emissaries were not able to get through to Arafat, so he was cut off from the PA. Mughniyeh also might have had potential plans to visit

The International Ramifications

Tehran sometime in January to celebrate the success of the ingenious *Karine A* scheme with the Iranians. Besides getting face time with IRGC chief Rahim Safavi and Quds Force chief Qasem Soleimani, he would have taken an opportunity to buy special Iranian-style gifts in Tehran for his daughter, Fatima, and his wife, Wafaa. (Fatima later received Iranian citizenship in recognition of Imad Mughniyeh's service to the Islamic republic.) Any thoughts of gifts and visits now would likely need to wait. Mughniyeh probably would not have planned on showing his face there for a while. He wasn't afraid of almost anyone, including the Mossad or the CIA, which he had outwitted for decades, but Khamenei was not a forgiving man and was not just anyone.

Mughniyeh was not cut off from Iran, but he would have known the relationship was now heavily strained. Of course, he would eventually be forgiven for the *Karine A* debacle. After almost twenty years of successes and nearly single-handedly building Hezbollah into an unofficial army for Iran from nothing, he was still irreplaceable. Also, it was not the first time the Israelis had thwarted plans by Iran or Hezbollah to smuggle weapons to Arafat or other areas bordering on Israel. But vast resources had been invested and dozens of operatives had planned, trained, loaded weapons, and piloted the ship for the greatest weapons-smuggling operation against Israel ever—that wasn't.

There would be a price to pay. The colossal failure might impact what funds and logistics support Mughniyeh could request for Hezbollah in the near future. His reputation with Arafat and the big plans for Iranian-PA cooperation were mostly thwarted. The disruption of the Iranian -PA relationship would have long-term consequences as the Islamic republic ultimately had to turn to Hamas and the Islamic Jihad to gain a footprint in the area. Both of these groups were distant second choices to its alliance with the PA, the largest Palestinian power. For example, in November 2019, almost entirely based on its limited firepower and depth, the Islamic Jihad quit fighting with Israel after two days.

But even if Mughniyeh held off on visiting Tehran, he would have still made contact with the Iranians. Mughniyeh generally spoke to foreign allies such as the top IRGC officials in person or through emissaries as he avoided being listened to by the Israelis' Unit 8200 or the Mossad. He would have instructed Haj Bassem or another top lieutenant to use his network of emissaries to contact the IRGC to confirm the failure of the *Karine A* mission.

Khamenei did not smile a lot in public. Instilling fear and awe of a "supreme leader" required his wearing serious or stern faces. And his religious principles were relatively ascetic. Given both his public statements and experts' estimates, he avoided being distracted by the Western wealth and perks that had brought down so many secular Muslim leaders. But sitting at a meeting of his national security team, he would not have been smiling then anyway. He would have known what the call would mean when it came in. Khamenei and anyone in the whole world who followed the news had learned from the globally televised Israeli press conference in Eilat of their shame and failure. Some of his advisers had been in disbelief and thought it was an Israeli hoax to shake out the true location of the weapons ship that they had failed to find. But the real nonpolitical intelligence professionals saw from the stash of weapons the Israelis put on display (many with the "made in Iran" label) that they had caught the real *Karine A* and its weapons.

They also had not heard any good news from their operatives who had gone diving for the tubes off the coast of Egypt. That meant they had probably found nothing. No one knew how, but the Israelis had bamboozled their best efforts again. When the call finally came and Mughniyeh's emissary spoke to IRGC commanders Soleimani and Safavi, they would have exchanged the initial pleasantries about Iranian and Hezbollah brotherhood. But Mughniyeh's emissary would have been reminded to tell his master Mughniyeh that he might be a daring genius, but the Iranians were still his masters and that they were furious. The Iranian spymasters would have been told that Haj Bassem and Mughniyeh's other operatives confirmed that the *Karine A* had fallen into Israeli hands. No weapons were floating off the Egyptian coast.

But Soleimani and Safavi had studied Israeli tactics and had

The International Ramifications

gathered intelligence. By all accounts, worst case, the Israelis were expected to wait and intercept the ship until it entered the Mediterranean Sea. IRGC and Hezbollah intelligence indicated the Israelis did not even have the capacity to capture a ship so far away from Israel's coast without running out of fuel. How could this have happened?

Lesser men than Mughniyeh might have met their end or at least ended their careers at this point. But Mughniyeh was different. He might get chewed out, but he was actually irreplaceable.

Soleimani and Safavi would have asked Mughniyeh's emissary about Arafat. The representative would have answered that Arafat would publicly distance himself from Hezbollah and Iran for the near future. The Iranian spymasters would have pushed for Mughniyeh to use his old ties to Arafat, going back to the 1970s, to rebuild the strained relations. After finishing speaking to Mughniyeh's emissary, Soleimani and Safavi would have gone for their own dressing down from maybe the only man on the planet who could talk down to them—Khamenei himself. Khamenei might have let them stir with some doubt about their fates for some time. Iran's supreme leader liked sometimes to exclude top officials from some key meetings and decisions to show his displeasure. This tactic almost led Iranian foreign minister Javad Zarif to resign in 2019 after being excluded from a meeting with Syrian leader Bashar al-Assad. Soleimani, however, was in that February 2019 meeting and very much at the height of his power. So despite the failure, Safavi continued to run the IRGC for several years, and Soleimani eventually recovered and continued to grow his own legend.

But Khamenei would never endorse Soleimani, Safavi, and Mughniyeh for carrying out a massive, daring weapons-smuggling operation such as the *Karine A* again. From then on, the operations would be smaller.

At some point, Khamenei and Arafat themselves and their various lieutenants used a variety of ways to coordinate their messages of denial of responsibility. Unlike Mughniyeh, who passed messages only through emissaries, these communications would also leave a trail that would be crucial in the ultimate battle for convincing the Bush administration that Arafat and the PA were in bed with Khamenei and the Iranians. At the same time, Israel's thwarting of the *Karine A* plot truly did torpedo the prospects of an Arafat-Iranian weapons alliance, but Iran would later send weapons to Hezbollah in Lebanon.

The Israeli Intelligence Case

Back in Israel, Jerusalem had trouble publicly convincing the world why capturing the ship was so significant. The Palestinians vehemently denied any connection between the ship and the PA, and the Iranians were also denying any connection to the plot. Arafat sent a personal letter to President Bush in which he disclaimed any knowledge of the ship. On January 4, when General Zinni asked Arafat about the ship, Arafat repeated that he didn't know about it and was ready to appoint an investigatory committee to get to the heart of the matter. In a January 8 talk with Colin Powell, Arafat again repeated his claim that he had no knowledge of the ship. An official statement from the PA emphasized that "the PA denies any connection whatsoever to weapons which were seized by the occupation forces deep at sea. The publication of the incident was designed to block implementation of the cease fire and to enable the continuation of Israeli attacks." All top-level Palestinian officials stuck to their message: the Israeli publication was a fabrication designed to thwart Zinni's peace mission. The international media raised doubts about whether the weapons were headed for the Palestinians, especially since the ship was captured so far away. It turned out that even if Mughniyeh's Red Sea and floating tubes strategy did not fool the IDF, it might fool the world and bolster the PA's and Iran's plausible deniability.

The international media also gave a serious platform to the Palestinians' denials and explored potential technical inconsistencies and holes in the many press releases Israel's public relations arm sent out. Most of the gaps were small or explainable, but any one of them could be exploited to increase doubt. What was really important was the disappointing official U.S. response. It started with a

The International Ramifications

New York Times article that quoted a senior Washington official who estimated that the weapons were headed for Hezbollah. The official added that the United States had no information to prove the claim that the weapons were headed for the Palestinian areas.

On January 4 U.S. State Department spokesman Richard Boucher did not connect the ship with the PA. Rather, he settled for a standard-sounding U.S. condemnation of any attempt by extreme actors to escalate tensions in the Middle East. He also noted that the U.S. administration was waiting for explanations from the PA about what had occurred.

But that was not all. Behind the scenes, the U.S. State Department and Bush's National Security Council, led by Condoleezza Rice, drafted a secret letter to Arafat that rebuked him somewhat while maintaining their diplomatic outreach to him. Vice President Dick Cheney's top aide I. Lewis "Scooter" Libby delayed the letter while Cheney and U.S. secretary of defense Donald Rumsfeld were out of town. Upon his return, Cheney took the issue to Bush, and the letter was never sent.

Collectively, there was still insufficient unity to bring about a major policy shift. Of paramount importance, Rice was still on the fence about the PA's and Arafat's culpability. So in the following days, there was no change either to the skeptical position of the United States or to its refusal to connect the ship to the PA, let alone Arafat. The start of a shift would only come on January 11.

The voices heard from Washington were disappointing and grating on Israeli ears. How could they convince the Americans that Arafat was at the heart of the weapons-smuggling enterprise?

"Let's send an intelligence delegation that can show the Americans the facts and the intelligence—not just spin and propaganda," Mofaz suggested to Sharon after a press conference on Friday, January 4.

"You need to go personally!" Sharon insisted.

"No! Just an intelligence delegation," Mofaz retorted. "I'll send Kuper and Meshita."

On this issue, Sharon and Mofaz simply were sitting in different chairs and looking over different fields of play—each with its own unique set of challenges. Sharon was mostly focused on the diplomatic goals of the mission and viewed Mofaz as far more versed than even senior intelligence officials in the diplomatic significance of everything that was happening. The IDF chief simply has more diplomatic responsibilities than intelligence officials, thought Sharon. In contrast, as an IDF chief, Mofaz believed that the proper tactical procedure was first to send an intelligence delegation to set the groundwork for his later visit. Mofaz also wanted to avoid being out of the Israeli arena except and until absolutely necessary because ongoing and new military threats required decisions to be made daily.

Mofaz finally convinced Sharon with that last point. As a retired major general and former defense minister, Sharon knew well the weight of responsibility for approving daily military operations. And he could still send Mofaz later if need be. "I approve," said Sharon.

On January 9 an intelligence delegation including Kuper, Meshita, and an official responsible for Israeli intelligence contacts with foreign agencies (whose identity is classified) flew to the United States. Stephanie also joined them. Kuper continued to be impressed with how focused and professional she was on the flight despite some of the pressures of her pregnancy.

Everything was put together in a rush, and the delegation's schedule was only finalized as they were landing. Thus far, CIA director George Tenet had refused to meet with them. Regarding Tenet's position on the Israeli-Palestinian issue, the Pentagon's then number 3 official, Douglas Feith, viewed it as "part of the problem with the crossroads of intelligence and policy always. People are not ready and are hesitant to accept information to the contrary because they don't want to give up their investment." Even Mossad director Efrayim Halevy's attempted intervention did not solve the problem. Only after Sharon personally called Tenet did he relent and agree to a meeting.

The delegation landed at dawn. With some difficulty, the members scrambled to get themselves organized at their hotel before they were whisked off to their meeting with Tenet, accompanied by the Mossad's attaché in Washington. That was when the first surprise came. Tenet was only willing to meet with Kuper and refused to meet with either Meshita or the Mossad representative. This was a meeting under protest. But what could the Israelis do?

The second surprise came when Kuper arrived: the meeting was not in Tenet's office but in the waiting room. Kuper sat and took information out of the files he had prepared. The only person in the waiting room was a secretary. Tenet came in, sat down, and crossed his legs. He then took a pipe out of his mouth, turned to Kuper, and said, "So what do you want?"

Kuper started to present the intelligence to him. It was neither philosophy nor propaganda. The facts assembled in the intelligence file meticulously described the structure of the weapons-smuggling network with Fuad Shubaki, Arafat's treasurer, at its head. The file described the connection to Iran and included the trajectory of the ship, the map used by Akawi, and other intelligence. Tenet started to listen and took notes. As Kuper was speaking, he studied Tenet's body language and his facial expressions, which seemed to give off the vibe that he was starting to understand there was something of significance here.

Then Tenet stopped writing, looked at his watch, and said, "Okay, I need to leave to see the president."

The meeting ended, and the delegation moved on to its next meeting, at the Pentagon. U.S. Department of Defense undersecretary for policy Douglas Feith led the meeting. By contrast, the room was jam-packed with officials. Meshita presented the operational side, and Kuper presented the strategic-diplomatic angle. Meshita and Kuper were extremely taken aback at first: not a single official in the room, including Feith, was aware of the details of the incident. The only official who was apparently up to date on the details of the operation was Defense Intelligence Agency Middle East region chief Bruce Riedel—and he missed the meeting. In that light, Kuper and Meshita were bombarded with questions about various details. Kuper felt that those present were not shocked that Arafat was involved in weapons smuggling. He did not need to convince them that Arafat was "the bad guy of the story." That was their point of departure.

Feith viewed himself and his staff as being "more open to some of these reports than were people at CIA and state who had developed a certain picture of Arafat. There were people at state and CIA who spoke respectfully or even reverentially of Arafat. That Arafat was a great statesman. Arafat had made an important commitment to peace. He was a hero of the Oslo process."

He continued, "They dealt with him with a kind of high opinion that did not prevail in my office. I think I knew a lot about Arafat and his history and I think I was much more in line with Rumsfeld's view and Cheney's view, which was that Arafat was a dishonest and corrupt person who did not deserve the high opinion that a number of people at state and CIA had for him.

"If I would get a briefing that said Arafat did something in secret that was inconsistent with things he was saying, that would not surprise me at all."

From the Pentagon, the Israeli delegation went to the U.S. State Department for a meeting with its Near East region chief Nicholas Burns. That same day, January 9, the department's spokesman confirmed that its officials had met with Israeli officials "to learn more of the details of their investigation into the issue" of the *Karine A*. Kuper and Meshita's feeling was that they had provided enough substantive details to convince the Americans that the PA and Yasir Arafat had initiated the weapons smuggling.

That night, Burns hosted the Israeli delegation at a Mexican restaurant in the Washington DC suburb of Bethesda. Burns received a call during the meal from the president's national security adviser Condoleezza Rice. Meshita was devoured by curiosity and wondered what Rice was saying to Burns.

Burns got off the call and addressed some of that curiosity, telling Meshita, "Tomorrow, the United States will put out a statement that it sees a connection between the senior PA leadership and the *Karine A* weapons smuggling."

The promised statement did not go out the next day, on January 10, but on Friday, January 11, as the delegation was leaving Washington and headed to England and France. In a statement capturing the spirit of Rice's perspective, U.S. State Department

The International Ramifications

spokesman Richard Boucher said, "We believe that there is a compelling case regarding the statement that senior PA officials and senior Fatah officials were involved in the operation to smuggle weapons, just as we think that Chairman Yasir Arafat has responsibility for senior PA officials." At the same time, Boucher said, "The U.S. does not have any evidence which directly connects Arafat to the smuggled weapons which were discovered when Israeli forces seized the weapons smuggling ship in the Red Sea."

"We're stuck," thought Sharon. "How can we convince the Americans that Arafat was the problem? How do we convince them that he was building a dangerous strategic connection with Iran?" He asked his advisers what they should do.

They all suggested that they needed to speak with Condoleezza Rice. The Israelis also needed to show her the documents about who planned the *Karine A* weapons-smuggling operation, who paid for it, and what weapons it contained. Sharon quickly concluded that he would send Mofaz to speak with Rice and the rest of the top U.S. decision makers.

Mofaz Visits Washington

Until the capture of the *Karine A*, Israeli leaders strongly believed that the reigning concept in the U.S. government was that Yasir Arafat was still an essential component for any diplomatic process or resolution. He was the undisputed and empowered national Palestinian leader with a full ability to control all Palestinian armed groups, so there would be no diplomatic solution without Arafat and his agreement. It was believed that he had no interest in promoting terrorism or in escalating conflict and, overall, that he was trying to move toward a peace deal he could live with.

Though the Americans did have some doubts about Arafat, they had not translated into concrete changes at the policy level. All attempts to convince the U.S. government that their kinder-gentler view of Arafat the peacemaker was misplaced had fallen on deaf ears. They were all greeted with the answer: "He's who we have to work with." In Europe, Arafat had even higher standing, as if he were an infallible king. By contrast, Israel was viewed as a nag that kept trying to wrongfully besmirch Arafat.

But the *Karine A* created a potential turning point. It could finally, at least somewhat, puncture the U.S. government's inflated view of Arafat. The members of the previous intelligence delegation to Washington DC, France, and England reported to Prime Minister Sharon that they thought they had convinced the expert-level officials that Arafat and the PA were directly involved in weapons smuggling and were connected to Iran.

Naval intelligence and the IDF's Planning Command worked around the clock for an entire week straight to prepare materials for Mofaz: maps, breathtaking pictures, diagrams, and other intelligence information. They clearly delineated the direct connection between Arafat and the weapons smuggling; the role of Arafat's moneyman, Fuad Shubaki; the names of all the Iranians involved; and the revealing testimonies of the ship's crew.

Mofaz himself, meanwhile, was under immense pressure to green-light additional operations. He barely had time to breathe. In the later afternoon on the day of his flight, Wednesday, January 16, he had a special meeting with Sharon and top officials to discuss the Second Intifada's leaders.

"Who is the commander in the field?" Sharon asked.

The defense minister responded that the leader was Marwan Barghouti.

"Capture him," Sharon ordered.

The meeting ended. Only Mofaz remained behind with Sharon. In a few more hours, the chief would fly to Washington. As his eyes lit up, Sharon said to Mofaz, "This is your operation. This operation has strategic importance." Mofaz listened and took it in carefully.

Sharon continued, "Like I already said to you, you will go to Washington in uniform. That will help you make a strong impression and grab their attention." Mofaz laughed to himself, and Sharon continued giving his guidance. His mantra was that Mofaz's mission was to incriminate Arafat. It was crucial that Israel's information went directly to President Bush and did not get stuck and intercepted by lower-level officials.

The Israeli Embassy in Washington organized a series of meetings for Mofaz for his two-day visit on Thursday and Friday, January 17–18. He would return to Israel Saturday night, January 20. The four top-level officials with whom Mofaz met were Secretary of State Powell, CIA director Tenet (round 2), Chairman of the Joint Chiefs of Staff Richard Myers, and National Security Council chief Rice. In addition, Mofaz met with other senior officials, including Deputy Secretary of Defense Paul Wolfowitz and Vice President Cheney's top adviser Scooter Libby.

The first meeting was with Condoleezza Rice, based on the sense that she was the one who most had Bush's ear. This meant she would be the first one to hear all of the classified and tantalizing information directly from the uniformed IDF chief. It was a closed and intimate working conversation with only Rice, Mofaz, and one of Rice's assistants. Mofaz unveiled a large map for her of the *Karine A*'s travels. Throughout the meeting, he presented her with additional pieces of intelligence information from his files. Mofaz did most of the talking. But Condoleezza would jump in at different points to compliment him on a successful operation or with a quick and supportive, "Yes, general," at the end of one of Mofaz's points. What did Mofaz tell her?

He opened by expressing his sympathy regarding the monstrous attack of September 11, 2001, noting that Israel and the United States were "in the same boat" in the struggle against terrorism. Then he pivoted to the general picture of al-Qaeda's terrorism globally and to Iran's tentacles, which extended both to Lebanon by providing longer-range Fajr rockets to Hezbollah and to the Palestinian Authority. He went into further detail about the intelligence regarding the Iranian-PA connections, including Arafat's agreement in principle to the presence of Iran's Islamic Revolutionary Guard Corps officers within PA territory. Next, he moved to intelligence showing how Arafat, the officials under him, and his forces in the field were all up to their necks in weapons smuggling.

What was the actual "meat" of the top-secret intelligence Mofaz shared? Much of it is still classified, but Mofaz had signals intelligence that repeatedly mentioned the names of IRGC members whom Israel's Unit 8200 and Mossad recognized.

He then showed Rice hard intelligence about how the Iranians physically assembled the floating tubes to hold the weapons. Mofaz also presented the information about where the Iranians had collected the weapons and the intelligence points used to prove that the IRGC had loaded the weapons on the *Karine A* at Kish Island. (Much of this information came from interrogating Akawi and other members of the *Karine A*'s crew.) Also, Mofaz shared with Rice readouts of conversations between Khamenei's IRGC and Mughniyeh's Hezbollah emissary, as well as readouts between that Hezbollah emissary and the PA's Mughrabi. All of them were focused on keeping the *Karine A*'s weapons-smuggling mission a secret.

But the most convincing point for Rice was a combination of human spying, signals intelligence, captured documents from Arafat's offices, and information from the interrogations of *Karine A*'s crew members that explicitly showed how Arafat and Khamenei coordinated their attempts to fool the United States into thinking Arafat was not connected to the smuggling plot. Evidence of this collaboration was simply too much for Rice to ignore. And all of the smuggling had one purpose: to further ignite and escalate the Second Intifada conflict.

"Arafat is the problem," Mofaz repeated as he showed how the PA was completely in bed with terrorists.

Condoleezza carefully followed Mofaz. Suddenly, she interrupted him. "Can I show the materials you have here to President Bush right now?" she asked politely.

Mofaz put on a face, acting as if he was hesitating, and told her that he needed to get a green light from Prime Minister Sharon. Condoleezza tried to reassure him, explaining that her intention was merely to take the material immediately to Bush and return it to Mofaz within the hour. This was along the lines of what Mofaz wanted, and he agreed to cut the meeting short. While Rice went to meet with Bush, Mofaz dashed over to the State Department for a short meeting. When he returned to Rice's office, she was already back from meeting with Bush.

"It was fantastic," she told Mofaz. "The president wants you to leave your files with him."

"Without the prime minister's approval, I can't leave them," Mofaz answered. Underneath, Mofaz was thrilled that the president was getting into the material directly, in depth, and with no intermediaries. This was exactly what Sharon had hoped he could achieve. But he kept a straight and serious face. He called Sharon from her office. He gave Sharon the good news and got his approval.

Sharon was giddy. He was ready to pop open champagne to celebrate. Nineteen years after Arafat had escaped him in Lebanon and weeks after the wily PA leader succeeded at keeping the *Karine A* affair at arm's length, Sharon finally had him cornered.

Mofaz turned to Rice to tell her Sharon had agreed to leave the intelligence information with her. Mofaz also had a chance to present information about Iran's nuclear program and Israel's policies for addressing it, and the two of them agreed to form a joint U.S.-Israeli task force to address the issue.

In later years, this joint task force, including the Mossad and the CIA, was reportedly responsible for assassinating a range of Iranian nuclear scientists; for the cyber virus Stuxnet, which ruined thousands of Iranian nuclear centrifuges; and for other actions to keep the Islamic republic's nuclear plans at bay. In January 2018 the Mossad pulled off one of the most daring operations in its history, appropriating most of Iran's secret nuclear files from the heart of Tehran and right from under its nose. Much of Iran's work on its nuclear program from 2002 to 2003 and later only became clear after this heist. To this day, Iran, the United States, and Israel remain in a standoff over the Islamic republic's nuclear program.

Mofaz was a bit surprised when Rice then said, "We won't act in Iraq before May 2002, and we'll coordinate with you." He immediately understood that this revelation was an expression of the high esteem and trust she held for him. It was also one of the earliest behind-the-scenes discussions between Israel and the United States concerning America's eventual invasion of Iraq in 2003.

That same day, January 17, Mofaz also met with Powell, Tenet, and Myers. He did not give them all of the files he had given Rice, but his message was clear and consistent: There is no hope for a diplomatic deal with Arafat, and there is a direct connection between Iran, which is working on nuclear weapons and long-range rockets, and the PA. Tenet was very skeptical about Mofaz's message regarding Arafat and the PA. Myers, an air force general, was very interested in the *Karine A*'s capture operation and emphasized strategic cooperation with Israel. Powell repeated his admiration for Israel's courageous operation over and over; however, it turned out that admiration would only go so far when it came to policy.

On Friday Mofaz received a report about a suicide bombing carried out by a PA-affiliated group against a city in the Tel Aviv corridor. Six people were killed, and dozens were injured. In response, the IDF took over Ramallah. On the flight back to Israel, Mofaz summarized the main points of the visit in his yellow notebook: The incriminating material had gone directly to Bush. U.S. officials understood that Iran and the PA were connected. There was an understanding of Israel's position that Arafat was a liar and a man of terrorism and that there was no way to reach a diplomatic deal with him. The U.S. government officially supported Israel's operation in the Red Sea as being legitimate. It agreed with Israel in viewing Iran's developing its nuclear program as a threat and understood that the PA was trying to smuggle weapons to escalate the conflict with Israel. Finally, there would be strategic cooperation on these issues between Israel and the United States. Mofaz himself also understood that what Israel needed to do now was to strike the PA's terrorism capacity in the broadest way possible and once and for all try to drain the swamp of suicide bombers. The United States would not oppose this action.

When Mofaz met with Sharon in Israel, he got a big bear hug. "You carried out a daring operation, and you personally paved the way for the start of a paradigm shift in the U.S. diplomatic approach to Arafat," Sharon said exuberantly.

The signs of Mofaz's successful meeting with Rice could be observed relatively quickly. By January 25 Bush was directly blaming Arafat for terrorism. He told reporters, "I am disappointed in Chairman Arafat. He must make a full effort to rout out terror . . . and ordering up weapons that were intercepted on a boat headed . . . for that part of the world is not part of fighting terror, that's enhancing terror."

Cheney added in a television interview with CNN on January 28 that "what's most disturbing isn't just the shipment of arms, it's the fact that it came from Iran. . . . So what we have here is Yasir Arafat . . . doing business with Hezbollah and Iran. . . . And it's difficult to take him seriously as an interlocutor in that peace process if he's going to conduct himself in that fashion."

Paradigm Shift in Bush Administration Policy

After the *Karine A* operation, officials at the Pentagon and the White House started to take control of Israel-related policy from the State Department. The change in its Middle East policy might have started as a trickle, but it emerged as a sustained wave. Since the visits of the Israeli intelligence delegation and of Mofaz to Washington DC, the Bush administration was listening more attentively to the Israelis' points.

Cheney and Rumsfeld had made a full and final shift against Arafat. Rice, following her meeting with Mofaz, had seriously started down that path, likely bringing Bush along with her.

Thus, the battle lines were drawn. Cheney, Rumsfeld, and their aides—including Libby, Feith, and others—would try to pull Bush in the direction of a divorce with Arafat. Tenet and, to a much greater extent, Powell would try to limit fallout from the *Karine A* to Arafat's lieutenants while maintaining him as the Palestinians' lead interlocutor with the U.S. government. They would suggest peace conferences, visits to the region, and a speech to cement the U.S. commitment to Palestinian statehood and a time line for the two-state solution between Israel and the Palestinians. Powell would tell Bush that he could not "do Iraq unless you have a major Arab-Israeli position taken. . . . You're viewed as being adrift." Cheney, Rumsfeld, and their staffs would try to block any rewards for Arafat and any speech that did not tar and further isolate him. Rice was in the middle but would steadily move toward Cheney and Rumsfeld, bringing Bush along with her—though Bush himself was already beginning to turn on Arafat. All of this would culminate in a historic presidential speech and dramatic policy shift in June of that year.

But it was still late January, and intervening events continued to slow the evolution of U.S. policy. After six weeks of making headlines, the Arab League on March 27 formally endorsed the Arab Peace Initiative, the most dramatic official regional peace offer that Israel's Arab neighbors had ever made. The central idea was that after Israel fulfilled all of the Palestinians' central demands, including the Palestinian refugees' right of return and a full withdrawal to the pre–Six-Day War borders of June 4, 1967, the Arab League would agree to peace with Israel. The Arab League Initiative did not stop the terrorist attacks against Israel; however, the historic peace offer still gave pause to those in the Bush administration considering a public divorce of sorts from Arafat.

Yet, the large crack in Arafat's armor from the *Karine A* saga became a gaping chasm during Operation Defensive Shield, a massive housecleaning of Palestinian terrorist groups in the West Bank. When the IDF raided Arafat's capital building, the Muqata, in March 2002, it obtained incriminating Palestinian documents that proved Arafat was incentivizing terrorism. They also indicated that he and his top lieutenants had planned and prepared the Second Intifada.

On April 1 Rice held a meeting to start considering a new approach to the Palestinians that was a combination of offering statehood recognition and being more demanding about renouncing terrorism. Starting with the documents Mofaz personally gave Rice in mid-January and continuing with the documents obtained during March's Operation Defensive Shield, the U.S. national security adviser shifted more strongly against Arafat. She even viewed Powell's visit to the region to gain Arafat's cooperation in early April as futile.

On April 4 Bush gave a speech on the issue that foreshadowed his later historic June speech:

The International Ramifications

The chairman of the Palestinian Authority has not consistently opposed or confronted terrorists. At Oslo and elsewhere, Chairman Arafat renounced terror as an instrument of his cause, and he agreed to control it. He's not done so. The situation in which he finds himself today is largely of his own making. He's missed his opportunities, and thereby betrayed the hopes of the people he's supposed to lead.

Yet this was not a clean break with Arafat, and the internal battle continued within the Bush administration.

On April 18 Powell and Cheney faced off against each other at a principals committee meeting of the senior U.S. cabinet secretaries. When Cheney told Powell, "Don't get completely consumed with Arab-Israeli issues," Powell replied, "You're dreaming if you don't think the Arab-Israeli conflict is central to the region—central to whatever we want to do in Iraq. Don't underestimate the centrality of the crisis."

Rice told her colleagues to take a new look at all the "fundamental assumptions of ours that may no longer be right" given the attacks of 9/11 and the changes in the region. So the pattern continued with Cheney pushing to finalize the break with Arafat, and Rice moving further in that direction.

On May 7, during Sharon's first official visit to Washington, the prime minister raised the *Karine A* incident with Bush. The president replied, "We understand that Arafat is the problem. It's started to become clear that as long as he's in power, the terror will continue. We'll find a way to address this." Arafat's lack of progress in rolling back terrorism beyond making speeches was highlighted that same day: Sharon had to cut his U.S. trip short after a suicide bomber killed fifteen Israelis and wounded more than fifty in a Tel Aviv club.

The U.S. administration's debate about a new policy direction hit a high point in June with nearly daily terrorist attacks resulting in large numbers of Israeli casualties and Israel's undertaking additional major operations in the West Bank. The central question was whether Bush should give a major policy speech on the Israeli-Palestinian issue and, if so, what its content should be.

Rumsfeld and Cheney rejected the idea of a speech that would give the Palestinians concessions or rewards while terrorism was still a daily event, but they accepted a speech that penalized Arafat and did not reward him in any way. On the other side, while opposing any break with Arafat, Powell continued to push Bush to give a speech that emphasized the two-state solution and a time line.

The speech went through thirty-six drafts. With only two days before Bush was supposed to speak in June, the administration was still furiously debating whether he should give the speech or drop it. Rice felt the pressure from the warring sides so intensely that she called Powell at his home and said, "I can't make this happen unless you are absolutely clear and forceful on the need for this."

Powell made a few Palestinian-friendly changes and called Rice back. He said, "Tell the president, I think he has to do this. We cannot just stand here staring at the sky." Thus, in helping bring Powell and others along, Rice helped Bush "get to yes" on making the speech.

At a key meeting, Bush made it clear to Deputy Secretary of State Richard Armitage, who repeatedly pressed Bush to take specific positions on final status issues in the peace process, that he was fed up with that approach. The president wanted "to change the way people think about the Arab-Israeli conflict." Feith called the exchange a "landmark moment."

In the end, Cheney and Rumsfeld embraced the speech, especially its call for a break with Arafat, while Powell viewed that break as a negative. Simultaneously, Israel continued to provide intelligence to the U.S. administration about Arafat's involvement with terrorism to help solidify its split with the PA leader and to move the United States to translate that into a concrete and public policy shift. In the final week before the speech, the U.S. administration received new intelligence that Arafat had authorized a payment of $20,000 to a terrorist group that had been responsible for a major suicide bombing only days before. On Saturday afternoon, June 22, Bush himself added to the speech the sentence officially calling for Arafat's removal for the first time. The payment may have been the nail in the coffin of the administration's support for Ara-

The International Ramifications

fat and may have led to Bush's determination to make that June speech, but the *Karine A* affair and the information that Mofaz gave to Rice had caused the paradigm shift.

On June 24, 2002, the U.S. officially broke with Arafat and dramatically and permanently shifted its policy regarding the Israeli-Palestinian conflict. Speaking from the Rose Garden of the White House lawn, Bush said:

> I call on the Palestinian people to elect new leaders, leaders not compromised by terror. I call upon them to build a practicing democracy, based on tolerance and liberty. If the Palestinian people actively pursue these goals, America and the world will actively support their efforts. If the Palestinian people meet these goals, they will be able to reach agreement with Israel and Egypt and Jordan on security and other arrangements for independence.
>
> And when the Palestinian people have new leaders, new institutions, and new security arrangements with their neighbors, the United States of America will support the creation of a Palestinian state whose borders and certain aspects of its sovereignty will be provisional until resolved as part of a final settlement in the Middle East.

The lot had been cast. A new era dawned for relations between the Bush administration and Arafat and for how the United States viewed the Palestinian issue.

Conclusion

Operation Noah's Ark for capturing the *Karine A*, without firing a shot and without injuring a single person on either side, was the first-ever naval commando operation to take over a moving ship with special forces both using ladders to climb aboard from commando boats while simultaneously fast roping down from helicopters. It was also possibly the first targeted military operation that Israel ever carried out that led to a major achievement and realignment at the strategic-diplomatic level. Many previous successful IDF operations achieved only limited successes at the tactical-operational-military level with no lasting diplomatic impact. After the *Karine A*, the IDF also conducted other successful operations to capture weapons-smuggling ships of the PA, Hamas, or Hezbollah, but they did not achieve new diplomatic results.

The capture of the *Karine A* continues to stand out as a unique moment. The operational success was self-evident in preventing the PA from receiving weapons that could have ravaged Israeli cities and ignited the Second Intifada's flames even further. But its greater significance was the resulting strategic-diplomatic realignment.

This paradigm shift had two main pieces: First, Arafat eventually ceased to be relevant in the eyes of the U.S. government. Second, the Bush administration accepted the Israelis' view that the Palestinians needed to end their terrorist attacks before the peace process could be pursued further. Put differently, the United States flipped the sequence of how to approach the Israeli-Palestinian issue. Until the *Karine A*'s capture, the U.S. peace process insisted first on ending the Israeli "occupation," and then the terrorism would end on its own as a natural consequence. Afterward, the administration accepted that the terrorism needed to end as a precondition to the diplomatic process.

The *Karine A* affair created the opening for this historic shift in policy. It led to the beginning of the end of the U.S. administration's trusting and relying on Arafat. Now the American leadership understood he was a liar.

What did top U.S. officials say about the *Karine A*'s impact on the massive policy shift? In August 2002 Undersecretary of State John Bolton, who would also later work as President Donald Trump's national security adviser in 2018–19, said:

> The *Karine A* had a critical impact and effect on Washington . . . the *Karine A* supplied dramatic proof and strengthened the feeling and trend of thinking in Washington that Iran was acting as a destabilizing force in a variety of areas and using multiple strategies: from developing weapons of mass destruction to distributing and supporting weapons smuggling for terror groups. . . . Without the clear evidence presented from the *Karine A* affair, it would

have been harder for the U.S. to harden its view of Arafat, even if it was already on the way to hardening its position.

Special Assistant to President Bush for the Middle East Elliott Abrams wrote that the *Karine A* affair's "eventual result was a new American view of Arafat, who was now placed in the post-9/11 context: He was a terrorist, working with Iran and Hizballah, at the moment when America was in a global war against terror."

The Pentagon's number 3 official Douglas Feith says, "The *Karine A* I think of as an important event, even a turning point for key Bush administration officials—the president, Cheney, Rumsfeld—a turning point in their attitude toward Arafat, the PA, and the Palestinians generally."

Feith concludes, "After the U.S. declared it was going to fight back in this war and leaders around the world were lining up to support us, here is Yasir Arafat in bed with the Iranians and continuing to develop his terror capabilities . . . and that put him on the enemy side in the war on terrorism."

Epilogue

The naval intelligence staff members displayed their profession-alism as they used systematic intelligence efforts sustained over several months to find the needle, the *Karine A*, in the haystack of thousands of commercial ships in the area. They successfully did so despite a disinformation campaign specifically designed to throw them off its course. The navy seals then took over the ship in the Red Sea, beyond Israel's standard operating zone, using new combat maneuvers both from the sea and the air. Did those in the IDF's high command who made the hard strategic decisions realize their military achievement would be key to blocking the PA from its plans to escalate the Second Intifada? Did all of the personnel involved realize their actions would lead to a historic shift in U.S. policy and the end of Arafat as the untouchable Palestinian leader?

What happened to the Israeli heroes of the operation?

The story of the Red Sea drama concluded, but the work of the operations' heroes continued. Naval intelligence continued its mostly anonymous work, just as the navy seals likewise continued to combat terrorism and assumed a critical role in the March 2002 Operation Defensive Shield. While six of its fighters who partici-pated in the *Karine A* raid eventually fell in combat against suicide bombers, most of the navy seals who participated in the operation moved up the chain of command. Chiny and Ram rose to become the commander of the navy in 2007–11 and 2011–16, respectively. Upon retiring from the navy in 2004, Yedidya became the chief executive officer of the giant Israeli defense company Rafael, and

Yoni Mann became a captain for El Al Airlines. Dan Halutz eventually became IDF chief of staff. Lieutenant General Mofaz, who understood early on the strategic diplomatic importance of capturing the *Karine A* and personally pushed hard to capture it—including taking bold and risky decisions to achieve that paramount goal—later became defense minister. Ariel Sharon remained prime minister until 2004 when he suffered a stroke, sending him into a coma from which he never recovered. The unstoppable Bulldozer finally gave way with his death in 2014.

Regarding the Palestinians, Yasir Arafat died on November 11, 2004, and was replaced by Mahmoud Abbas (also known as Abu Mazen). Imad Mughniyeh continued to be Hezbollah's military leader and a prime supporter of expanding Iranian influence in the Middle East until February 12, 2008, when the Mossad and the CIA finally caught him and took him out with a car bomb in Damascus, Syria. Iranian supreme leader Ayatollah Ali Khamenei still has an iron grip on his country. His top lieutenants are still promoting Iran's influence throughout the Middle East, and Soleimani was the architect of much of the chaos in the region until he was killed on January 3, 2020. His replacement, Esmail Ghaani, continued threatening Israel and other countries throughout the spring and summer of 2020.

And what of the young hero Anat? She continued in naval intelligence for quite a few years but retired after her third child was born. As of the fall of 2019, her children were in the twelfth, ninth, and sixth grades. Anat eventually concluded that she almost would need to abandon them to expend the necessary time and energy to rise in the ranks of naval intelligence. Intelligence is an essential unit. There are no standard vacations, and extra duty is built into the schedule to monitor certain emergency operational channels on holidays. Anat wanted to help the country and was extremely competitive, but having kids changed her priorities. She wanted to help them get dressed in the morning and to put them to bed at night. She was unwilling to pay the price of losing time with her kids to continue. After retiring, she had a fourth child and works now in a high-tech company whose hours are not as crazy as those of naval intelligence.

While presidents have changed in the United States, the central problems underlying the *Karine A* incident—that is, terrorism and Iran—have only become more threatening. In 2006 the Palestinian terror group Hamas took power in Gaza, and Lebanon is mostly ruled by the Shiite terror group Hezbollah. Radical Islamic terrorism has grown.

Iran, which had viewed the *Karine A* as part of its trend of facilitating terrorism, is still aspiring to achieve regional hegemony in the Middle East. In the summer of 2019, Iran got back into the terror-at-sea business, capturing a range of ships of U.S. allies, including from the United Kingdom. In February 2020, the United States intercepted the Iranians' attempt to smuggle weapons to their Houthi allies in Yemen as Iran continued its efforts to destabilize that country. Iranian proxies in Iraq also continue to attack U.S. bases there. Despite its cunning and lies, Iran became the United States' central problem in the Middle East and the biggest threat to its allies and global interests in that region. With the embargo on selling arms to Iran expiring in October 2020, the U.S. secretary of state and the rest of the U.S. national security team must confront an Iran that is far more dangerous and confident than that which Powell and Rumsfeld had to face.

APPENDIX A

Key Points in the *Karine A* Story

The First Half of 2001

Early contacts about joint smuggling operations were established between Iranian and senior PA officials with Hezbollah serving as the middleman.

May 2001

The Israeli Navy captured a small fishing boat in the Mediterranean Sea called the *Santorini* as it tried to smuggle weapons from Hezbollah in Lebanon to Gaza. The volume of weapons was small, but, importantly, they included SA-7 Grail shoulder-fired antiaircraft missiles that the PA planned to use to shoot down Israeli aircraft. Popular Front for the Liberation of Palestine leader Ahmed Jibril organized this operation. Although not directly connected to the *Karine A*, it foreshadowed the network of international cooperation between the Palestinians and outside terrorist groups to acquire game-changing weapons. The capture of the *Santorini* was one reason why the PA decided to try to smuggle weapons on the *Karine A* via the Red Sea instead of through the Mediterranean Sea.

June 2001

Having acquired a fishing boat a few months earlier, Omar Akawi purchased another in Egypt. Later, it was decided to use them for receiving and moving weapons that would eventually be smuggled to Gaza.

July 2001

Hezbollah and Iranian operatives conducted joint activities to make floatable sealed containers that could be dropped and store weapons just under the water's surface until they were collected by fishing boats. At the same time, the operatives made efforts to find divers. On July 29 a meeting was held with Iranians, Hezbollah members, and senior Palestinians to continue to clarify and discuss the details of smuggling weapons into the Gaza Strip for the PA's use.

August 2001

The PA's weapons-smuggling network started looking into purchasing a large cargo ship. Eventually, it bought the ship *RIM K* on August 31 from a Lebanese company. An Iraqi middleman made the actual purchase on behalf of Adel Mughrabi.

September 2001

On September 12 the ship was registered under a Togolese flag, after which its name was changed to *Karine A*. On September 15 the ship sailed south through the Suez Canal. On September 28 the ship arrived at Port Sudan. It remained docked there until October 3, and part of the crew was replaced during that time.

During the month of September, a crew, including a diver trained for handling the containers, was organized for the ship.

October 2001

The ship arrived at one of the ports in Yemen. Omar Akawi took charge of the ship along with additional new crew members, with the final crew numbering thirteen. It included eight Egyptians from the same village, mostly machinists and service providers; a Jordanian engineer; and four Palestinians, including Akawi. They took care of various additional registration and documentation issues while at the port in Yemen.

November 2001

At the end of November, the ship left Yemen for the Persian Gulf. On November 24 it arrived at a port north of Dubai in the Persian Gulf. There, Adel Mughrabi met the crew and paid their wages.

December 2001

On December 8 the ship left the port north of Dubai and sailed to an island just off the coast of Iran. On December 9–10 the *Karine A* broadcasted the code "Sultan," which was the sign for an Iranian ship to meet up with it as part of the smuggling process. During those days, the Islamic Revolutionary Guard Corps, along with Hezbollah operatives, loaded the crates of weapons that had been brought in from Iran onto the *Karine A*. On December 11 the ship left the Persian Gulf and headed for the Red Sea. In mid-December, U.S. intelligence started to assist the IDF in finding and monitoring the ship's progress, making key contributions in keeping the mission on track. On December 17 the ship passed through straits bordering Yemen and the Horn of Africa on a northern trajectory. From December 18 to 29, the ship docked at another port in Yemen to have an electrical problem fixed. It left that port on December 29 on a northern trajectory to cross back through the Suez Canal.

January 2002

On January 1, 2002, surveillance aircraft located the ship in the middle of the Red Sea on a northern trajectory. On January 2 surveillance identified the exact name of the ship, which was still headed north. In the early morning of January 3, the Israeli Navy Seals captured the *Karine A*, found many of the concealed weapons, and redirected the ship toward Eilat. On January 4 at 8:00 p.m., the *Karine A* docked in Eilat.

On January 9–10 and January 17–19, two Israeli military delegations visited Washington DC. During the first meeting, two top Israeli intelligence officials laid the groundwork for the second by the chief of staff of the Israel Defense Forces. The IDF chief convinced U.S. national security adviser Condoleezza Rice to present intelligence directly to President George W. Bush that proved the Palestinian Authority's and Yasir Arafat's complicity in the *Karine A* affair and their connection to Iran and Hezbollah.

Late January–June 2002

From late January 2002 until June 2002, Rice, Vice President Dick Cheney, and Secretary of Defense Donald Rumsfeld maneuvered the administration into an eventual open break with Arafat and a complete policy shift regarding the Israeli-Palestinian conflict.

APPENDIX B

The Ship's Capacity and Weapons Cargo

The *Karine A* carried a limited volume of commercial goods that were of minimal value. The purpose of this legitimate cargo was to help conceal the ship's main cargo—the weapons meant for the Palestinian Authority in the Gaza Strip.

The volume of weapons and ammunition, at fifty-four tons, was sealed in the eighty-three containers that were stored in three-meter-long crates. At the time, it was the largest cache of weapons the Israeli Navy had ever captured.

The weapons were exceptional both in volume and in their game-changing quality. Some of the rockets could have opened up larger Israeli cities to a new level of destruction and mass casualties, and some of the weapons would have allowed the Palestinian Authority to destroy IDF tanks, aircraft, patrol boats, and other vehicles critical to maintaining deterrence on the Gaza border.

Rockets and Related Parts

Four launching tubes for 122 mm rocket launchers and sixty-two rockets with a twenty-kilometer range had the capacity of striking the Israeli cities of Ashkelon (one of the largest in the country's south), Sderot, and Netivot, as well as all of the many villages near the Gaza border. Around forty launching tubes for various rocket launchers along with approximately two thousand mortars with ranges of up to eight and a half kilometers would have allowed the Palestinians to strike the many villages near the Gaza border.

Anti-Tank Weapons

Six Sagger launchers and ten missiles, 346 RPG-16 anti-tank grenade launchers, fifty-one RPG-7 grenade launchers, 209 more standard rockets, and 119 Tandem rockets would have provided a combination designed for a one-two punch against IDF mobile units. The first attack would have disabled any shielding or defensive elements, and the second would have destroyed the IDF unit itself. The ship also held around 211 YM-III Iranian anti-tank mines and around 311 regular mines.

Light Weapons

The *Karine A* carried around eighteen PK 7.62 mm machine guns, 212 AK-47 Kalashnikov rifles, around thirty Dragunov sniper rifles with a 450-meter range and PSO-1 telescopic sights, and approximately seven hundred thousand rounds of 7.62 mm ammunition for small arms.

Explosives

Around 2,100 blocks of C-4 explosives were found on board. The blocks were an advanced form of plastic explosives that were water and shock resistant, meaning they did not need to be handled as carefully as other more unstable explosives. These explosives have been used in terrorist operations against civilian airplanes. The *Karine A* also had 2,300 kilograms of blocks of TNT and 735 grenades.

Naval Equipment

Two Zodiac boats with external Yamaha twenty-five-horsepower engines, cylinders, and diving equipment were also found on board.

The Israeli Navy used the *Karine A* itself for training exercises for a time and later sold it to India for use as scrap material. The port of Eilat also erected a monument to mark the *Karine A*'s capture and the displaying of its weapons at the port.

APPENDIX C

The *Karine A*'s Crew and Leading Players

The Crew

The *Karine A*'s crew numbered thirteen men: eight Egyptians, one Jordanian, and four Palestinians. When interrogators finished with the Egyptians and the Jordanian, Attorney General Elyakim Rubinstein eventually ordered their release during the second half of 2002. The four Palestinians had been connected since the 1970s with either Fatah's naval units or their successor, the Palestinian Authority's Naval Police.

OMAR AKAWI

The ship's captain for its final voyage, Omar Akawi was part of the second graduating class for the navy of Fatah out of Karachi, Pakistan. He had served in a variety of roles, such as on the crew of the Fatah ship *Moonlight* when it was used in operations against Eilat in 1984. He was close to senior PA officials and had long been involved in smuggling on the organization's behalf, including purchasing ships for smuggling to Gaza.

Days after his capture, Israel showed Akawi on television confessing to having acted on behalf of Fatah and the PA. He was indicted and eventually given a twenty-five-year sentence.

RIAD ABDULLAH

A PA naval police officer, Riad Abdullah was credentialed as a commercial ship engineer. In the *Karine A*'s last voyage, he served as the chief engineer. He was close to senior PA officials and had also been involved in past sea-based smuggling operations to Gaza. He was indicted and given a seventeen-year sentence.

AHMAD HARIS

A PA naval police officer, Ahmad Haris was close to a senior Hezbollah official as well as the point man for passing messages with Hezbollah. He was indicted and given a seventeen-year sentence.

SALEM AL-SANKARI

A diver, Salem al-Sankari was a veteran of Fatah dating from the 1970s when it was based in Lebanon. He had been involved in two attempted terrorist attacks against commercial ships in the 1980s.

During the second attempt in 1985, he was arrested but was later released as part of a prisoner exchange with the Popular Front for the Liberation of Palestine. He was drafted for the *Karine A* smuggling operation for his diving skills, and he traveled to Lebanon to be trained in handling the special Iranian floating containers.

He was arrested during the IDF's capture of the *Karine A*, but in January 2004, he was released again in a new prisoner exchange with Hezbollah in which three dead IDF soldiers' bodies and a captured Israeli civilian were returned.

Involvement of Senior PA Officials

FUAD SHUBAKI

Brig. Gen. Fuad Hindi Hajdi Shubaki (also known as Abu-Hazam) was the head of finance for the Palestinian Authority's security services and was Arafat's right-hand man. During the Second Intifada, his security services were one of Arafat's central arms for smuggling and carrying out terrorist operations against Israel.

Shubaki financed and organized the *Karine A* weapons-smuggling operation. He was also involved, though to a lesser extent, in weapons-smuggling efforts from Jordan and Egypt.

After the *Karine A* was captured, under U.S. and Israeli pressure, the PA arrested Shubaki and "detained" him in Arafat's Muqata compound. In May 2002 Israel and the PA reached an agreement that a group of Palestinians who had assassinated an Israeli minister would be detained at the Muqata and that Shubaki would be moved to a jail at Jericho, where he would be supervised by British policemen. In 2006, when Hamas won the Palestinian parliamentary elections, the British policemen left Gaza. In response, Israel came and arrested both the Palestinian assassins of the minister as well as Shubaki. In 2009 an Israeli court gave him a twenty-year jail sentence.

ADEL MUGHRABI

A veteran operative in Fatah's terrorist operations against Israel, Adel Mughrabi was a trusted aid of Fatah's military chief Khalil al-Wazir (also known as Abu Jihad). Due to his operational background, Mughrabi was put in charge of many PA clandestine and weapons-smuggling operations. For the *Karine A* smuggling operation, he was in charge of purchasing the ship, changing its registration status to make it harder to track its trajectory, recruiting its crew, and briefing the key crew members on the true mission. He also coordinated with officials at ports in Egypt, Sudan, Yemen, and the United Arab Emirates. Further, he organized developments with Iranian and Hezbollah officials.

FATHI GHAZEM

Fathi Ghazem was a former bodyguard for Yasir Arafat. In the 1980s, he started dealing with Fatah's naval issues and was later appointed deputy chief of the PA Naval Police in Gaza. In that role, he helped direct smuggling into Gaza. He was in charge of the Palestinians of the *Karine A*'s crew and had been designated to direct three Gazan fishing boats to collect the eighty-three floating tubes of weapons off the Egyptian coast.

SOURCES

Primary Sources

A large amount of material in this list was classified until it was declassified for purposes of this book.

IDF chief—original intelligence material provided to U.S. president George W. Bush via U.S. national security adviser Condoleezza Rice; personal journal and real-time notes of his meetings with Israeli prime minister Ariel Sharon and other top officials; internal transcripts of meetings of the Israeli high command over which the chief of staff presided.

IDF forward commanders—recordings of real-time communications with the navy seals at sea before, during, and after their capture of the *Karine A*.

Israeli intelligence—internal transcripts of meetings of junior to senior officers from multiple levels of Israeli intelligence agencies and operational agencies; raw items of intelligence, including cables and other items; satellite imagery following the *Karine A*; and intelligence collection orders and plans relating to different agencies, including communications between the different arms, from the Mossad, to Unit 8200, to naval intelligence, and to the IDI.

Shin Bet—internal transcripts of the interrogations of the many Palestinian and related persons involved in the attempt to smuggle weapons to Gaza.

Open Source Information

Abrams, Elliott. *Tested by Zion: The Bush Administration and the Israeli-Palestinian Conflict*. Cambridge: Cambridge University Press, 2013.

Feith, Douglas, and Lewis Libby. "The Trump Peace Plan: Aiming Not to Make a Deal but to Make a Deal Possible." Ramat Gan: Begin-Sadat Center for Strategic Studies, July 15, 2020.

Public statements by the U.S. State Department.

Various Arabic-language, Hebrew-language, and English-language articles in the media mostly in the two weeks after the capture of the *Karine A*.

Interviews

A large number of those listed as interviewed on the record are also mentioned in the book. Some individuals mentioned in the book have been interviewed off the record. In those cases, they do not appear on this list, and any quotes by them in the book have come from third parties with whom they spoke.

Anat, Lieutenant Junior Grade
Ben-Besht, Rear Adm. David "Dudu"
Ben-Eliezer, Binyamin
Benisch, Lt. Cdr. Michael
Ben-Porat, Beni
Ben-Shalom, Maj. Reuven
Dan
"Dudu"
Feith, Douglas
Friedman, Dror
Gal, Lieutenant Commander
Gil, Captain
Halamish, Col. Yuval
Halutz, Maj. Gen. Dan
Itamar, Lieutenant Colonel
Kobi, Captain
Kuperwasser, Brig. Gen. Yossi
Mann, Lt. Col. Yoni
Marom, Rear Adm. Eliezer "Chiny"
Meshita, Real Adm. Hezi
Mofaz, Lt. Gen. Shaul
Palti, Col. Zohar
Peretz, Hanania
Rothberg, Capt. Ram
Shimon, Lieutenant Commander
Sisso, Lt. Cdr. Yehuda
Tal, Lieutenant Commander

Tamir, Major
Tiron, Zvi
Yaari, Adm. Yedidya "Didi"
Yaron, Commander
Yoki, Commander
Ziv

12-30-21